ANATOMY
OF FAILURE

ANATOMY
OF FAILURE

Why America Loses Every War It Starts

HARLAN K. ULLMAN

NAVAL INSTITUTE PRESS | ANNAPOLIS, MARYLAND

This book was made possible through the dedication of the
U.S. Naval Academy Class of 1945.

Naval Institute Press
291 Wood Road
Annapolis, MD 21402

Library of Congress Cataloging-in-Publication Data
Names: Ullman, Harlan, author.
Title: Anatomy of failure : why America loses every war it starts /
   Harlan K. Ullman.
Other titles: Why America loses every war it starts
Description: Annapolis, Maryland : Naval Institute Press, [2017] |
   Includes bibliographical references and index.
Identifiers: LCCN 2017024947 (print) | LCCN 2017050192 (ebook) |
   ISBN 9781682472262 (ePDF) | ISBN 9781682472262 (epub) |
   ISBN 9781682472262 (mobi) | ISBN 9781682472255 (hardcover :
   alk. paper) | ISBN 9781682472262 (ebook)
Subjects: LCSH: United States—Military policy. | National security—
   United States—Decision making. | Presidents—United States—History—
   Case studies. | United States—History, Military—Case studies. |
   Militarism—United States—Case studies. | Defeat (Psychology)—
   Case studies. | Strategy.
Classification: LCC UA23 (ebook) | LCC UA23 .U1415 2017 (print) |
   DDC 355/.033573—dc23
LC record available at https://lccn.loc.gov/2017024947

Print editions meet the requirements of ANSI/NISO z39.48-1992
(Permanence of Paper).
Printed in the United States of America.

25 24 23 22 21 20 19 18   9 8 7 6 5 4

Book design and composition: Alcorn Publication Design

Contents

Preface

Since the official end of the Cold War in 1991, remarkably, the United States has been at war or engaged in significant military conflicts and interventions for over two-thirds of the intervening years. Tens of thousands of American soldiers, Marines, sailors, and airmen have been killed or wounded in these conflicts. Wars and conflicts in Iraq in 1991; Somalia, 1992–93; the global war on terror, and Afghanistan, 2001–present; Iraq, 2003–present; and Syria and Yemen since 2016 represent a total of nineteen of the past twenty-six years in which this nation's armed forces have been engaged in combat!

Using the end of World War II in 1945 as a second starting point and including the Korean (1950–53) and Vietnam Wars (from 1959—when the first Americans were killed—to withdrawal in 1974), Americans have been in battle for thirty-seven of the past seventy-two years, or well over 50 percent of the time. The record has not been impressive. Korea was a draw. Vietnam was an ignominious defeat, vividly encapsulated by the poignant image of the last Huey helicopter lifting off the roof of the embattled American embassy in Saigon.

The only outright victory of the past six decades was the first Iraq War in 1991, in which President George H. W. Bush had the sound judgment to limit the objective to ejecting Saddam Hussein and his army from Kuwait and then to withdraw the bulk of our forces from the region. Tragically for the nation, Bush's son, George W. Bush, presided over arguably the greatest American strategic catastrophe since the Civil War, the second Iraq war—a conflict that led to the rise of the Islamic State and is still being waged today, without an end in sight. The reader can evaluate the outcomes of the other interventions cited above.

Several observations that can be made about this history of repeated failure are almost as dismal the record itself. First, few Americans are even aware of or concerned over how long this nation has been engaged in armed conflict over recent decades. It is quite a staggering length of time for a country that prides itself on its "exceptionalism" and its "peaceful" efforts to spread democracy around the globe. Second, few Americans even ask why, given what we believe is the greatest military in the world, our record in war and military interventions is so failure prone. Third, we ourselves must ask: What can be done, in light of general public indifference, to ensure success whenever the nation employs military force in major conflicts or interventions?

This book examines the more significant American uses of force over the past six decades to understand why we lose wars (and fail in interventions) that we start. It also argues the absolute need to adopt a valid framework for making decisions—what I have termed a "brains-based approach to strategic thinking." While some may regard this term as arrogant, the fact is that too often we have failed to exercise fully the grey matter between our ears, with disastrous results.

To succeed, sound strategic thinking must transcend or minimize the vagaries of politics, ideologies, simplistic campaign slogans, wishful ideas, and the inexperience that have (as the forthcoming chapters will argue) handicapped the nation's last three commanders in chief and almost certainly will affect the current one. From these analyses, the book derives means for how to win, how to succeed in applying force.

To make this argument more vivid, vignettes about major events are interspersed throughout the text. To some, they will be controversial. To others, these vignettes will underscore on a personal level the larger reasons for failure and the damning impact of the absence of sound strategic thinking. Each vignette is an accurate summary of actual events, to the best of my recollection. A few circumstances have been altered to protect sensitive information or sources.

As with any work, shortfalls and errors are the responsibility of the author alone. The only responsibility of the reader is to keep an open mind in understanding why we lose the very conflicts we start.

Harlan Ullman
Washington, D.C.
September 30, 2016

ANATOMY OF FAILURE

Introduction

A Simple Truth Shaped by Moments of War

Presidents, politicians, and publics have failed to grasp this simple truth: for more than half a century, America has lost every war it has started. Likewise, America has also failed in military interventions it has initiated, interventions undertaken for reasons that turned out to be misinformed, contrived, baseless, ignorant, or just wrong.

In extreme humanitarian crises, especially those involving genocide and mass slaughter of innocents, decisions over whether or not to intervene with military force rather than with only aid and assistance are agonizing. More often than not, such humanitarian interventions bring temporary, not long-term solutions—the relief of the Kurds in northern Iraq in 1991 and the North Atlantic Treaty Organization (NATO)'s ultimate engagement in the Balkan wars of the 1990s being notable exceptions.

Tragically, intervention for the right reasons may still fail. Somalia in the early 1990s and, particularly, Libya in 2011 are poignant examples of failure. In some cases, administrations see no choice except to intervene, regardless of risk and the unlikelihood of success. In others, such as the catastrophe now enveloping Syria, all the options range between bad and worse.

When examined critically, objectively, and dispassionately, the reasons and factors that have led to failure in applying military force are self-evident and unarguable. However, too often we are blind to or dismissive of these realities. Vietnam and Iraq (after the 2003 invasion) are the clearest and most damning examples of failed military interventions. Afghanistan is almost certainly going to follow suit—and it is a war in which the United States has been engaged for more than three and a half decades.

Yet, the proposition that wars we start, we lose has been ignored by a succession of presidents of both parties and, for far too many decades, by the American public, especially following the great victories of World War II and the Cold War. "War" in this book is defined as the use of military force in a major conflict, not metaphorical declarations of war against inanimate enemies, such as drugs, crime, poverty, and other social ills—"wars" that, by the way, have also failed, particularly the ill-named "global war on terror."

The purposes of this book are to alert future leaders and publics: to inform them about disastrous wars of the recent past started by us and to propose solutions and actions to prevent such failures from recurring—or to minimize the consequences—through sounder strategic thinking. Where the use of force went badly awry, it was through the failure of decision makers, who allowed unsound and flawed strategic thinking to drive bad decisions.

This book has its origins in the Vietnam War, in 1965. I was serving as a Swift Boat skipper in the northernmost part of the Republic of South Vietnam. Over time (I was there from 1965 to 1967), even a junior naval officer could not ignore the recurring displays of arrogance, naiveté, ignorance, ineptitude, and incompetence by the senior American political and military leadership in waging that conflict. Despite the heroism and commitment of those who fought and died in Vietnam, the war, like most wars, would have been tragicomic in its idiocies and irrationalities had it not been so deadly serious. And have no doubt: America started this war, which would turn into a quagmire.

The Gulf of Tonkin Resolution, passed two votes short of unanimously in both houses of Congress in August 1964, gave three presidents virtual blank checks to wage war in Vietnam. Tragically, that authority was based on the utterly false premise that Hanoi had purposely ordered two separate attacks on American destroyers in international waters off the coast of North Vietnam—the second of which never occurred.

Battlefield tactics exploiting the massive American superiority in firepower and mobility became surrogates for strategy in Vietnam. This confusion of ends and means had fatal consequences. One was excessive reliance on numerical and quantitative measures to rationalize the tactics. This circular logic was manifest in the perverse establishment of "body count," which became the metric of success. Because the numbers of enemy dead showed we were winning, then ipso facto, we had to be winning.

✦

The year 1965 begins my chronicle for understanding and identifying the anatomy of failure. Like many of the millions of Americans who served in or during the lengthy Vietnam War, I was particularly affected by certain events. Three dramatize on a personal level how and why we lost in Vietnam and too often would make similarly grave errors in the future. Each demonstrates the folly of using force without understanding the interplay of ends and means or applying sound strategic thinking—failures that guarantee defeat. Of course, they also illustrate how all wars reflect human weaknesses and unintended consequences.

The first incident demonstrates that wars cannot be successfully waged in isolation or in compartmentalized fashion by individual services and agencies. The absence of coordination is inexcusable and ultimately proves fatal. The second underscores the huge gap that often exists between those on the front lines and the politicians and commanders hundreds or thousands of miles away. (It also reinforces the Napoleonic axiom that luck matters.) The third and final vignette is the most powerful: when ends and means are not related owing to flawed strategic thinking and fallacious reasons for having gone to war in the first place, the effort will become morally and politically corrupt.

In 1965, the Vietnam War was escalating, and the Navy called for volunteers to serve in Southeast Asia. The Navy, engaged in the air battle over the North and uncertain how it would join the ground war and the fight in the rivers and offshore in the South, began with a modest (and largely pointless) operation to stop North Vietnam from infiltrating arms and men by sea. The intent of what was called Operation Market Time was to monitor the coasts of South Vietnam with a combination of maritime aircraft, warships, and small patrol craft called "Swift Boats." Swift Boats were fifty-foot aluminum-hulled craft designed by Sewart Seacraft for servicing oil rigs in the Gulf of Mexico, especially in rough weather. Powered by two Cummins diesel engines, a Swift Boat could make thirty knots in average or better sea conditions.

Swifts carried twin .50-caliber machine guns in a forward mount above the pilothouse; an "over and under" 81-mm (three-inch) mortar that could fire an explosive round about two thousand yards; and a third .50-caliber machine gun mounted above the mortar tube. The crew was equipped with AR-15 automatic rifles, 79-mm grenade launchers, and other small arms. The aluminum skin barely kept out the sea, let alone enemy bullets and shrapnel. Crews were usually five or six, or larger, depending on the mission.

The flaw in this strategy was that North Vietnam already had an effective logistical land route to the South, called the Ho Chi Minh Trail. This trail, deep in the interior of Southeast Asia, did not need seaborne routes. But the Navy was anxious to get its share of the action—even though there was little action to be had.

My very modest training at the naval base in Coronado, California, included a superficial course in Vietnamese culture, a course that in my case had only one high point—a lecture by retired Army lieutenant colonel John Paul Vann. Vann was an extremely controversial former officer who later became the de facto commander of Vietnam's II Corps area (the Central Highlands, north of Saigon) and the only civilian to be awarded a Distinguished Service Cross for gallantry during the 1972 Easter Offensive. Vann was to be killed in June 1972, when his helicopter smashed into trees on a night flight in II Corps.

At this training session, Vann described the North Vietnamese and Vietcong in glowing terms and disparaged our South Vietnamese allies. When asked why he regarded the enemy so highly and our allies so poorly, he hesitated for a moment and replied, "I guess God put all the good guys on the other side."

Classroom instruction was followed by SERE training (survival, evasion, resistance, and escape) in freezing temperatures high in California's mountains—ideal preparation for the heat and jungles of Vietnam. After that, several Swift Boat crews, including mine, boarded chartered civil airliners at Travis Air Force Base, outside San Francisco, for the long transpacific flight to the Tan Son Nhut air base, near Saigon, Republic of South Vietnam. But it did not happen that way.

Arriving at Clark Air Force Base in the Philippines, expecting to continue on, we were notified that our tickets ended there. Despite Priority One flight status and what we were told was an immediate operational requirement to get us in-country "pronto," no one had bothered to book us on the next leg, to Saigon. Neither begging nor strong language had any effect. At best, the Air Force could get us to Saigon in about two weeks, following the airlift of a huge USO (United Services Organization) entourage of Hollywood and other celebrities and noncombatant personnel. (Entertaining the troops under the doubtful assumption that it will raise morale seems to be part of every war we fight.) Even worse, the bachelor officer and enlisted quarters at Clark were full up—there was no room at the inn.

"Where the hell do you expect four Swift Boat crews to stay—in tents on the parade field?" the exasperated officer in charge—me—asked a nonplussed and slightly disoriented airman.

"Oh no, by far the best place and much better than here on the base is the nicest whore house in Angeles City," called the House of the Angels. And that is where we went, cooling our heels, if that was the appropriate phrase. While we tried our best to get to the war, persistently harassing the ticketing office to move up our flights, the crews were not enthusiastic about advancing our departure date. The rooms were quite comfortable, and unlike in the BOQs (bachelor officer quarters), their air conditioning worked. Food was good, beer and booze were plentiful and cheap, and sailors were not bored by their accommodations. With no direct means to contact naval headquarters in Saigon, we were stuck at Clark. One of the few recreations at Clark was the Officers' Club. There, I fell into the clutches of Air Force F-4 Phantom fighter pilots on rest and recreation ("R

& R") from the 389th Tactical Fighter Squadron, stationed at Phan Rang in South Vietnam.

As we Swifties had the inside track on the local scene, given our billets, a half dozen or more of the pilots joined me in a tour of Angeles City. The pilots had been flying missions in-country for about two or three months. As Americans tried to be in those days, each was overly aggressive and anxious to get back "into the fight." After some hard drinking, the entourage returned to the Clark Officers' Club, where there were two bars. The downstairs bar was entered "at one's own risk" and was not too different from some of the joints in Angeles City. At some stage, an altercation broke out between one of the Air Force pilots and a Marine.

When the scrape was broken up, the Marine was quick to disappear and the Air Force pilots were escorted out of the bar by a bevy of large bouncers. The pilots were not happy with their dismissal and tried to reenter the bar forcibly. Fights broke out with the club bouncers. The Air Police were summoned. Being slightly more sober than my comrades, I attempted to separate the combatants. The APs arrived. Bad language led to a further exchange of blows, and a three-way donnybrook broke out among the Air Police, the bouncers, and the pilots. The APs and bouncers outnumbered the pilots and manhandled each of them, one by one, into the waiting paddy wagon. Realizing this would not be good for my new friends, I demanded that the senior airman summon the officer in charge.

Though I was seemingly coherent, and wearing a Navy tropical white uniform that was not commonplace on an Air Force base, the young Air Police officer in charge was confused. Exploiting that confusion, I invented an outrageous story about how these pilots were soon off on a highly classified, above-top-secret, extremely hazardous mission over North Vietnam. This could be their last fling, so to speak. That was the soft sell. For the hard sell, I, as a representative of Gen. Marmaduke Smedley, had the authority to place everyone in custody if need be.

The "we who are about to die" line may or may not have worked. But the threat of awakening the general with such a bizarre name (the first to come to mind) surely did. Fumbling to find the imaginary phone number in the right pocket of my tropical white shirt, I said, "Here's the general's personal phone number. He will not like being disturbed this late." Whether the young officer believed me or not, he chose leniency rather than the threatened wrath of my general. The officers were released—and, being young and dismissive of authority, waited only a few minutes before reentering the bar. This time they were on their own.

(I later exchanged very occasional letters with one of them. Thirty-five years later, long after I'd forgotten the incident, that pilot, then 1st Lt. Gene Quick, turned up in Washington and called. We arranged a get-together, and after Gene and his wife arrived, he got around to telling the story. My wife was disbelieving. Yet I suspect some elements were true. Welcome to Vietnam—almost.)

After much pleading and begging, finally we were airborne, landing at Saigon's Tan Son Nhut air base ten days late. It was 3 a.m., and Vietcong mortars were peppering the field, already illuminated with star shells. Our only orders were to call "Tiger 345," headquarters of Commander, Naval Forces Vietnam, on an antiquated field phone. The other two hundred or so passengers were quickly collected and hustled away to safety. We remained huddled in the empty hangar, hungry, frightened, and tired, listening to mortars exploding nearby and automatic weapons occasionally firing while I cranked on the phone, which was straight from a World War II movie, desperately trying to reach Tiger 345.

Wars in those days were obviously fought, in Saigon, on an eight-to-five basis. Thus, there was no answer from Tiger 345 until well after the sun had risen and the mortar attacks had subsided. A soft, female Vietnamese voice answered the phone. The way she pronounced "Tiger 345," with both a Vietnamese and English lilt, is etched into my memory. An hour later a dilapidated yellow school bus arrived, with mesh wiring over the windows to prevent someone from lobbing a hand grenade or Molotov cocktail into the ancient vehicle.

The briefings in Saigon were as useful as our SERE training had been. Soon we were flying north to "I Corps" (that is, the zone assigned to the South Vietnamese army's I Corps, the northernmost of four) in Da Nang and PCF Division 101. All of us were new to

Vietnam and to war. We officers were young, arrogant, invulnerable (we foolishly thought) to the enemy, and thoroughly inexperienced and unprepared for war.

◆

The first of my three vignettes was an incident that occurred on the evening of August 10–11, 1966. Three Swift Boats and four crews had been detached to a small base just inside the mouth of the Cua Viet River in the northernmost reaches of I Corps, almost in the shadow of the Demilitarized Zone separating the South and North. A Vietnamese junk base located a few kilometers away was supposed to provide some security. But the most worrisome part of a generally defenseless position was that we were colocated with the U.S. Marine Corps' largest fuel depot of petroleum, oil, and lubricants (collectively called POL) in that part of the country, protected by an understrength guard unit.

Had a North Vietnamese or Vietcong rocket hit the fuel dump, the smoke, we joked, would have been visible in San Francisco. Still, despite the presence of local enemy units, no one in the chain of command seemed particularly worried about security. There was very little boat or junk traffic in the canals or to seaward on the ocean. As officer in charge, I dedicated one boat to "over-watch" duty, patrolling at night a few hundred yards from the base as added security. Its task was to detect any infiltration against either our undefended base or the vulnerable POL site and, if necessary, shoot on sight.

On that night, our boat drew over-watch duty. The only radar contacts were two U.S. Coast Guard WPBs—eighty-two-foot-long cutters—also on patrol. Around midnight, two jets overflew us. These could only be American, as the North Vietnamese air force never ventured south. Moments later, fire erupted in the vicinity of one of the WPBs. It appeared that the jets were strafing the boat— USCGC *Point Welcome*.

Knowing these were not North Vietnamese fighters, we rang up flank speed and closed the cutter. We arrived too late. Two Air Force B-57 Canberra bombers had, incredibly, mistaken *Point Welcome* for an enemy PT boat and made several strafing runs. The skipper, Lt. (jg) David Brostrom, had been killed while heroically shining a searchlight on the cutter's U.S. ensign, hoping the aircraft would see it. A second crewman, Engineman Second Class Jerry Phillips, had also been killed.

We began picking up survivors who had jumped overboard. Meanwhile, our Vietnamese allies ashore had seen the attacks and, thinking we were the enemy, began firing at us with .30- and .50-caliber weapons. Fortunately, and courageously, Coast Guard chief petty officer Richard Patterson had taken command and fought to save *Point Welcome*, managing to turn on enough lights to convince our allies to stop shooting. A second WPB joined us in dealing with wounded.

Charges were filed against the Air Force pilots. "Friendly fire" was unfortunately the rule, not the exception, and virtually no coordination existed between the different services operating in the region. The Air Force needed pilots, and the charges disappeared. Other friendly-fire incidents occurred, particularly ashore. Miraculously, no one among our crews was killed or wounded by friendly fire during my tour, either at sea or operating close ashore (although I was almost sunk by a misdirected broadside fired, ironically, from the destroyer USS *Uhlmann*).

Thirty-one years, to the month, after the *Point Welcome* tragedy, a very close American friend living in England arrived in Washington with combat photographer Tim Page. They were in town for the CNN/Newseum salute, a huge exhibit, to photojournalists on both sides who died during the Vietnam War.

Over dinner and drinks, Tim, inquiring about my time in Vietnam, asked what had been my most harrowing experience. I recounted a summary of the *Point Welcome* episode. Page's face went ashen. "Tim, are you all right?" my friend asked worriedly. Page remained stunned for a moment. Recovering slightly, he looked at me and asked, with emotion, "Did your crew wear red ball caps?"

I looked at him askance. "I beg your pardon?"

"Yes," he replied, his color returning. "Red ball caps. And didn't you go by the call sign 'Red . . .' something or other?"

"Ah yes, Red Baron . . ." I said—and then I was speechless. "Yes, Tim, I did, and I was."

Tears running down his cheeks, he said in a voice filled with awe, "You saved my life! I was aboard *Point Welcome*."

As with Gene Quick, sometimes events catch up with you.

✦

The larger failure was clear even to a young "jaygee." Vietnam was fought as three or four separate wars by at least four different armies and air forces and operational commanders. Coordination was avoided by setting geographic boundaries to prevent or reduce friendly fire, rather than addressed by operational requirements. The Central Intelligence Agency further confused coordination. Throughout the country, the agency maintained a separate air force and paramilitary ground forces, as well as a small contingent of patrol boats, operating out of Da Nang.

A subset of the lack of coordination and command was the absence of fire discipline, exacerbated by a gross excess of available firepower. The body count became the metric for success and, too often, the basis for medals and good fitness reports. Aggressiveness was the order of the day. Hence, Air Force pilots were incentivized to mistake *Point Welcome* for a North Vietnamese PT boat even though none ever ventured south. "Shoot first" may not have been the explicit order of the day, but few units acted otherwise.

The lack of jointness and of a single, integrated operational chain of command would be addressed twenty years later with the Goldwater-Nichols Act, passed in 1986. However, integration of all cross-agency capabilities in what would be called a "whole-of-government approach" still has not been fully addressed. Future failures would arise in the Afghan and second Iraq interventions, where underresourced civilian agencies were unable to deal fully with the "What next?" questions involved in bringing stability and security to those regions. "Stovepiping" of departments and agencies still persists, limiting the effectiveness of U.S. policies when all arms of government are vital to success.

✦

The second vignette was an incident that spoiled Christmas Eve, 1966. A supposed truce was meant to halt fighting over Tet, the lunar new year, a well-known Buddhist holiday coinciding with

Christmas. The command in Saigon issued strict orders to return fire only when certain the enemy had fired first. But wars, especially this one, rarely celebrate holidays. We in the field knew that the Vietcong and the North Vietnamese army (NVA) had often disregarded truces and that we had to be prepared for any attack or probe, no matter the orders from Saigon. PCF Division 101 was based and housed on a floating barracks barge. The barge, an APL in Navy jargon, was anchored in Da Nang Harbor, about five hundred yards from the nearest shoreline.

Since there was little to do on Christmas Eve except drink beer and eat extra food rations, drawing duty as the "ready boat" was no hardship. Earlier in the year, my crew had rescued U.S. Marines pinned down by enemy fire on the Cap Batangan (a peninsula south of the Marine base in Chu Lai, at the southern tip of I Corps). Cap Batangan was a formidable Vietcong stronghold with caves that were layers deep and centuries old. The village of My Lai was on Batangan. Upward of five hundred Vietnamese men, women, and children were to be massacred there in March 1968 by a U.S. Army unit in one of the worst atrocities of the war.

In naval gunfire support, there are two types of shore-bombardment missions, direct and indirect. Direct fires engage targets that are in sight. Indirect fires are against targets not visible to the firing platform but identified by map coordinates or a spotter. Navy warships have fire-control computers that make indirect fires very accurate.

Swift Boats lacked any form of computer, so indirect fires were not only infeasible but, in this case, would place the Marines pinned down on Cap Batangan at great risk. We simply could not guarantee where our mortar rounds might land. As the Marine captain to whom this was being explained replied on the radio, "If this doesn't work, don't worry. It will be too late so start shooting now!"

Using "seaman's eye" to aim the mortar barrel in the direction of the enemy and guessing at the range, we fired about forty rounds without ever seeing the target. The Vietcong were either scared away or the 81-mm rounds did some damage. The Marines radioed back that, judging from the blood trails, we had hit the targets. Miraculously, our rounds hit no Marines. The lesson, one that is inherent in war, was to be prepared for any and every eventuality—especially those least expected and above all those that authorities dictate cannot be done.

Now, just before midnight on Christmas Eve, Marines ashore in Da Nang reported that Vietcong were probing their front lines. My boat got under way in case fire support was needed. Cruising to about a hundred yards off the beach, we soon received urgent calls for fire from the Marines and our South Vietnamese allies. Our Swift Boat too was receiving incoming fire. The probe turned out to be real, because it was not uncommon for friendlies ashore to shoot at us believing we were enemy—a lesson that should have been learned at the *Point Welcome* debacle. It had not been.

We fired a combination of star shell—illumination rounds—and high explosives. After about twenty explosive rounds, we loaded a star shell into the mortar at the stern and fired. The round could have been defective, or it might have been hit by incoming fire. That made no difference. The magnesium-laden round exploded just outside the mortar tube and above the ready-service ammunition locker, which still contained twenty or thirty mortar rounds.

The loader, Gunner's Mate Third Class Ernie Franzia, was caught in the explosion and received agonizing burns on his right arm. The mortar operator was Chief Boatswain's Mate Charles Norris, standing behind the gun. Norris' job was training the mortar with its bicycle-like handles. Exhibiting enormous courage, Norris stood his ground, traversing the mortar away from the ready-service locker to prevent the ammunition from detonating. Miraculously, Norris was largely unscathed, although parts of his uniform were smoking from the white phosphorous.

I grabbed a CO_2 fire extinguisher from the front of the boat and raced aft to contain the burning magnesium flare, no doubt in my mind that we were about to be blown to pieces. While I was emptying the CO_2 bottle on the blaze, I turned to Chief Norris, who was holding on to the smoldering mortar for dear life, and blurted out, "This is some fucking way to spend Christmas Eve, isn't it, Chief?"

Napoleon was absolutely correct: in war, luck counts. Although the 81-mm mortar and stand were partially melted, the ammunition in the ready-service locker did not detonate. Fortuitously, a Navy hospital ship was just under way from Da Nang Harbor en route to Hong Kong. Within minutes, we were alongside, offloading Franzia, whose burns turned out to be painful but not debilitating. The sailor enjoyed a ten-day R & R in Hong Kong before the hospital ship returned to Da Nang.

Meanwhile, we headed for the APL and brought the wounded Swift Boat alongside. The crew was somewhat emotionally drained by this episode. I told them to stand down. I found another boat and crew in case a second call for fire was received. The replacement crew had arrived in Da Nang literally earlier that day. The skipper was Lt. (jg) Alex Krekich, someone I knew from the Naval Academy who graduated a year after me and had been a star lineman on the Navy football team. It being Christmas and with crew new to Da Nang, the only sober member was Krekich.

When the second call-for-fire mission came—as predictably it did—we made for the shoreline in the new boat. Since Krekich's crew was largely hors de combat, Al was singly manning the stern mortar, his massive body loading, pointing, and firing as I relayed instructions from the cockpit. After a few rounds, the mission ended. We were thanked, and we headed to the APL for some needed Christmas cheer. The rest of Christmas Eve passed without incident. Poor Al, who went on to be a vice admiral, must have thought that if this was his first day in Vietnam, what would the remaining 364 be like? Still, this was not the best way to spend Christmas Eve for anyone!

Chief Norris had been incredibly brave. I probably would have leapt overboard. I recommended him for a Silver Star, the nation's third-highest award for valor, and a Purple Heart, along with one for Franzia. I was stunned and enraged when the awards were later disapproved on the grounds it had been during a "truce" and Americans would never violate such an agreement.

This reinforces just how remote Saigon was from the fighting. In every war, similar complaints are common. However, Vietnam was particularly marked by self-delusion about the war in the high command and the political leadership. It did not change until the

Tet Offensive of early 1968 forced an agonizing reappraisal of the war. Reality would begin to take hold, even if it was six more years before the United States finally withdrew. Christmas Eve of 1966 is a reminder of how distant Saigon was from the realities of the war and of the crippling impact of delusion.

Years later, I was still trying to get recognition for the chief's heroism, with the help of Adm. Elmo "Bud" Zumwalt. The Navy finally awarded Norris a Bronze Star. Whether Norris actually received the medal, I do not know. But his gallantry probably saved our lives, as well as the boat.

◆

The third vignette represents perhaps the most incisive explanation of why we lose wars. It taught that killing one's way to victory—which seems today to be the strategy in the war on terror—does not work, period. Operation Phoenix was the CIA plan to terrorize and eliminate subversive Vietcong and NVA elements operating clandestinely in the South. No one knows the exact number of people killed by Phoenix; about 50,000 is the best estimate. Most of the "wet work" was carried out by Western and South Vietnamese mercenaries (we called them "mercs"), advised and controlled by CIA and other U.S. paramilitary forces.

In early 1967, in a scene reminiscent of *Apocalypse Now*, I was invited to the trailer of an Army brigadier general. Also present was an unnamed civilian I assumed to be CIA. An enlisted man passed around drinks and then the standard rare-roast-beef lunch. "You have been selected to conduct a very important and highly sensitive mission," the brigadier said, after swallowing a hefty portion of beef. "You come highly recommended for your competence and aggressiveness in action."

It was clear that this was going to be a soft sell. Having once been assigned a ludicrous mission to go well into North Vietnamese waters to attack the heavily defended "Tiger Island" (a mission that by the grace of God was aborted at the last minute), I had visions of an equally foolish operation flitting through my mind. As in most wars, common sense was often missing in Vietnam. I worried that this was going to be another foolhardy mission.

This mission, however, seemed too ordinary for such a sales job. The task order was to insert a dozen Vietnamese "special forces" soldiers into a village not far from My Lai on Cap Batangan at night and then extricate them before sunrise. The purpose of the insertion was "above my pay grade." But it did not take an Eisenhower to surmise that this team was part of Phoenix and that its purpose was to "terminate with extreme prejudice"—the term of art in those days, meaning to kill—suspected enemy agents.

A few weeks later, when there was no moonlight, the mission got under way, in a manner of speaking. Midmorning, a bus drew up to the pier at Chu Lai where our boat was moored. Chu Lai was also the headquarters for the 7th Marine Regiment and air wing. Two Westerners identified only by first names led twelve Vietnamese, armed literally to the teeth with bandoliers of ammunition, hand grenades, automatic weapons, pistols, and knives. I asked the head mercenary for a numbers count; he grumbled "Twelve," displeased I would even raise the question. But thirteen Vietnamese had come on board. It was not difficult to pick out the thirteenth man: he wore only sandals, shorts, and a white T shirt. Turning on him as if he were the devil incarnate, one of the mercs demanded to know who he was. "The bus driver," the now thoroughly frightened man replied in Vietnamese.

"We need to get rid of him," the merc said. "This can compromise the mission." Being highly suspicious of the mission in the first place, I strongly disagreed. "No, we will take him with us and let him go when we return." The two CIA spooks muttered their objections but had to accept, grudgingly, my authority.

At about 10 p.m. we closed to about a hundred yards of the targeted village and offloaded the team into two rubber rafts to paddle ashore. We drifted as silently as we could on one diesel engine, to avoid detection. The Vietnamese special forces should have needed no more than ten minutes to paddle to the shore. Half an hour later, after considerable radio talk—tactically dangerous and not hard to detect—the Vietnamese team finally reported it was ashore. We took a position about five miles out and waited.

I had persuaded the 7th Marines in Chu Lai to provide us with an interpreter. This Marine, who spoke excellent Vietnamese, had made several patrols with us. Because most of the patrols were boring, we had struck up a friendship during the long hours under way. The Marine was a corporal, in his thirties—old for so junior a rank. He had had a rather excellent, if not unblemished, career. He had qualified for Marine Force Recon, the elite of the Corps. He had been a staff sergeant, with remarkable language skills, including fluent Russian and Chinese. Ordered to the U.S. embassy in Moscow as a specialist interpreter and a member of the Marine Guard, he had fallen in love with a Russian he said was the most beautiful woman he had ever met.

After that, his story was less clear, if not suspicious. He had had an affair with this lady, whom, he said, he married. The embassy had uncovered the romance, strictly prohibited for staff holding top-secret security clearances, which he did. The Marine complained that the embassy had claimed she was a "swallow"—meaning a KGB agent assigned to seduce foreign officials. The corporal maintained she was not.

In any event, he was punished, demoted, ordered out of Russia to Vietnamese language school, and then sent to Vietnam for a thirteen-month tour. Asked what he was going to do about his "wife," he said he was going back to Moscow on his first R & R to find her. Soviet authorities, he had been told, had detained her. I suggested he might be wasting his time. He had been promoted to corporal and was now serving as a very competent interpreter. As a Force Recon Marine, he was skilled in combat arms. While his story was suspect, he was nonetheless quite an impressive Marine, physically and intellectually.

About 4 a.m., the Vietnamese radioed that they had completed their mission and were returning to the Swift Boat, which had moved closer ashore. The distance it had taken them considerable time before, they covered in a few minutes in a commandeered junk, obviously having left the rubber boats ashore. The junk pulled alongside, its captain crying and screaming in Vietnamese. While the two mercs were helping their team aboard, the corporal whispered to me, "Sir, we have a big problem. The Vietnamese claims these guys shook down the village, stole watches, money, and medicines and raped several women."

"And he could be making this up," I said.

The corporal spoke to the Vietnamese junkman, asking for proof. The villager simply said to search the raiding party. This was going to be a very wrought situation, as the mercs were growing increasingly anxious about this extended discussion with the junk captain. Turing to the mercs, I told them to move the Vietnamese team to the Swift's stern. Then I turned to Gunner's Mate First Class Eugene Sands, who was manning the twin .50-caliber machine guns in the turret above the pilothouse, and whispered, "Gunner, lock and load."

In the dark and quiet, the staccato click-click of .50-caliber rounds being rammed into firing positions sounded like claps of thunder. Not much concerned with what was happening ashore, I said, "Gunner, fire a burst over the heads of the mercs and Vietnamese at the stern." A .50-caliber bullet is half an inch in diameter and travels at several times the speed of sound. When a round passes overhead, the shock wave is physically painful. "If any of them go for their weapons, don't miss." Then the Marine and three of my crew disarmed the twelve Vietnamese and their two handlers. The Marine told the Vietnamese to strip.

Each one of them was laden down with booty—money, wrist-watches, jewelry, medicines, silks, and anything that had seemed of value. One of my men scooped up the contraband and asked me what to do with it. I told him to give it to the boatman and shove him off. The poor Vietnamese bus driver we had temporarily detained could believe too easily what was happening. We bound the fourteen men with plastic wrist restraints, ordered them to sit down and keep silent. One of the crew, Ernie Franzia, who had been wounded Christmas Eve, kept a loaded M-16 pointed at the prisoners with Engineman First Class David Rees in reserve. The corporal joked, "You think I got into trouble in Moscow. What the hell are you going to do, now that you've taken on the CIA?"

That was a very good question. After reporting what had happened, we were ordered to return to Da Nang, not Chu Lai—a longer journey. A furious CIA station chief was waiting at the pier. The discussion was not pleasant. I was a Navy lieutenant, and he was the equivalent of a one-star general, but that made little difference. I lost my temper and—according to my crew, who were biased—I tore the CIA chief verbally to pieces. That was not clever.

For some time, I was in serious trouble. My report and the charges I filed were buried. The CIA did not have me on their most friendly list. For reasons that are not central to this book, the deputy head of Phoenix, Ambassador Robert Komer, was someone I knew. Through his good offices, I was removed from whatever list would have led to reprisals. Some, but not all, of the excesses of Phoenix were addressed.

I recall once seeing at the Chu Lai air base "enhanced interrogation techniques" at work. Several suspected Vietcong were loaded into a Huey helicopter and flown to an altitude of about a thousand feet, where one of the prisoners was pushed out through an open door. Newsweek carried on its front cover a photo of this Vietcong hurtling to the ground. In such cases the other suspects usually confessed to any- and everything, almost always untruthfully. These extreme interrogation practices would not disappear after Vietnam.

As with Phoenix, the Taliban and terrorist insurgents in Afghanistan and Iraq have been hunted down by a combination of JSOC (Joint Special Operations Command) and Predator drone strikes. Similarly, in the fight against the Islamic State, special forces and drone and air strikes reportedly have killed at least 40,000 jihadists in Syria, Iraq, and Afghanistan, as well as a handful now in Pakistan.

◆

Nearly fifty years lie between these experiences in Vietnam and the current battle against jihadists and Islamist radicals. Today's military operations and commando raids are far more tightly controlled; they must be approved by legal counsel in advance. The United States makes every effort to minimize noncombatant casualties and limit collateral damage—far different from the free-fire zones of Vietnam and reliance on horrid body counts to measure progress. However, collateral damage still occurs.

One wonders what has changed over time. Since wars were first fought, Clausewitz' "fog and friction" have made the easiest of tasks impossible in the stress of battle. Confusion, uncertainty, and fear were and are commonplace. There is no doubt that today's American military is by orders of magnitude more professionally competent, committed to service, and able than the largely drafted Army that fought in Vietnam. But the lack of understanding of either the enemy or the culture of Vietnam was repeated during the Afghanistan intervention in 2001, Iraq in 2003, and Libya in 2011. Ignorance of the local situation and of the culture has been so chronic as to seem embedded in our decision-making DNA. Too often, American leaders have believed that the enemy always thinks as we do. All these are symptoms of flawed strategic thinking.

Overreliance on technology, whether massive firepower or selective drone strikes, continues. While no one would wish our forces ever to go to war with anything less than the best weapons and supporting systems, to ensure that no fight was "fair," killing our way to victory doesn't work any more than it ever did. Huge resources were put into attempting to win "hearts and minds" in Vietnam. These efforts failed. Why were these examples of failure ignored or dismissed decades later? That question has always been one of the most disturbing legacies of the only war I ever fought.

My crew was lucky. Despite close scrapes, only two of my crew were wounded, neither seriously. One PCF Division 101 boat capsized and was lost only yards off the beach on the Cua Viet River. The division suffered only a handful killed in action. Fifty-eight thousand other Americans were not so fortunate. Ironically, the first operation in which I recall supporting the Marines was called "Last Chance." Meant to refer to the enemy, too often the code name applied to how we were fighting that war.

I was to have plenty of time to brood on the sixteen or seventeen months I had spent training for and deployed in Vietnam. Shortly after I returned home, late one night a car full of teenagers rammed my convertible, sending me to the hospital for a year, six months of it in intensive care. Only the skill of surgeon Dr. Robert Mullin and his staff and the wonder drug Keflin saved my life. It is doubtful that I would have survived if I had sustained similar injuries in Vietnam. When I was sufficiently recovered to think cogently, I began the long journey of analyzing why we won and lost wars. The reader can now understand why these Vietnam experiences form the basis of this book.

✦

Nearly a decade after leaving Vietnam, I was a young Navy PhD in political science and international finance (rather than with a technical degree, more useful for a technologically driven service). In June 1975, I found myself assigned to the faculty of the National War College in Washington, D.C., the most junior officer at the nation's most senior war college. Students were largely colonels and Navy captains, with a sprinkling of senior members of the Foreign Service, CIA, and a few other civilian government agencies. Virtually all the military students had served and fought in Vietnam. Many of the civilians had likewise been stationed in Southeast Asia.

When the topic of Vietnam arose, most of the military students became sullen and defensive. We had lost. Every student in uniform felt a shared responsibility. It was not a good time, and it was made worse by President Nixon's resignation over Watergate the year before and by the poignant image of the last Huey helicopter lifting off the roof of the U.S. embassy in Saigon as the North Vietnamese army paraded through the capital.

Three and a half years at National gave ample time to analyze why we had lost in Vietnam and to dissect the anatomy of that failure. It also put me in contact with the government's best, people who would play major future roles in defense, foreign policy, and national security. Colin Powell, the future chairman of the Joint Chiefs of Staff, would become the best known and most admired. However, many other graduates in the bicentennial National War College class of 1976 went on to distinguished careers in the military and other branches of government. That class was known as the "Great Americans," in evocation of the much-loved War College commandant, Maj. Gen. James Murphy, U.S. Air Force, who used the phrase frequently.

But if 1965 was not, as Frank Sinatra once crooned, "a very good year," no one could have imagined then (or even today) that how the Vietnam War was fought and ended would become, sadly, the template for the future, the precursor of more American failures through misapplication of its military. More than half a century later, what should have been learned from losing that war has skipped generations of leaders, perhaps implying a missing gene or two in America's strategic and political DNA.

Starting or needlessly provoking wars or military interventions without legitimate and credible rationales and sound strategic thinking makes failure inevitable. Yet, too often, this obvious route to failure has been America's way of making war. The question is whether America's elected leaders will continue to be trapped in the insanity of repeating the same actions and yet expecting different outcomes. At some stage, Americans must realize how tough the job of president is and demand of the candidates specific plans for coping with this harsh reality, not accepting empty or flawed promises. Sadly, that pressure is not likely to affect future elections. It certainly did not in the 2016 elections. Worse, Americans, oblivious to the absence of sound strategic thinking that has infected too many White Houses, have no means or leverage to encourage future presidents to respond to this recurring malady. If in a small way this book can publicize that message, perhaps—and that is a big caveat—someone might listen, maybe even lead.

One

An Analytical View of Why We Fail

Las Vegas at the Skybridge Strategic Alternatives Annual Conference (SALT), May 2015. Harlan K. Ullman (HKU) is presenting his book *A Handful of Bullets: How the Murder of Archduke Franz Ferdinand Still Menaces the Peace.*

Conferee: "You just made the case that the biggest threat to society is failed and failing government. Can you also explain why it is that the United States has lost every war it has started since 1945? Is it because government fails, or something else?"

HKU: "Your question is my next book. The simple answer is that no matter who or what party is in power and whether the president is seasoned or inexperienced, ideology, political expediency, and failure to pose and answer difficult questions or to challenge basic policy assumptions too often dominate and become surrogates for sound strategic thinking. Nor do we always fully understand the issues and consequences of action and inaction. Vietnam was the most blatant example. The second Iraq war is another. And the intervention in Libya in 2011 is a third.

"Every time we initiated using force without just cause or legitimate provocation, the results at best damaged our security and at worst were far more destructive. Unfortunately, every administration since Vietnam, less one—that of George H. W. Bush—ignored or did not understand this reality.

"Without a major revolution in how the nation provides for the common defense and its security, do not
expect the future will prove any more successful than
the past five decades when we decide to commit force to
protect or advance our interests. The most worrying possibility is that this propensity to start wars and use force
for the wrong reasons may now be deeply embedded in
the nation's DNA.

"That does mean we should not use force when we
must. But we must be certain when we do use force that
it is for the right reasons and in our national interest."

Over the last century, why has the United States, despite overwhelming industrial and military superiority, lost the wars it started
without just cause? Evidence of failure is unmistakable from the
Vietnam War and its 58,000 American dead to the more recent deba-
cles in Iraq, Afghanistan, and Libya. They are unlike World Wars
I and II and a Cold War that if mishandled could have led to thermonuclear Armageddon. America then was responding to external
threats that started or provoked these conflicts: the kaiser's Germany
in 1917, Hitler and Japan's military junta two and a half decades later,
and the Soviet Union in the aftermath of World War II.

At best, Korea was a draw, even though the North was the
undeniable aggressor when it invaded the South in June 1950. The
attacks of September 11, 2001, that destroyed New York's Twin Towers and part of the Pentagon in Washington, D.C., warranted a strong
response. But the "global war on terror"—a misnomer—so far has
failed by exacerbating, and not neutralizing, the dangers posed by
violent Islamist extremism.

✦

In identifying and dissecting reasons for these failures, we ask: Why
over the past decades have successive administrations of both parties, despite asserting that force was a last resort, too often turned to
force as the *first* resort of policy, ignoring or marginalizing other tools
of government? A corollary question about this record of failure is,
Why, since the end of the Cold War, have the United States and both
of its political parties seemed incapable of applying sound strategic

thinking and judgment, of treating the causes and not the symptoms of crises, threats, and challenges to security and well-being—and always with predictable and unwanted results?

Has this propensity for failure become permanently grafted onto America's political DNA? Is failure a product of a political system that is seemingly unable or unwilling to govern, that has elected for the past two dozen years presidents who were insufficiently ready or prepared for the exceedingly difficult demands of the office they assumed? Or do today's multifaceted, complex, and numerous challenges, some of which defy solution, simply exceed the capacity of any individual and administration, no matter how capable, to respond effectively?

Failure or success in foreign policy is often, to quote the Duke of Wellington, "a close-run thing." But even before the end of the Cold War, Vietnam should have made clear that when the United States intervenes and starts a war for mistaken reasons, especially the most flawed reasons, it will fail. Since the end of the Cold War, interventions in Iraq, Libya, and most likely Afghanistan have repeated these unfortunate outcomes. These failures have also provided ample ammunition for critics with which to assail the foreign policy and strategy of every administration.

Presidents dating back to George Washington and their administrations have been accused of having no strategy, the wrong strategy, or simply an ineffective strategy on which to base foreign policy. Vitriolic debate over foreign policy is neither new nor unique to today. Before the attack on Pearl Harbor on December 7, 1941, Americans by an overwhelming majority resisted and resented Franklin D. Roosevelt's efforts to side with Britain after Hitler declared war on civilization and occupied virtually all of Western Europe in 1940. The Vietnam War too deeply divided America. Still, it took years for Washington to recognize that the war in Southeast Asia was lost and withdrawal inevitable.

Over the two and a half decades since the end of the Cold War, in terms of the most significant foreign-policy issues, failure has been too frequent. If the United States is to change this dangerous reversal of fortune, to fashion more effective strategies, what can or must be done? Or has the likelihood of failure, not success, become the new normal?

A crucial question must be asked and answered, especially by those seeking to hold high office. Why and how have American strategies involving the use of force succeeded in the past, and why have they failed? Given the challenges and threats of the twenty-first century, fuller understanding of the reasons for and factors in success—and, perhaps more important, for failure—is imperative. The process of enhancing the chances for success may be better informed by focusing first on failures.

Regarding the repetition of past failures, Afghanistan is, unless God or luck intervenes, on course to follow suit. A corollary is, Why has the consistent American preference for promoting regime change proven so disastrous? Answers very much lie in the people we elect to the presidency.

The job of the president is extraordinarily difficult, so difficult that those taking office for the first time do not fully appreciate how agonizing and sometimes impossible the duties are. President John F. Kennedy famously quipped that there is "no school for presidents." Perhaps there should be. However, the nominating processes and campaign are surely not it. The Constitution lists only four requirements for the presidency: be a natural-born citizen, be at least thirty-five years old, have lived in the United States for fourteen years, and win a majority of votes in the Electoral College.

Each of the post–World War II presidents, from Harry Truman to Richard Nixon, with the exception of JFK, was reasonably prepared to assume that high office. While Truman may not have possessed obvious, outward qualifications for the presidency and had been excluded by Roosevelt from many decisions, including the Manhattan Project to build the A-bomb, few presidents read more history or knew more about every prior presidency. Dwight D. Eisenhower, Nixon, and Gerald Ford likewise were seasoned. The young Kennedy's charisma and selection of the so-called best and brightest for his team offset his lack of experience. Jimmy Carter was the first president whose resume could be called into question regarding his fitness to assume the office on Day One.

While it is easy to dismiss Ronald Reagan, he had twice been governor of a state with a gross domestic product larger than those of most countries and had presided over the Screen Actors Guild for many years. Without question, George H. W. Bush was as qualified as any president in recent history when he entered the Oval Office; how he and his administration dealt with the implosion of the Soviet Union, made Europe "whole, free, and at peace," and ejected Saddam Hussein from Kuwait in 1991 are textbook cases of the application of sound strategic thinking and judgment. Unfortunately, the four presidents since were by no means elected because of their resumes and qualifications.

Bill Clinton was a brilliant politician and inherited the best hand of any president in recent memory. The George H. W. Bush administration had righted the economy, and Clinton would be the beneficiary. Desert Storm and the sensible and correct decision not to occupy Iraq had exorcised the demons of Vietnam. The implosion of the Soviet Union had ended the Cold War and the threat of mutual annihilation, opening huge opportunities for the advancement of global stability and prosperity. Clinton was lucky, but his first year in office was chaotic. While his administration was able to avoid major international crises, his deciding to expand NATO without determining how to deal with Russia over the long term, taking seventy-eight days to resolve the Kosovo crisis, and dallying with an intern were indelible blots on his record.

George W. Bush similarly lacked experience and qualifications for the office. Two terms as governor of Texas—a position with far less authority than in most states—could not equip the younger Bush for higher office. Observing his father's twelve years in the White House as vice president and then as president might have been instructive. It was not. Bush learned, and by his last year or two he finally understood how to be president—but it was too late. The damage done in Afghanistan and by the Iraq invasion was irreversible. Indeed, many have argued that the Iraq war was the greatest geostrategic calamity created by the United States since the Civil War.

Barack Obama was even less experienced than George W. Bush. In contrast to Clinton, Obama inherited the worst hand of any president since FDR took office in the Great Depression. The financial crisis of 2008, Iraq, Afghanistan, the global war on terror, and disintegrating relations with Russia would have challenged a Washington, Lincoln, or a Franklin Roosevelt.

With the inauguration of Donald J. Trump in January 2017, a president took the oath of office without a single day of political experience in government or, indeed, of managing a large public corporation responsible to shareholders and boards of directors. He now has a board of 535 directors on Capitol Hill and about 320 million shareholders, in the form of the American public. Insufficient time has passed to make any judgments about success or failure in the Trump administration. However, the flurry of executive orders the president signed in his first weeks in office and the chaos and confusion that resulted were not good precursors. His promise, on which he ran, to grow the economy by at least 4 percent a year, create millions of jobs, repeal and replace "Obamacare" with a better product, and reform the tax system will have its day of accounting in November 2018, with the by-elections for Congress.

Still, one of the major causes of failure and success is the occupant of 1600 Pennsylvania, personally. It is misleading to believe that if presidents surround themselves with capable advisors and cabinet secretaries, that talent will compensate for their own lack of experience. Possibly—but talent can never substitute for character and judgment.

All of this raises a question. Over the past seven decades, many leaders from both American political parties have lacked the ability to govern wisely, successfully, or sensibly: Has the proclivity for foreign-policy failure become ingrained, as if from the air they breathe? Can it be true that a political system of checks and balances and divided government invented by the best minds of the eighteenth century no longer works in the twenty-first? Or have the challenges and crises of today just become intractable, whose solutions would elude even the most informed and able of leaders?

Here are a few preliminary answers. The current broken condition of the political process makes it highly likely that leaders who are insufficiently prepared for high office and unequipped to grow quickly enough into the job will be elected or appointed anyway. The brokenness of government might condemn even the best of leaders, with basic understanding of the complex issues and threats facing the nation, to fail. The good news is that no existential threat to the United States (other than the specter of an environmental calamity) exists: no matter how much politicians try to make China and Russia into latter-day Nazi Germanys or Soviet Unions, barbarians will not come crashing through the gates anytime soon. The bad news is that "anytime soon" is not forever.

A bitterly charged and destructive partisan environment magnifies the likelihood of failure. Ubiquitous social media give access and a platform to virtually anyone with a smart phone. A round-the-clock news cycle and reporting media that are often skewed to the far left or right often result in the presentation of rumor and speculation as fact and biased opinions as truth. And priority given by a political system to winning elections and reelection rather than to governing is symptomatic of failure in the making.

Furthermore, in a twenty-first-century environment in which virtually all points of the globe are instantaneously connected and events are interrelated far more than ever before, huge "bandwidth" problems have developed. This means that White Houses and presidents often are simply overloaded with crises and issues, all with 24/7 media scrutiny. Time has become an enemy. Setting priorities becomes difficult when the media cycle constantly spews out mini-crises and bad-news stories that demand immediate attention. The tyranny of a twenty-four-hour news day means that spending sufficient time on each and every crisis, no matter how significant, is impossible. And no president can afford to delegate responsibilities that involve life-and-death decisions. The buck most certainly stops in the Oval Office, as Harry Truman often observed.

Finally, no good or practical solutions may exist to certain of the crises, challenges, and dangers of the world we inhabit. With the demise of the Soviet Union, President George H. W. Bush became the first commander in chief to inherit "the New World Order." However, it is not clear that President Bush or his very able advisors, struggling to make the post-Soviet world safer than the one it replaced, were fully aware of the consequences or impact of the changed and changing conditions. In any case, in 2017 Bush's New World Order seems to have mutated into a condition of No World Order.

The central recommendation of this book is an approach to strategic thinking that informs good judgment. Sound strategic thinking combines three elements. First is the necessity of deep understanding and knowledge of the circumstances surrounding and encompassing the issues. In Vietnam, Iraq, and Afghanistan, White Houses simply ignored, denied, or lacked the understanding and knowledge on which they needed to base policy. This absence of understanding and knowledge has sadly become a recurring theme, from the Libyan debacle of 2011 to the war on the Islamic State (IS).

Second, administrations have failed to understand the changing strategic environments of their times. For example, today's foreign-policy intellectual framework remains embedded to a considerable degree in twentieth-century and Cold War thinking. The interconnectivity and interrelationships of the twenty-first century, products of the shift from a bipolar world to one of many conflicting and yet shared interests among a large number of engaged parties, have not been assimilated.

"We," meaning we Americans, too often allow outdated concepts to prevail when they no longer even apply. This was true of JFK and the flawed thinking that produced both the Bay of Pigs fiasco in April 1961 and a total misreading of Soviet intentions that led to the Cuban Missile Crisis. One of the most outdated concepts that survive in the twenty-first century is the twentieth-century view of deterrence, a view that no longer fits. Deterrence in this century is not solely dependent on the force of arms and the threat of thermonuclear war, the obliteration of society as we have known it. Deterrence instead depends on good ideas and sound strategic thinking, whether in dealing with a more aggressive (or frightened) Russia or with Islamist terrorists who have perverted a great religion to fit political aims. Obsolete concepts can be as dangerous as, or more dangerous than, an absence of concepts. Their absence, or ignorance generally, may at least constrain and limit engagement—a reluctance that would be far more prudent than action that ultimately is reckless and counterproductive.

Regarding the Islamic State, many nations—Russia, Iran, the other Gulf states, the European Union, Turkey, and the United States, among others—have a common interest in defeating that enemy. Yet many conflicting issues, such as over Ukraine, terrorism, radicalism, and Israel, are at play. As Lenin pithily observed, "There are contradictions, comrade." Indeed, resolving these contradictions over policy is akin (as in Syria) to untying many Gordian knots at the same time.

Third and last, policy outcomes must be achieved through affecting, influencing, and even controlling the will and perception of the target or adversary. That takes an appropriate, well resourced, and comprehensive strategy that makes use of *all* policy tools and is never overly reliant on military force as a surrogate for missing or fragile components of government. Also, that strategy must not rest on flawed assumptions or assumptions that have not been rigorously challenged. Too often slogans and sound bites have been allowed to masquerade as strategy. Consider two of these sound bites: "hybrid war" and the "global war on terror." This book will later explain that each of these sound bites is antithetical to sound strategic thinking, that each applies simplistic descriptions of very difficult and complex issues.

To be effective, policy must begin with identifying outcomes that can be realistically achieved and then proceed by linking means with ends and available resources. Too often the proposed outcomes are vague or unobtainable. Worse, the assumptions that lead to policy choices are often untested or not fully challenged, taken as truths instead of hypotheses. Vietnam, Iraq, Libya, and Afghanistan are tragic examples of the consequences of disregarding these basic tenets of strategic thinking.

It is the very telling of this story of repeated failures (and occasional successes) that is this study's central value and importance. Only through recognition that American actions and policies have too often been disastrous can any change occur. Recognition of the disease is the first step in curing it. Understanding what has succeeded illuminates the reasons for failure.

The dual themes of this book and its analysis are how failure to employ sound strategic thinking or derive comprehensive knowledge and understanding of the conditions where force may be used has proven fatal. This diagnosis may seem rather straightforward and uncomplicated, but as Albert Einstein suggested, solution to a difficult problem should be made as simple as possible (though no simpler).

Two

John Fitzgerald Kennedy, the USSR, and the Path to Vietnam

Robert Strange McNamara (RSM) and Harlan K. Ullman (HKU) at lunch in early 2000.

HKU: "Thanks for meeting with me again today."

RSM: "My pleasure. I know that we have disagreed in the past over Vietnam. In retrospect, at this stage, I think you were right. But that is history."

HKU: "Actually I wanted to talk about the Soviet Union and the Penkovsky Papers. These as you may remember were copies of the Soviet General Staff's top-secret publication called *Military Thought* that documented the great debate in the Soviet Union over nuclear strategy and how much was enough, from about 1959 to 1961. Oleg Penkovsky was a GRU/military intelligence colonel, discontented because he had not been promoted to general. He managed to microfilm these articles and got them to Britain's MI-6 through an agent posing as a journalist in Moscow, one Greville Wynne."

RSM: "Yes, I was aware of this material."

HKU: "It was obvious that Nikita Khrushchev had finally decided that an arms race with the West was draining the Soviet economy. Following Eisenhower's lead of adapting a strategy of 'massive retaliation' and reliance on nuclear weapons, which were less expensive than conventional forces, Khrushchev began cutting Soviet defense spending and of course the army. *Military Thought* presented this debate in real time, followed in due course by unclassified Russian journals publishing arguments on both sides of the debate."

RSM: "The CIA had this material. However, the conclusion was that this was disinformation. Jim Angleton [James Jesus Angleton, then head of counterintelligence] rejected the material for that reason."

HKU: "But we knew that Angleton was paranoid and like Dulles [Allen Dulles, then head of the CIA] was not prepared to analyze the Soviet Union objectively."

RSM: "We realized that after the Bay of Pigs. Dulles got fired, and Angleton was retired. However, that made no difference."

HKU: "What do you mean?"

RSM: "The president had decided that we were going to rearm and increase our forces dramatically. He ran on that promise and made good on it. It is why we basically doubled the size of our nuclear forces and then shifted to the strategy of "flexible response" so we could match the Russians at every level of conflict, from guerilla war up to nuclear. Strength was the only way to deter the Soviets, a lesson we all learned from Hitler and the run-up to World War II."

HKU: "Even though it was clear that Khrushchev was cutting his forces? Why did we ignore that? And even though Kennedy ran on a 'missile gap,' to the right of Nixon, when the missile gap was entirely in our favor?"

RSM: "As I said, it made no difference. President Kennedy had made up his mind. And while the 'missile gap' was not as bad as we thought, we were taking no chances and increasing our forces."

HKU: "Of course, no one would ever disagree with the president, even if that got us into Vietnam and perhaps extended the Cold War by a decade or more?"

RSM: "Don't forget. It was the generals who advised us on going ahead with the Bay of Pigs invasion and, of course, on increasing defense."

HKU: "And no one dissented from the generals, because they were agreeing in principle with what JFK wanted to do."

RSM: "Yes."

HKU: "Regrets?"

(Robert McNamara reversed his views on Vietnam twice before he died in 2009, first claiming responsibility and admitting failure and then arguing the opposite.)

✦

In his rousing inaugural address, delivered on January 20, 1961, John F. Kennedy promised "to pay any price and bear any burden" to protect and defend freedom and liberty. The new and young president's charisma was contagious. Camelot and the New Frontier took Washington by storm.

Even at the age of forty-three, Kennedy was widely perceived as having what was later called "the right stuff." Kennedy had been groomed and educated by his father, Joseph P. Kennedy, who himself had committed political suicide trying to convince President Franklin D. Roosevelt, as his ambassador in London, that Britain could not stand up to Hitler and that war was a foolish choice for America. The elder Kennedy would become a liability for FDR and be treated accordingly.

While at Harvard, the younger Kennedy had written *Why England Slept* as his senior thesis. His father had the thesis rewritten and published in 1940, and it sold some 80,000 copies. The book argued against appeasing Hitler. In many ways, the book was the cornerstone of Kennedy's later thinking that the Soviet Union and its tyranny had to be matched with force so as not to repeat the tragedy of the 1930s, the rise of Nazi Germany. When Kennedy became president, most of his cabinet and his advisors had served in World War II. All were supportive of his thesis that appeasement would ultimately fail. Kennedy regarded himself as the ultimate "Cold War warrior."

Planning for the Bay of Pigs invasion to overthrow Fidel Castro and his communist regime in Cuba began in late 1959 and early 1960, during the last year of the Eisenhower administration. The Guatemala coup in 1954, engineered by the CIA, had succeeded, and the shah had resumed, also with CIA "engineering," Iran's Peacock Throne the year before, when Prime Minister Mohammed Mossadegh had been overthrown in a coup. For these reasons, CIA director Allen Dulles and his deputy for operations, Richard Bissell, were highly confident that Castro could be removed by an invasion force of Cuban freedom fighters supported by CIA-paid mercenaries.

Eisenhower had been briefed on the final plan after the election, in which Kennedy had bested Ike's vice president, Richard Nixon, in a very close and hotly contested race. Kennedy had run to the right of Ike and Nixon in asserting that Eisenhower's "strategic new look" policy of reliance on nuclear deterrence and "massive retaliation" left the nation and the NATO alliance vulnerable to Soviet conventional forces. Kennedy also claimed, falsely, that a "missile gap" existed, that the United States was trailing far behind the Soviet Union.

While the Cuban invasion was in the final planning stages, first as Operation Pluto then as Operation Zapata, Kennedy sought immediate increases in defense spending, through several supplemental spending bills. Ultimately, U.S. strategic nuclear forces would be set at 1,054 intercontinental ballistic missiles (ICBMs), 41 Polaris missile submarines with a total of 656 missiles, and about 650 long-range bombers. Further, nuclear targeting would be centralized in the new SIOP, or Single Integrated Operational Plan, which coordinated American nuclear firepower among the 3 military services. In addition, the United States was fielding thousands of shorter-range or tactical nuclear weapons for its Army, Navy, and Air Force.

The service chiefs were calling for "more" nuclear armaments without providing a rationale for how much was enough. McNamara recognized the absence of reasoning to justify these increases. But what "analytical" proof could he offer to stem the appetite of his generals for more nuclear weapons? The answer, at the time, was none. So some measure was needed. If the United States could destroy about a third of the Soviet population and about half of its industrial capacity, McNamara arbitrarily assumed, the Soviet Union would be deterred from any aggression. He then produced a graph with "assured destruction" curves that flattened out at the force levels he believed were enough, meaning that inflicting more damage was not cost-effective and was thus unnecessary.

McNamara had concluded that with the budget and strategic weapons increases approved by JFK, the United States had more than enough nuclear forces. He did not want the services to request ever more money for systems he argued were unnecessary. Whether this argument was cynical or commonsensical remains debatable. Regardless, the strategy would become wrongly known as "MAD," for Mutual Assured Destruction, once the Soviets matched and then exceeded the United States in numbers of deliverable nuclear missile warheads. However, in 1961, no one had thought that far ahead. Nor did that thought process appear when McNamara gave his "no cities" speech in 1967. The argument McNamara made then was that the targets for U.S. strategic nuclear weapons should be the Soviet Strategic Rocket Forces, a view that ushered in the so-called damage-limitation strategy. This meant the first priority in the event of war was to destroy as much of the Soviet Union's nuclear force as possible, in order to "limit damage" to the United States and its allies.

On April 4, 1961, Kennedy was presented the final plan for Operation Zapata and the landing of about 1,400 CIA-trained Cuban exiles at the Bahía de Cochinos, or Bay of Pigs, later that month. The CIA and the Joint Chiefs assured Kennedy that the invasion would trigger a popular revolt in Cuba against Castro and his regime. Whether President Eisenhower concurred with the invasion or cautioned Kennedy about it, before and after leaving office, remains unclear.

On April 17, the invasion was launched. It was a disaster. Only U.S. airpower could rescue the landing force, now trapped and helpless, from the Cuban defenders. And there was doubt airpower would work. Despite pleas from the Cuban invading forces at the Bay of Pigs and their CIA mentors for air support, JFK determined to cut his losses. The invasion and exiles were abandoned. The Kennedy administration was humiliated. At the press conference immediately following the debacle, Kennedy remarked that success had many fathers while failure was always an orphan.

The Bay of Pigs and Kennedy's rearmament program to close a nonexistent missile gap forced a huge debate in the Soviet Union over Khrushchev's new defense strategy. The Soviets well understood that the United States was far ahead of Russia in both nuclear and conventional weapons; the Soviet military rightly complained that the United States had greatly increased its lead in defense capability. Khrushchev had already begun cuts in conventional forces in 1960, on the basis of Eisenhower's strategy of massive retaliation, which emphasized nuclear forces. However, the rush of the Kennedy administration to rearm was a direct and potentially fatal challenge to Khrushchev's plans. In October 1961, the Extraordinary XXII Party Conference was convened to reevaluate Soviet defense policy in light of the new American administration's muscular actions and very threatening increases in its military forces. This imbalance, the generals argued, could only be countered by reversing Khrushchev's defense spending cuts and greatly strengthening Soviet military power.

Khrushchev was put on the defensive. If resources were to continue to be shifted to the civilian sector and away from defense, Khrushchev needed a means to mollify his generals and respond to the rapidly growing gap between the military capabilities of the superpowers. The economy could not fund both the civilian and defense sectors.

This debate was duly reported in *Military Thought*, the top-secret publication of the Soviet General Staff. The relevant articles were microfilmed by Oleg Penkovsky and surreptitiously passed to British intelligence, which code-named the material the "Ironbark" files. The CIA was fully informed. Penkovsky would be caught. He would be executed for his treason—one story has it that Penkovsky was thrust alive into a blast furnace.

What would Khrushchev do? His bluster, such as in his January 1960 speech calling for "wars of national liberation," was directed against the Chinese, not the West. Khrushchev realized that policy statements alone would never check the new defense policies of the Kennedy administration or calm the generals. A shrewder alternative was needed. Khrushchev had intimidated, bullied, and badly frightened Kennedy at the Vienna summit in June 1961, over Berlin and Laos. There Khrushchev had threatened a separate peace with East Germany, which would have precipitated a crisis over the jointly occupied city of Berlin. The Soviet leader believed he had the measure of the young president, regarding Kennedy as highly inexperienced and very weak.

Khrushchev's strategic thinking was clear: How could the American advantages in strategic nuclear weapons be reversed and checked? His plan was brilliantly simple: deploy shorter-range Soviet nuclear missiles to Cuba. Once in place, these missiles would threaten the American East Coast. In a single move, the Soviet Union would have outflanked and neutralized the U.S. nuclear strategic advantages and thereby become less dependent on long-range missiles. Billions of rubles would be saved, and the shift to the civilian sector could proceed.

Khrushchev knew that the United States had stationed short-range Jupiter missiles in Turkey, virtually on the border with the USSR. The Soviet Union would be following suit, and that would make it impossible for Kennedy to object, especially if the Soviet missiles could be secretly deployed to Cuba and revealed as a fait accompli. Ironically, Kennedy had already ordered the Jupiters withdrawn from Turkey, a decision that the Defense Department had not implemented.

Khrushchev prevailed, and the plan was put in train. The Soviet Union began building missile sites in mid-1962. In September, U-2 overflights of Cuba photographed the sites. In October, the Cuban Missile Crisis exploded. The danger was clear and present.

If Khrushchev refused to remove the missiles, the unthinkable possibility of nuclear war was no longer unthinkable. Khrushchev was convinced, on the basis of the Vienna meeting, that even if Kennedy discovered the missile activities he would back down. Khrushchev could not have been more wrong in his understanding of how Kennedy would react.

The story of the Cuban Missile Crisis need not be repeated. A small group of advisors led by Robert F. "Bobby" Kennedy—called the "EXCOM," for executive committee—was formed. Kennedy's generals called for air strikes to destroy the missile sites. Particularly vocal was Gen. Curtis Lemay of the Air Force. But none of Kennedy's military leaders could guarantee, with 100 percent certainty, the elimination of all the missiles. Diplomacy won out. The solution came in the form of a naval blockade, purposely called a "quarantine," to prevent Soviet merchant ships from entering Cuba carrying, presumably, nuclear-related material. It was Khrushchev and not Kennedy who, in the words of Secretary of State Dean Rusk, blinked first. Caught in the act and not prepared to risk war given the significant advantages the United States enjoyed, Khrushchev had no alternative except to remove the missiles. The secret quid pro quo was agreement that the United States would never invade, threaten, or attack Cuba. Also, the United States would finally carry out the president's previously ignored order to remove Jupiter missiles from Turkey, without fanfare or public comment.

The missile crisis was universally perceived in the West as a significant victory for the Kennedy administration and for the president. In the Kremlin, this "hare-brained scheme" of Khrushchev's set the Politburo against him. Khrushchev was now on borrowed time. In November 1964, a palace "soft coup" replaced Khrushchev with Leonid Brezhnev. Worse for the West, the Soviet Union reversed direction on defense cuts, embarking on a major rearmament campaign that persisted until the USSR finally imploded a quarter of a century later.

Kennedy also sought a nuclear test ban, for environmental reasons more than the sake of disarmament. But another, disastrous problem was looming for Kennedy, Vietnam—and Vietnam would not proceed as smoothly as had the missile crisis. In late 1961, Kennedy had sent two trusted advisors to Vietnam: his deputy national security advisor, Walt Rostow, and Maxwell Taylor, a retired Army general. (Taylor would return to active duty and become Kennedy's chairman of the Joint Chiefs and ultimately ambassador to South Vietnam.) Rostow was optimistic about the war and that the United States and South Vietnam would defeat the insurgency. Taylor was far more pessimistic. As David Halberstam reports in *The Best and the Brightest*, when the advisors delivered these highly contradictory findings, Kennedy asked, "You two did visit the same country, didn't you?" Communism was asserting itself in Southeast Asia, and Laos was emerging as a crisis. The Vietcong were a growing threat to Saigon.

The United States had made modest investments toward supporting the South, beginning with the Eisenhower administration, which sent about seven hundred advisors to the Republic of South Vietnam in the mid-1950s. Since the Truman administration, American foreign policy had been based on George Kennan's theory of containing communism. In Southeast Asia, the fear of communist expansion was predicated on the so-called and very flawed domino theory—that if one country fell to communism, the rest would collapse as well, like dominoes. This was another slogan that did real damage.

In Europe, dominoes had indeed fallen, and an iron curtain had descended across Eastern Europe. The United States had begun creating alliances to surround and contain the Soviet Union. The first and most important was the North Atlantic Treaty Organization (NATO), founded in 1949. In 1955, the Southeast Asia Treaty Organization (SEATO) was formed to prevent further communist expansion in the region. By the time Kennedy came to office, however, the effort to check communism in Southeast Asia was floundering.

In South Vietnam, the government of Ngo Dinh Diem was failing. Diem was a Catholic in a Buddhist country, a nation rife with corruption and religious differences. Successes by Vietcong guerrillas mounted. Public protests over Diem's repression of Buddhists threatened the viability of his rule. To support the increasingly embattled Diem, Kennedy accelerated the flow of aid and gradually increased American military advisors to more than 16,000 by 1963. Nevertheless, and despite demands that Diem reform and curtail corruption, little positive action occurred, and the political and military situations continued to deteriorate.

In June 1963, a Buddhist monk set himself afire in protest. Diem's sister-in-law, Madame Nhu Tran Le Xuan, callously remarked that if "the Buddhists wanted another barbeque, I would provide the gasoline." Meanwhile, the South Vietnamese military, led by Gen. Duong Van "Big" Minh, realized that Diem could no longer govern the nation. A coup was needed, and the army began planning one. The CIA and Washington were aware of the plot. Kennedy gave tacit approval to the plotters; the United States had no other option or any means to thwart a coup. From the beginning, the intent of the coup was only to remove, not assassinate, the president.

In September 1963, a frustrated President Kennedy declared in an interview with Walter Cronkite on Vietnam that

> in the final analysis, it is their war [the South Vietnamese]. They are the ones who have to win it or lose it. We can help them, we can give them equipment, we can send our men out there as advisors, but they have to win it, the people of Vietnam, against the Communists. . . . But I don't agree with those who say we should withdraw. That would be a great mistake. . . . We made this effort to defend Europe. Now Europe is quite secure. We also have to participate—we may not like it—in the defense of Asia.

On November 1, 1963, the coup was launched. In the confusion, Diem was killed. Big Minh became the first of a long line of generals and one air marshal to run the country. Unsurprisingly but unfairly, much of blame for the coup and Diem's death was shifted to Washington. Three weeks later to the day, Kennedy was murdered in Dallas.

The disastrous Bay of Pigs invasion, the Cuban Missile Crisis, and the ousting of Diem were all marked by unsound strategic thinking and insufficient understanding of the situation. Kennedy and his generation were very much products of the Great Depression and World War II. A wholesome naiveté persisted in which good would trump evil, as manifested in that war. Americans very much regarded themselves as "the good guys," as if in a Hollywood western.

Despite the isolationist views that had sprung up in the interwar years and dominated U.S. foreign policy for much of that period, American idealism would in the future shape much of the foreign-policy thinking. This idealism led to groupthink in the belief that politics notionally ended at "the water's edge," when they did not. Groupthink concluded that the Soviet Union was simply a new version of the fascism and authoritarianism that had erupted in World War II.

Kennedy's cabinet was refreshingly bipartisan. Dean Rusk, secretary of state; Republicans Robert McNamara, secretary of defense, and Douglas Dillon, secretary of the treasury; Stuart Udall, secretary of the interior; J. Edward Day, postmaster general; and Orville Freeman, secretary of agriculture—all had served in the military during World War II, many in combat. Thus, it was not surprising that similar rather than diverse views were brought into the White House regarding the Soviet Union.

Trust in government was real. During the Cuban Missile Crisis, Kennedy dispatched to French president Charles de Gaulle photographic evidence of Soviet systems in Cuba. De Gaulle dismissed any need to see the evidence, saying he trusted the word of the American president. Americans took pride in the democratic process. Cynicism and despair were as yet only latent; while social conditions, including segregation, were often despicable, a sense of domestic crisis was only just forming. Similarly, the military was popular. Ike had been an admired leader. Kennedy's generals and admirals had distinguished wartime records. Their views were respected and accepted even when it turned out they were wrong.

Third, the tendency to "mirror-image"—that is, to see others as we see ourselves—was commonplace. As the distinguished Harvard academic Stanley Hoffmann has expressed it, we believed others should think strategically as we do or be brought up to our level. Hence, when the CIA brought forward its Operation Zapata, both Dulles and Bissell had (undeserved) reputations for success. In hindsight, much of the coup plotting of the Eisenhower years to counter the Soviets had unexpected and sometimes tragic results. But no one was prepared to challenge the establishment.

Meanwhile, the CIA leadership exaggerated what it thought were past successes but were not. The Bay of Pigs would be modeled after what happened in Iran in 1953 and the overthrows in Iran and Guatemala the next year. No "red teaming" took place. The experts must have got it right. Otherwise they were not experts. As a result, the Bay of Pigs went forward on the basis of assumptions that were as flawed as those underlying Hitler's decision to invade Russia or Japan's to attack Pearl Harbor.

Similarly, Kennedy's Cold War–warrior ideology led to blunting Soviet ambitions with raw military power in order to close a missile gap that did not exist. Ideology had replaced sound strategic thinking. Worse, this unsound strategic thinking and reliance on ideology heralded what would happen forty years later, in the decision to invade Iraq in response to weapons of mass destruction that did not exist.

The Kennedy administration ignored the intelligence available in the Penkovsky Papers in part because the counterintelligence chief, James Jesus Angleton, was paranoid and distrusted everything. But it did so largely because Kennedy, as McNamara would recall, had campaigned on the promise to rebuild defense. Facts and the evidence made little difference. Ideology and preconceived notions prevailed. Those flaws have persisted.

Kennedy's rearmament and Khrushchev's response collided, creating the Cuban Missile Crisis. Yes, that crisis was a tactical political victory for the United States. Strategically, it probably extended the Cold War for years. On one hand, one could argue that the Soviet decision to reverse Khrushchev's minimum-deterrent thinking and pour billions into defense ultimately bankrupted the country and caused it to collapse. Yet, on the other hand, if Kennedy had understood Khrushchev's strategy and rationale, had not run on a nonexistent missile gap, and had chosen to ignore the exiles' plans to invade Cuba, perhaps the long-term result would have been for the better.

Ignorance, in the form of a lack of knowledge and understanding, is not an excuse for failure, and it is anathema to achieving success. That failure further trapped us in Vietnam. Whether or not Kennedy would have escalated the Vietnam War as his successor did is unknowable. However, increasing advisors to 16,000 from under a thousand, tacitly supporting the coup against Diem, and believing the "domino theory" all suggest JFK would not have ended that commitment to Southeast Asia. In any case, JFK was not one to challenge the basic assumptions on which his policy decisions rested.

As in the Cuban Missile Crisis and in its dealings with the Soviet Union, and despite its experienced diplomats and insightful academics, America has been plagued by an absence of cultural intelligence. The White House was profoundly wrong in predicting Castro's and the Cuban people's reaction to the Bay of Pigs invasion. American leaders believed Russians and others thought like them and that American strategic thinking had a universal appeal—which it certainly did not. Similarly, Americans were ignorant of Vietnam, the weaknesses of the South, and the persistence of the North. Common failures of understanding would be repeated over the next fifty or more years. The lingering question and answer from the Kennedy years is, Why have we not learned? For we have not.

Similarly, borders do not limit the need for sound strategic thinking and full understanding of issues. Khrushchev's concept to outflank American strategic nuclear superiority was clever, if not ingenious. But it failed, because Khrushchev completely underestimated Kennedy and the ability of the United States to detect the construction of the sites before they became operational. Personalities count, and leaders can never forget that in making judgments.

Three

Lyndon Baines Johnson and the Vietnam Catastrophe, Richard Milhous Nixon, and James Earl Carter

The Family Quarters, the White House, March 1967.

President Lyndon Johnson was increasingly distressed by the state of the war in South Vietnam. Casualties were growing. The North remained intransigent despite the expanded bombing campaign called Rolling Thunder. Over half a million American soldiers, Marines, and sailors would be sent to Vietnam, the total reaching 550,000 in 1968.

To comfort himself, Johnson asked the secretary of defense to invite four young officers, representing each service, to the White House, where Johnson would engage them in a conversation about the war. McNamara directed the chairman of the Joint Chiefs of Staff, Gen. Earle G. "Buzz" Wheeler, U.S. Army, to follow up. He in turn passed the request to Gen. William Westmoreland, commander, U.S. Forces Vietnam, who then ordered one of his many assistants to comply.

On a cool evening in March, three young officers entered the West Wing of the White House in khaki uniforms. Speculation was that the fourth officer had been killed in action. In fact, however, the young Army captain had gotten drunk in Saigon, where he had been given a special three-day R & R in preparation for this meeting.

With Johnson were his defense and state secretaries, Robert McNamara and Dean Rusk; General Wheeler, chairman of the Joint Chiefs; Walt Rostow, national security advisor; and half a dozen senior civilian and military aides.

Johnson ushered the three into the spacious living room of the family quarters, which few outsiders see, shook their hands vigorously, and bade them take their seats.

LBJ: "I am delighted and honored to meet with you. You are the best of the best, and when we finish this conversation, I have some medals to award you that you sorely deserve. But I want this to be a candid conversation, boys. As we say in Texas, 'This is a no bullshit zone.'"

Johnson turned to one of the three, a naval officer. "We last met at the Naval Academy several years ago, didn't we? I recall I gave you your diploma as a distinguished grad." Johnson's staffers had done their homework.

"Yes sir, Mr. President, you indeed gave me my diploma. It was an honor."

LBJ: "Ok, let's cut to the chase."

The three young officers looked at each other, wondering how candid "candid" meant. The naval officer had no doubts.

"Mr. President, I take your word about no bullshit. Mr. President, in Texas terms, we are getting the shit kicked out of us in Vietnam. No matter what you are being told, the other side is tough, capable, and will not quit. We have two choices . . ." The naval officer paused, glancing at the senior advisors around the president, their expressions fixed and glaring.

"Mr. President we can get out or get in—that means taking the fight to the other side, blockading Haiphong and the other ports, and sending an amphibious force to land around Vinh [a city midway up the coast of North

Vietnam] cutting that country in half. That and only that will force Hanoi to quit or negotiate."

Johnson swallowed hard. The two other officers looked at their brown shoes, uncertain how the president, with his notoriously short temper, would react. Johnson got up and put his arm around the naval officer. Then, for the next hour, he and his staff tried to explain to the trio why the strategy would work and why the United States would win. None were convinced.

Years later, Robert McNamara and I recalled that meeting. He asked if I ever heard Johnson's reaction. I said no. Smiling, McNamara said that after we junior officers were escorted out of the family quarters, Johnson turned to one of his trusted aides and complained, "Why the fuck did I think that would work?"

✦

Lyndon Baines Johnson became the thirty-sixth president of the United States on board Air Force One at Love Field in Dallas, Texas, hours after Jack Kennedy was murdered on November 22, 1963, in Dealey Plaza. Johnson was just fifty-four years old.

If anyone was ever prepared for the presidency, it was Johnson. Elected to the House of Representatives from Texas in 1937 (in a vote he barely won, earning him the nickname "Landslide Johnson"), he moved to the Senate in 1949. Before becoming vice president in 1961, LBJ spent six years as majority leader. Called by biographer Robert Caro the "master of the Senate," Johnson was a very powerful and effective leader and legislator.

Johnson served during World War II in the Navy, where he was awarded the Silver Star, the nation's third-highest decoration for valor. He was, notably, the only one on the mission in question, in which he acted as an observer, to be so decorated. For years he always wore the miniature bar connoting a Silver Star on his left jacket lapel. His many critics and opponents always questioned the validity of the award.

Johnson's major domestic successes were huge ones, including Great Society legislation and the Equal Rights bill, which would turn into the Voting Rights Acts of 1964 and 1965. Johnson was an unexpected champion of the poor, the disadvantaged, and of minorities. Had it not been for Vietnam, Johnson arguably could have been one of America's greatest presidents. He certainly was, regarding domestic policy.

In Vietnam, however, conditions had not improved with the accession of Gen. Big Minh to the presidency. Throughout the first half of 1964, Johnson was receiving reports from MACV (Military Assistance Command Vietnam) in Saigon calling for greater American involvement and engagement. Then, on August 2, the Navy destroyer USS *Maddox* (DD 731), off the North Vietnamese coast as part of an intelligence and surveillance operation called the DESOTO (DeHaven Special Operations off TsingtaO) patrol, was attacked by at least four North Vietnamese torpedo boats.

Maddox engaged them, firing nearly three hundred five-inch rounds of ammunition. About fifteen minutes after *Maddox* radioed for help, F-8 Crusaders from the carrier USS *Bonhomme Richard* (CV 31) attacked the retreating North Vietnamese PT boats. Kept secret at the time were a series of attacks against the North by the South Vietnamese in cooperation with the CIA, under a covert program called "Operation 34-A." Clearly, and as later was revealed, the local North Vietnamese commander mistook *Maddox* for a participant in a 34-A raid then in progress nearby.

Two days later, *Maddox,* in concert with a second destroyer, USS *Turner Joy* (DD 951), back on patrol, radioed that they were under attack. But that attack never took place. Probably unaware of the proximity of and confusion with 34-A attacks, Johnson and his administration readily and uncritically believed the reports. This was the opportunity Johnson had been seeking to escalate the war against the North and so force Hanoi to the bargaining table.

With only two dissenting votes, Congress passed the Gulf of Tonkin Resolution, authorization for the president to take whatever action he believed was in the national interest in Vietnam—in essence, a de facto act of war. That resolution would lead to a decade-long involvement in Vietnam that cost 58,000 American lives and those of hundreds of thousands, if not millions, of Vietnamese.

In January 1968, North Vietnam and its Vietcong allies launched the massive Tet Offensive against and across the South. By any military measure, the month-long battle was decidedly won by U.S. and South Vietnamese forces. However, Tet was decisively lost in the living rooms of America: television-news icon Walter Cronkite declared the war lost. Several months later, Johnson, distraught over the war, would irrevocably remove himself as a candidate for president. Five years later, in 1973, Johnson was dead, no doubt a victim of that war.

Why the United States and its South Vietnamese allies lost has been analyzed to excess. Clearly, Vietnam was a war that Washington chose to escalate on the basis of an incident that never took place—a situation that would repeat in 2003. Escalation was tantamount to starting a war in that it turned a limited engagement into a full-scale conflict. But America was never actually prepared to escalate its commitment or take the risks necessary for winning this war.

The reasons why America would fail in Vietnam were obvious both before the escalation and after it was clear that the war would be lost. Had strategic thinking been judiciously applied in 1964, the outcome might have been different. Of course, given that Johnson was running against the more conservative Barry Goldwater that year, one could cynically argue that resolve, in the form of a strong response to a North Vietnamese "surprise attack," neutralized some of the senator's appeal to the right wing. But few analysts have referred to the election as a reason for Johnson's immediate action to request the resolution and escalate the war.

As for understanding why America would fail: in the first place, the "domino theory" and the corollary that the communists reasoned as we do and thus would defer to this gradual escalation were entirely wrong. If America lost on the Mekong, we would not be fighting, as LBJ predicted, "on the Mississippi." There was no master plot invented by and run from Moscow in which the Soviet Union and the Maoist government in Red China could defeat the United States. The Sino-Soviet schism that Kennedy's second national security advisor, Walt Rostow, had predicted in *The Prospects for Communist China* was ignored. Nor was the historical rivalry between Vietnam and China ever taken into account.

The combined absence of both knowledge and understanding was fatal. The American leadership never comprehended that the battle in the South was more than a single civil war fought between Saigon and Hanoi. The National Liberation Front (NLF), or Viet-cong, sought to overthrow the current government in the South but not necessarily to unite it with the North. The North understood that it could seduce the NLF and then dispense with it. The Tet Offensive destroyed much of the NLF's capacity and leadership, allowing the North ultimately to invade the South with a conventional army and unite the country.

The American leadership believed that superior weaponry and technology could overcome a relatively primitive and unsophisticated enemy. The United States had huge firepower superiority in every conventional category. Only, Vietnam was not a conventional war. After the battle in the Ia Drang Valley in late 1965, Gen. Vo Nguyen Giap created a "hug the belt" strategy in which North Vietnamese forces operated in such proximity to American forces as to neutralize the latter's superiority in airpower and artillery by raising the risk of causing American casualties in friendly-fire incidents.

The United States attempted to quantify victory. Hence, the dreaded body count became the metric of success. The United States could never kill its way to victory. Furthermore, the United States did not fight only one war. Because tours of duty were limited to twelve or thirteen months, personnel rotation meant that multiple wars were being waged, on a twelve-to-thirteen-month basis—something that never happened during World War II, when service personnel fought "for the duration." Also, the American command-and-control arrangements in Vietnam were often operationally irrational.

The United States had three or four different armies in the field, four air forces, and an independent operation, in the form of the CIA. The Marine Corps was assigned I Corps in the northern quarter of the country; the Army had the remaining three-quarters, including the Delta, where Marine amphibious capability would have been far better suited. The Vietnamese army was reinforced by local and regional and popular forces (RF/PF). The CIA employed large numbers of mercenaries, especially in Operation Phoenix, discussed earlier.

In addition to the South Vietnamese air force, the U.S. Army, Air Force, Navy, and Marine Corps had their own air forces, operating largely independently in assigned geographic areas, to prevent "blue on blue" engagements and friendly-fire casualties and to give individual services maximum flexibility in fighting their respective wars. There was no single, coherent, integrated American air campaign plan. While operating out of Danang and the Cua Vet River in northern I Corps, Swift Boats regarded as a major threat the U.S. Air Force, which occasionally strafed U.S. Navy and Coast Guard units misidentified as North Vietnamese patrol boats. But the fundamental miscalculation was failure to understand the staying power of the North Vietnamese and their commitment to unifying the country. The United States also failed to heed the famous Chinese military strategist Sun Tzu, who, writing two and a half millennia ago, argued that the best strategy was to defeat the enemy's strategy.

That is precisely what North Vietnam, under Ho Chi Minh's leadership, did. The North planned to win by not losing. Hanoi appreciated that outlasting the Americans was the key to victory. At some stage, American support of the war would fade. As a North Vietnamese general famously told his American opposite numbers at one of the Geneva conferences on ending the war, "You won every battle and we won the war!"

The conclusions are clear. First, know your enemy and his strategy. We did not. Second, do not let ideology, mirror-imaging, or conflation of tactical success and strategic victory obscure judgment. Do not allow intelligence to be distorted either to reflect groupthink or serve political expediency. Ruthless objectivity and questioning of basic assumptions are essential.

Third, cultural intelligence is prerequisite for success. Unless or until the United States better understands the cultures and perceptions of friends and adversaries, success in foreign policy or war will be achieved only by luck. This warning applies to intelligence. The United States was taught that again in 2003: just as the second Tonkin Gulf attack never took place, Iraq did not possess weapons of mass destruction. Belief that the North could never sustain the losses and casualties from the bombings was dead wrong.

A subset is cultural arrogance. Many in the White House and the military could not believe that the physically small Vietnamese could defeat the much larger and stronger American fighting man. Also, the force of will counts most—it does not require huge strength to pull a trigger, set a punji spike, or activate a mine.

Fourth, do not allow technological superiority to dominate strategy or produce optimistic assessments that in reality are wrong.

Finally, the organization and command and control of U.S. forces, which involve all arms of government, remain too ambiguous today. Part of this problem rests in the National Security Act of 1947 as amended, which does not reflect the twenty-first century and surely did not contribute to success in Vietnam. Keeping agencies separate and "stovepiped" is a prescription for failure.

Lessons of Vietnam still apply. The more a whole-of-government approach is impeded by bureaucratic organization, the more difficult, if not impossible, achieving success becomes. The conclusion from Vietnam is brutally simple—we lost, they won. And we started it.

◆

Richard M. Nixon assumed office on January 20, 1969. Nixon was uniquely qualified for the office. Elected to the House and then the Senate, Nixon had served as vice president under Dwight Eisenhower for eight years. Losing both the presidential election of 1960 and that for the California governorship in 1962, Nixon understood and learned from defeat.

In 1968, Nixon ran against Lyndon Johnson's vice president, Hubert Humphrey, and a much divided Democratic Party. The party had been almost ripped asunder by the assassination of Robert Kennedy earlier that year and by its disastrous Chicago convention, accompanied by substantial riots and protests. Nixon promised that he had a "secret plan" to end the Vietnam War, a war that had become hugely unpopular with a large majority of the American public. In fact, Nixon had no secret plan. He did, however, have better ideas for dealing with the Soviet Union and China.

Nixon was to be bitterly criticized for expanding the Vietnam War into Laos and Cambodia—the "secret war." Nixon's view was that the North Vietnamese had unobstructed use of the Ho Chi Minh Trail, which meandered through Cambodia. Nixon's plan was to cut off that route. Of course, the domestic reaction to the Cambodian incursion was explosive, and it was vastly intensified by the Kent State massacre in May 1970. There, Ohio State National Guardsmen panicked and opened fire on students protesting the war, killing four and wounding nine. The combination subjected the Nixon administration to blistering attacks. Domestic opposition to the war grew, and casualties in Vietnam mounted. Nixon's "secret plan" morphed into Vietnamization—that is, turning the war over to our allies in Saigon and reducing our presence.

One sad conclusion is that "secret wars" and "secret plans" do not always work. Often, security withstanding, transparency (or at least honesty) is critical. One wonders if President Trump's advisors who believe the media are the "opposition" understand this.

The brilliance of Nixon's foreign policy lay in the pivot to China. Using the rift between Beijing and Moscow as strategic leverage to improve relations with both, Nixon gambled that the two erstwhile enemies could help the United States extricate itself from Vietnam. One achievement of Nixon's triangular politics would be a pair of historic 1972 arms control agreements with the Soviets. The Anti-Ballistic Missile (ABM) Treaty limited defensive weapons, and the Strategic Arms Limitation Talks (SALT) executive agreement capped the number of offensive warheads both sides could maintain. But prior to that, Nixon made the historic trip to China in early 1972.

Nixon had charged his national security advisor, Henry Kissinger, to be his secret negotiator with Moscow and Beijing. Kissinger's intellect and sophistication, largely shaped by his European heritage, were vital in establishing relationships with Leonid Brezhnev and the Kremlin leadership and with Mao and the Chinese. By late 1971 both parts of the plan were working.

Only Nixon—the fierce anticommunist—could have pulled off a reconciliation with China. A Democrat or liberal Republican would have been savaged by the right wing. But Nixon's credentials were so strong as to inoculate him against right-wing criticism. The Strategic Arms Limitation Talks with Moscow were nearing conclusion. Meanwhile, the North Vietnamese were well aware of Nixon's triangular diplomacy and the pending February 1972 visit to Beijing.

Hanoi was completing plans for what would be called the "Easter Offensive," also known in Vietnamese as the "red fiery summer." On March 30, 1972, the North sent about 300,000 PAVN (People's Army of Vietnam) troops in a massive conventional assault on the South. Hanoi had no intention of conquering the South at that stage but only to weaken it as much as possible, convince the American public that the war could not be won, and strengthen Hanoi's negotiating position at Geneva.

Nixon, betting that Moscow needed the arms agreements more than the support of North Vietnam, ordered Operation Linebacker I—an equally massive plan to blunt and reverse the Easter Offensive, largely through air- and sea power —and the mining of Haiphong Harbor, to prevent resupply by sea. His bet was sound. In May, Nixon traveled to Moscow, where he signed the ABM Treaty, which limited both sides to two launcher sites, and an executive agreement to limit offensive warheads. The ABM Treaty would be approved by the Senate; the "executive agreement" format for nuclear arms reductions was purposely used to avoid a Senate vote. The agreement could have been controversial and might not have received the needed two-thirds majority.

The Easter Offensive continued until mid-October, when the badly bloodied North Vietnamese finally withdrew from the South. Having achieved the opening to China and the arms pacts with Russia and halted the North Vietnamese offensive, Nixon rode to an electoral landslide in the November elections, overwhelming Senator George McGovern. To prod negotiations in Geneva and secure the release of American prisoners of war held by Hanoi, Nixon authorized the "Christmas bombing" of 1972. Despite widespread protests in America, Hanoi blinked, and the Geneva agreements were signed in early 1973.

During these foreign-policy successes, however, a cancer threatened the presidency. On May 17, 1972, the Washington, D.C., police arrested five men attempting to break into the Democratic National Committee headquarters in the Watergate Hotel. That burglary and subsequent cover-up would explode into congressional hearings the next year. These hearings ultimately would end the Nixon administration. Nixon's administration had indeed broken the law and abused its power by covering up these criminal activities. Nixon would be forced to resign in August 1974, by when it was clear that Congress would impeach him and the Senate would convict him. His vice president, Gerald Ford, who had replaced the disgraced Spiro Agnew (who had resigned in 1973), assumed the presidency.

Before Nixon was forced to resign, however, the October 1973 War of Atonement, or Yom Kippur War (marking Judaism's most sacred holiday), brought the United States and Russia to a crisis level not seen since Cuba in 1962. Egypt and other Arab states had preemptively attacked Israel. The Egyptian army crossed the Suez Canal into Sinai, which had been occupied by Israel since the 1967 war. In a second front, the Syrian army threatened to cut Israel in two in the north by attacking through Kunitra, just south of the Golan Heights. Weary of expensively mobilizing its army on threat warnings that proved wrong, Israel had stood down and was taken by surprise.

In fierce fighting in the Sinai, Israeli forces counterattacked bravely but without air cover and were repulsed by the Egyptians. A bold Israeli brigadier, Uri Uri, leading a tank assault against superior numbers, checked the Syrian assault in the north. Israel finally stabilized the overall battle. In large measure, this was due to a massive air resupply of ammunition, weapons, and aviation fuel by the United States. (The chairman of the U.S. Joint Chiefs, then Adm. Thomas H. Moorer, later told me, when he was my suitemate at the Center for Strategic and International Studies, that for every gallon of gasoline that reached Israel, it took seven or eight gallons to fuel the air transports.) Soon the battle reversed.

Rumors of an unstable Nixon, beset by the pressures of Watergate, circulated. Secretary of Defense James R. Schlesinger became so concerned about Nixon's mental condition that he informed the military that any and all orders from the White House would be directed through him, as the second most senior official in the chain of command specified by the Unified Command Plan.

Nixon ordered the setting of DefCon 3 (that is, raising the nation's "defense condition," or preparation for conflict, up two levels from the peacetime DefCon 5)—a signal to the Soviets not to intervene in the conflict. Moscow did not intervene, in part because Egyptian president Anwar Sadat had ejected some 25,000 Russian troops from the country that summer and Moscow now had few forces nearby that it could use. The war ended days later, expedited by Kissinger's shuttle diplomacy. While it appeared that Egypt and Syria had been defeated by Israel at the last moment, Sadat's strategy had been brilliant. By sending forces into the occupied Sinai to seize occupied Egyptian territory, Sadat had sown the seed of an ultimate reconciliation between Cairo and Jerusalem and a peace treaty that still stands today.

Nixon and his principal aide, Kissinger, had wrought remarkable achievements vis-à-vis China and the Soviet Union. Both men understood global politics and were well versed in history. Both were experienced. And both had the sophistication to carry out a well-thought-out but risky strategy. The same cannot be said about the secret plan to end the Vietnam War.

No matter who won the 1968 election, rectifying the tragic errors that had led to the Vietnam debacle was politically impossible. No one would have been prepared to consider escalating the war to the extent of invading and mining the North. Nixon reasoned that a delaying action in Vietnam was essential to his strategy toward China and the Soviet Union. Had he in January 1969 launched Linebacker I, mined Haiphong, and initiated a more intense air campaign in the North, Hanoi could conceivably have been forced to the peace table.

But would the American public have been behind him? After Tet 1968, rejection of the war by Walter Cronkite, and LBJ's decision not to seek reelection, taking more radical steps in Vietnam would be a political bridge too far. That said, many more Americans would be killed during Nixon's watch, as well as greater numbers of Vietnamese.

As for Nixon himself, he surely was adept at strategic thinking. Character flaws and an acute sense of inferiority were personality disorders, and they would prove fatal to his presidency. It is not that Nixon started wars, notwithstanding his expansion of the Vietnam conflict. The tragedy is that it had been in his power to end the war much sooner. That did not happen, as Nixon believed a withdrawal would have destroyed U.S. credibility with both China and the Soviet Union. However, if Nixon applied the motto of Britain's Special Air Service—"Who dares wins"—to Vietnam, as he did to China and Russia, perhaps that war might have been terminated much earlier and on better terms

◆

The White House West Wing basement and the Office of the Deputy National Security Advisor (DNSA), June 1977.

DNSA: "You know that we are interviewing for the National Security Council Staff."

HKU: "Yes."

DNSA: "Do you think you are qualified?"

HKU: "Qualified for what? Is there a specific position or assignment that is open?"

DNSA: "We are not sure yet. We are just interviewing people."

HKU: "I see. Well, I have huge respect for your boss, Zbigniew Brzezinski."

DNSA: "Do you know him?"

HKU: "No, but we have met once or twice."

DNSA: "What do you think of him?"

HKU: "He has one of the most brilliant and well-informed minds in the business. He is not always correct. But his views must be listened to."

DNSA: "How so? Where do you disagree?"

HKU: "Dr. Brzezinski brilliantly argued that convergence would draw the East and West closer as the Soviet Union had to reform and modernize. He was absolutely correct about the need for the Soviet Union to reform. But that could cut both ways. I always thought that any autocratic system, and especially one as dysfunctional as Russia's, was brittle.

"And I also disagree with our strategy—not necessarily Dr. Brzezinski's—that if war came, it would be a replay of World War II but in Central Europe. War in the minds of the Soviet General Staff would be a fight to the finish, to use their language. And nuclear weapons almost certainly would be used. The West refuses to accept that proposition and insists war could be contained on the conventional level.

"The good news is that I don't believe Brezhnev and the Politburo want war any more than we do, and we need to do more to push a smart détente on our terms— something that post-Nixon, -Watergate, and -Vietnam will be exceedingly tough."

DNSA: "I see. Let me take that aboard and move on. We are in the process of redefining the NSC. Do you have any ideas?"

HKU: "Yes, but I am very much a creature of the Vietnam War and the incredibly stupid way we fought it and were organized for it. You know this was the most stovepiped war in history, with each of the services given a little bit of responsibility and no one in charge. The same was true for the CIA."

DNSA: "You know that we have put Admiral [Stansfield] Turner in charge of the CIA."

HKU: "Yes. I know the admiral and had a lot to do with him when he was assigned by Admiral [Elmo] Zumwalt as president of the Naval War College in Newport [Rhode Island] in 1972 or '73, while I was at graduate school at Fletcher."

DNSA: "What did you think?"

HKU: "Turner revolutionized and modernized Newport. The only objection I had was that he stopped the curriculum at the end of World War II, thinking that Vietnam was still too emotional for the students. I disagreed. Because it was so emotional and current, it needed to be part of the program, at least so that we do not recreate those blunders."

DNSA: "Would you like to work here?"

HKU: "I cannot answer that. It is always a privilege to work directly for or close to a president. But I would need to know what my responsibilities and authorities were. I would also need to meet with Dr. Brzezinski. I am a bit worried that the president hasn't spent much time in politics and national security—what, four years in the Georgia senate and four years as governor. Plus, as a Naval Academy graduate myself, I am not sure that school is the best background for a president. Being selected for nuclear training, as the president was, can be a bit intellectually constraining, especially with Admiral Rickover exercising such micromanagement as a mentor. You know the president. What do you think?"

DNSA: "I think we will get back to you. Thanks for coming in."

No one ever got back to me.

✦

Jimmy Carter, the nation's thirty-ninth president, was raised in rural Georgia. After attending local colleges, he entered the Naval Academy, graduating with the class of 1946. A future chairman of the Joint Chiefs, William Crowe, and a future CIA director, Stansfield

Turner, were classmates. Carter went into submarines and eventually was selected for nuclear-power training under the watchful eye of Adm. Hyman Rickover, director of Navy Nuclear Reactors. Carter regarded Rickover as one of his major influences, outside his parents. But after Carter entered nuclear training in March 1956, his father died, and Carter with his wife Rosalynn and their three children returned to Plains, Georgia, and the family peanut farm.

It was tough living, and the Carter family was forced to seek public housing. However, Carter improved his lot economically and was able to serve two terms as a Georgia state senator, from 1963 to 1967. Four years later, he won the governorship of Georgia, serving until 1975, after which he would be nominated as the Democratic Party's candidate for president, winning a close election against Gerald Ford in 1976.

Washington and the United States were not happy places in 1976. Vietnam, Watergate, the energy crisis, and double-digit interest and inflation rates had stricken the country. The mood was sour. Internationally, the Soviet Union appeared to be on the ascent. These were tough times to be president. Carter promised that as president he would never lie to the nation. He was anxious to establish a clean slate after Watergate and Vietnam. On his second day in office, he pardoned all of the Vietnam draft evaders, which did not please Americans still embittered over the war. His National Security Council (NSC), under the impressive intellectual leadership of Dr. Zbigniew Brzezinski, began laying out the new national security approach.

Carter was going to reverse the interventionist years of Eisenhower and Kennedy and undo the damage of Vietnam and Watergate. He wanted to reduce defense spending and engage the Soviet Union, both competitively and in reducing tensions, as well as limiting arms races. On August 26, 1977, he signed out his top-secret national security strategy, PD/NSC 18. (PD stood for "presidential directive.")

- Counterbalance, together with our allies and friends, by a combination of military forces, political efforts, and economic programs, Soviet military power and adverse influence in key areas, particularly Europe, the Middle East, and East Asia.

- Compete politically with the Soviet Union by pursuing the basic American commitment to human rights and national independence.
- Seek Soviet cooperation in resolving regional conflicts and reducing areas of tension that could lead to confrontation between the United States and the Soviet Union.
- Advance American security interests through negotiations with the Soviet Union of adequately verifiable arms control and disarmament agreements that enhance stability and curb arms competition.
- Seek to involve the Soviet Union constructively in global activities, such as economic and social developments and peaceful nonstrategic trade.

In the same document, Carter called for reducing and ending U.S. presence on the Korean Peninsula and for about 3 percent annual real growth in defense spending, both for America and its NATO allies. Carter would also issue documents to begin negotiations to return the Panama Canal to Panama. These initiatives would meet strong opposition.

Unfortunately, Carter and his policies were perceived as representing an American retreat and retrenchment from foreign affairs and the nation's position as the leader of the free world. No doubt, Carter was an internationalist. But his policies and aims were ambivalent regarding the Soviet Union. Arguing for negotiation and engagement with Moscow, on the one hand, while challenging Russia over its influence abroad and its disregard for human rights, on the other, was an inherent contradiction. Such policies required more than the usual deft diplomacy and sophistication, qualities that could not be invented out of thin air. Reconciling the inherent contradictions would prove impossible.

Carter did not, however, fall into the trap of starting wars. He engineered the Camp David Accords, securing peace between Israel and Egypt, a diplomatic triumph for which he deservedly won the Nobel Peace Prize. He also entered into SALT II negotiations with Russia. However, the negotiations over returning the Panama Canal and withdrawing U.S. forces from South Korea were extremely controversial. Carter abandoned the idea of exiting Korea.

By 1979, Carter was seen as weak both at home and abroad. He reshuffled his cabinet early that year. And late 1979 would prove disastrous for the president. On November 4, 1979, Iranian so-called students stormed and occupied the American embassy in Tehran; 54 hostages were seized and held in captivity for what would be 444 days. On Christmas Day 1979, Soviet troops rolled into Afghanistan. Carter was in political shock, admitting he had not believed that Moscow would invade Afghanistan.

The preference for negotiation and compromise with the Soviets had failed. As for Iran, the fact that an ancient exiled cleric living in Paris could have engineered a revolution there and toppled the shah—one of the closest allies of the United States—earlier that year had been bad enough. But the seizure of an embassy in complete violation of international law was unacceptable. Yet Carter could do virtually nothing about either. He banned American participation in the 1980 Summer Olympics, held in Moscow, as if a boycott were a harsh punishment. However, Carter did set in motion a rescue plan to retrieve the hostages. It was called Operation Eagle Claw.

"Desert One" (as the operation became known, for the code name given a landing zone deep in Iran) failed tragically. Of the eight helicopters sent to the aircraft carrier USS *Nimitz* (CVN 68) for this one mission, none had been flown before by any of the Marine pilots assigned, meaning they had no opportunity to acclimate to these particular "helos." At launch, two had mechanical problems. A third returned to the carrier, having been caught in an unexpected sandstorm—a storm so severe, in fact, that it was an extraordinary feat of airmanship on the part of the pilots even to undertake the mission.

On reaching Desert One, the helos landed and began refueling, still in the sandstorm. One of the helos collided on the ground with a C-130, causing a fire and explosion. Eight servicemen were killed.

The president aborted the mission. The helos were left behind, and the team evacuated by another C-130. Ironically, two of the captured helos are still serving with the Iranian navy.

The debacle ended any chance of Carter's reelection. Carter was seen as a decent but weak man overwhelmed by the responsibilities of the office. In the Democratic primary, Carter, challenged by Senator Edward M. Kennedy, narrowly won the nomination with barely more than 50 percent of the primary votes. In the general election, he was routed by Ronald Reagan.

If Carter did not start any wars, his foreign policy ran aground through a lack of presidential competence. The Camp David Accords were so important that they alone far outweigh the less fortunate outcomes. Carter's intentions were good, but it is not clear that he fully understood sound strategic thinking. His intellectual framework was much more along the lines of an engineer's practicality. He also had an idealist's view of the future. Vision and action were therefore disconnected from strategy, despite the best efforts of his national security advisor, who was a prolific and very innovative strategic thinker.

Carter was also damaged by the absence of what became known as "jointness" in the military. In 1986, well after Desert One and other military failures, the Goldwater-Nichols Act was passed, in the face of stiff service opposition. The new law did a great deal to break down the stovepipe structure dividing, rather than integrating, the four services. It would take time, however, for the law to take hold.

Faced with the threat of the Soviet Union marching south across the Zagros Mountains to capture Iran's oil assets, Carter authorized the Persian Gulf Study, which led to the formation of the Rapid Deployment Joint Task Force (RDJTF). Its first commander, Marine Corps general and later commandant P. X. Kelley, declared the task force neither rapid, joint, nor deployable. Nevertheless, this force ultimately became Central Command, with responsibilities that spanned from the Middle East to Pakistan.

Future presidents need to recognize that idealistic or ideological views must be tested by reality. When they are disconnected from reality, the likelihood of failure is pronounced. And as long as presidents are elected without the requisite experience, judgment, and ability to learn, the prospect of failure looms large. This is a sad truth, one that all but one of subsequent presidents needed to learn—and did not.

Four

Ronald Wilson Reagan

Evil Empires and Star Wars

Early 1982, the E Ring of the Pentagon.

Vice Chief of Naval Operations (VCNO): "As you know, we need to prepare briefing books for CNO-designate Adm. James Watkins, currently Commander, U.S. Pacific Fleet."

HKU: "Aye, aye, sir. Any guidance?"

VCNO: "No, just use your good judgment. As you may know, Admiral Watkins is well connected in California politics. His mother was speaker of the House or held some other high elected position. She is close to President and Mrs. Reagan."

HKU: "Well, as you know, many of us have been highly critical of the absence of an in-depth evaluation of Reagan's call for a six-hundred-ship Navy. I know the Secretary of the Navy, as we were at graduate school around the same time. He has been a formidable proponent of expanding the Navy. I am just concerned that we lack the correct strategic context to make the case. And despite the large increases in defense spending, I do not

see how the Navy and Marines can afford this enlargement in the out-years."

VCNO: "That is why I wanted you to prepare a brief,
with an overview letter I will sign out. That letter should
be short—not more than a few pages. And how soon can
you finish it?"

HKU: "A few days."

VCNO: "OK, come up and see me when you have it."

A week later in the VCNO's office:

HKU: "Admiral, here it is. Just three big ideas. First
and most importantly, we need a maritime strategy that
can coordinate war plans and contingency operations,
make the case for the larger Navy and Marine Corps,
and give the fleet a plan of action around which our programs, training, recruitment, and procurement can be
structured.

"I know the current CNO is content with his plan
for Sea Strike as a strategy. [Sea Strike was an operational plan to attack Soviet naval bases on the Kam-
chatka Peninsula in the Pacific with four carrier battle
groups.] But that is a campaign plan for an attack on
the Soviet homeland with naval forces, rather than a
broader strategy. We need not embarrass CNO. But we
need a better context."

VCNO: "What else?"

HKU: "Planning and coordination between the fleet
commanders and Washington is nonexistent. The commanders submit their priority lists, which, you know, are
usually ignored. Then they bitch and get some of what
they want. This is not planning or strategy."

VCNO: "I agree. We will set in train some fixes for that."

HKU: "Finally, unless we take dramatic action, the six-hundred-ship Navy is completely unaffordable. We can get there. But there isn't enough money in the budget to sustain it. The secretary has been shrewd in cutting procurement costs. That is not the problem. It is operations, maintenance, personnel, and training costs that will kill us.

"Attached are ideas for implementing each of these three recommendations. But I have some concerns."

VCNO: "Go on."

HKU: "The Reagan administration is more concerned with getting to six hundred ships than in sustaining them. Whatever strategy we devise, the civilians no doubt will embrace it as a marketing plan to sell the six hundred ships to Congress and the public. That is fine. But sales is not the best basis for designing a military strategy. We are not General Motors selling a car."

VCNO: "You wrote your dissertation on the Soviet military, did you not?"

HKU: "Yes, sir."

VCNO: "Well, after the new CNO settles in, he's got an idea about strategic defenses. Your views might be helpful."

HKU: "One more thing about strategy. We have always planned for a conventional war—refighting the Battle of the Atlantic against Soviet wolf packs. That's not the way the Russians think.

"The Russians see a war with us as a fight to finish. Nuclear and thermonuclear weapons are part of that fight. If we send carrier battle groups and submarines in a war, it is almost certain the Soviets will use nuclear weapons, even a nuclear area bombardment in the oceans, aimed at disrupting our missile subs.

"As you well know, a high-altitude nuclear blast will provide enough EMP [electromagnetic pulse] at very long range to knock out our electronics and blind us. That is why our strategy needs to recognize this type of thinking and why we need to begin hardening our 'big decks' [carriers] against EMP. That signal alone will be read by the Soviets.

"I have no idea what the White House and the president think about this. They are pretty hard-line anti-Soviets, with Dick Allen as the first national security advisor and Bill Casey at CIA. Quite frankly, while this is way above my pay grade, this scares me. The Soviets have huge internal and economic problems. Their leadership is geriatric. I can remember some time ago serving on the faculty at the National War College when the CIA director, Bill Colby, would lecture year after year predicting that Brezhnev had months to live. Yet, the CIA was wrong. And Brezhnev's potential successors are not in any better shape."

VCNO: "I won't comment about the White House. About understanding the Russians, I agree with you. But changing decades of thinking and of war plans will not be easy. I agree that our view of strategy and the Russians' are different. But turning that reality into action will be our toughest task."

Ronald Reagan became the fortieth president of the United States at noon on January 20, 1981. His most vocal supporters called for a "Reagan Revolution," based on a combination of fiscal conservatism and his reputation as a strong anticommunist. The combination would lead to major breakthroughs with the Soviet Union in arms control, notably the Intermediate Nuclear Force Treaty (INF) and the nearly miraculous (or foolhardy) effort at the Reykjavik Summit five years later with Mikhail Gorbachev to eliminate nuclear weapons. Reagan and Gorbachev held a total of four summits and laid the groundwork for the Strategic Arms Reduction Treaty (START I) approved in 1991.

Reagan was also famous for his speeches and memorable phrases. He declared the Soviet Union "the evil empire," a comment he retracted in Moscow in 1988 at his last meeting with Gorbachev. In March 1983, he announced his Strategic Defense Initiative (SDI), popularly and irreverently known as "Star Wars." And in 1987 in Berlin, Reagan offered his famous challenge: "Mr. Gorbachev, tear down this wall."

Despite the president's formidable rhetoric, not all of his ideas drew praise. Experts such as Lt. Gen. Brent Scowcroft, twice national security advisor, criticized the "tear down the wall" statement as meaningless, absent any leverage or means to enforce the demand. That same critique would arise thirty years later, when a future president would demand that Bashar al-Assad must step down from power and draw a "red line" around the use of chemical weapons. Assad dismissed both orders.

As 1981 dawned, Reagan promised "Morning in America," a successful campaign slogan conveying the message of a new beginning for the country. Americans were largely taken with a sense of "malaise," a word Carter had never used, and pessimism that had accumulated over the past decade. The defeat in Vietnam, an economic misery index that combined double-figure interest rates and inflation, the oil embargoes and energy crises, the American hostages still held in Iran, the failure of Desert One rescue attempt, and the seeming Soviet challenge to the United States as the leading superpower—all this made for a somber national mood.

Reagan's plan for his revolution was, in today's world, bumper-sticker and Twitter length: cut taxes, cut government, and rebuild defense. And so he did. While his defense secretary, Caspar Weinberger, had been known as "Cap the Knife" in an earlier incarnation as Nixon's head of the Office of Management and Budget, at the Pentagon his job was to spend a great deal more money. Huge sums were directed to the Pentagon to enable it to outpace the Soviet Union in military power. One of Reagan's principal aims was to build a "six-hundred-ship Navy."

By increasing defense spending, some supporters believed, Reagan was forcing the Soviets to follow suit. Ultimately, the assertion went, that spending bankrupted Moscow and collapsed the USSR. At best, this was highly wishful thinking. As will be explained later, the geriatric Soviet leadership would finally die off, bringing the relatively youthful Mikhail S. Gorbachev into power. It was Gorbachev's attempt to reform the Soviet Union through *perestroika* (restructuring) and *glasnost* (openness) that broke the inherently brittle and irrational system, consigning the USSR to oblivion, not Reagan's defense plans.

Part of the so-called Reagan Doctrine was to challenge communism and the Soviet Union globally. His CIA director, William Casey, had full license to undertake covert action. The Reagan administration would deploy ground forces overtly to Beirut and to Grenada, with disastrous consequences for the former and confusion for the latter. Covertly, the CIA began in Latin America the illegal mining of Nicaragua's harbors, and Reagan's NSC produced the Iran-Contra fiasco, which nearly ended Reagan's presidency. The effort to arm the Afghan mujahedeen with Stinger missiles and other weapons for use against the Soviets proved tactically effective and strategically shortsighted. It enabled the Taliban to overthrow the Najibullah regime and seize power in 1996.

With the Iran-Iraq War raging, intense hostility between Tehran and Washington induced the Reagan administration to consider Saddam Hussein a de facto ally. The United States provided Iraq substantial intelligence data on Iran. An infamous photo was taken of Donald Rumsfeld, Reagan's envoy to Baghdad, in what appeared to be a jovial meeting with Saddam. During the "tanker war," Iran attacked these huge ships in the Persian Gulf, threatening to disrupt or halt the flow of oil. In response, the United States cleverly and effectively reflagged Kuwaiti tankers under U.S. colors to protect against and prevent Iranian attacks against them. Called Operation Earnest Will, reflagging began in 1987 and lasted for about a year, ensuring that oil flowed from the Gulf.

In 1987, Iraqis, flying French-made Mirage fighters, fired Exocet missiles that struck and nearly sank USS *Stark* (FFG 31), a U.S. Navy missile frigate on patrol in the Gulf. Iraq apologized for the mistake, and its apology was accepted. In July of the following year, however, the guided-missile cruiser USS *Vincennes* (CG 49) inexcusably shot down an Iranian civilian airliner, Iran Air Flight 655, shortly after it cleared the Iranian coast, killing all on board. While the United States ultimately apologized, the *Vincennes* incident made an already grim relationship with Iran understandably worse. Fortunately, although tensions in the Gulf were fierce, and despite the nearly decade-long Iran-Iraq War, broader conflict in the Gulf between Iran and the United States was averted. After that war ended, Saddam mistook the lack of a strong American response to his threat against Kuwait as a green light to invade that country in August 1990. The next administration would have to deal with that invasion.

Reagan was deceptively smart and a brilliant politician, with his magnetic ability to connect with the public. His career as an actor served him well. Reagan was seen as immensely likable and decent, qualities that no doubt helped save his presidency during the very illegal Iran-Contra fiasco. In fact, Reagan's administration was scandal ridden almost from the outset. More members of his administration were charged with or convicted of a range of crimes and misdemeanors than in any White House in memory, even Nixon's. The scandals extended across several departments.

These malfeasances portrayed Reagan as either incompetent or uninterested in exercising the necessary oversight and accountability. Whether this was a matter of trusting when trust was not deserved or delegating too much authority as a de facto means of governing is not clear. Indeed, one of Reagan's best throwaway lines was highly suggestive: "Hard work never killed any body. But why take the chance!" Also, the assassination attempt barely ten weeks into his presidency that nearly claimed Reagan's life surely slowed the new administration's grasping of the reins of power.

Reagan himself remained an enigma. On one hand, he was regarded as disengaged and often laid back. He seemed to lack the killer instinct when it came to firing subordinates. On the other hand, he could be tough and aggressive when necessary. When the air controllers went on strike in 1982, Reagan fired them. He was never the ideologue that opponents maintained he was. His philosophy was laden with pragmatism and common sense.

Reagan worked very closely and well with the Democratic House speaker, Thomas "Tip" O'Neill, in a relationship that must be envied in today's destructively pernicious political environment. Reagan slashed taxes. But, his fierce rhetoric to the contrary, he also raised taxes, when fiscal deficits threatened the economy. He was a pragmatic idealist and conservative. Ideology was fine, when tempered with reality.

If Reagan had vision, warmth, charm, and charisma, strategic thinking was never his strong suit. Space precludes an exhaustive review of his eight years. However, Beirut and Grenada in 1983, Iran-Contra several years later, Afghanistan, and his love-hate relationship with the Soviet Union can be used as lenses through which to examine his strategic thinking.

Reagan had another flaw as noted—his disdain for management and oversight. Nothing demonstrated Reagan's lack of management skills more than his laissez-faire approach to his key advisors. He allowed his first chief of staff, James Baker, and his first treasury secretary, Donald Regan, to swap jobs. Regan may have done well heading Merrill-Lynch on Wall Street, but he was an ineffective chief of staff. He was ultimately fired after a series of mistakes and run-ins with First Lady Nancy Reagan.

The president was even more cavalier and aloof in his selection of national security advisors. That seeming indifference was to erupt in the Iran-Contra fiasco, which contaminated Reagan's presidency. Reagan's first national security advisor was Richard Allen, who was forced to resign after a year in office over allegations of improperly handling and accepting money from Japanese sources. That money was, inexplicably, stored in Allen's White House office safe. In defending Allen, President Reagan called the furor over the stashed money blatantly political foul play to discredit the White House and his administration.

As a replacement, Reagan appointed Judge William Clark, a member of his "kitchen cabinet" from the California state house. Clark had absolutely zero foreign-policy experience. One senior member of the NSC staff (and Clark's replacement as national security advisor), Robert "Bud" McFarlane, recalled that Clark once showed him a map of Europe, with allies denoted in blue and adversaries in red. Clark told him that their job was to "keep the blues blue and turn as many of the reds blue as we can."

When McFarlane replaced him, Clark went on to be the secretary of the interior. McFarlane was a retired Marine lieutenant colonel with extensive NSC experience. His downfall would come when he attempted to recreate the Nixon-Kissinger triangular diplomacy with Russia and China in a complicated (and as it would prove, dangerous and bizarre) plan to retrieve American hostages from Iran and recycle the proceeds from a prohibited arms sale to Tehran to the Contras, guerillas in Nicaragua, in Central America. All of this was illegal and political malfeasance.

Another Marine on the NSC staff, Lt. Col. Oliver North, whom McFarlane regarded "like a son," was entrusted with this convoluted diplomacy. The plan had four parts, all fatal. First, Iran would receive banned weapons in exchange for releasing American hostages. Second, these weapons would come from Israel, to which the United States would provide replacements. Third, payment for the weapons would be laundered to the Contras. Fourth, the Contras would use the arms to overthrow the Nicaraguan government, seen as hostile to American interests.

The plan was unworkable and totally illegal. Two Boland Amendments, passed by Congress and signed into law by Reagan, prevented any funding of the Contras. Shipping American arms to Iran was prohibited, even though technically these weapons were to have been supplied by Israel. When this story leaked, the scandal almost ended Reagan's presidency, and it did lead McFarlane to a suicide attempt, which fortunately failed.

Prior to "Iran-Contra" becoming public, McFarlane left the White House for the private sector and a choice position at the Center for Strategic and International Studies. McFarlane was replaced by his deputy, Vice Adm. John Poindexter, who unknowingly was sitting on this political time bomb. When the Iran-Contra bomb exploded, Poindexter's mentor and a former Chief of Naval Operations, Adm. James Holloway III, took the national security advisor to lunch at Washington's Metropolitan Club, a block and a half from the White House.

Over lunch, the admiral asked Poindexter if he had retained a lawyer. Poindexter looked baffled and asked why would he need one. The more experienced Holloway replied, in what was clearly an order, "Admiral, if you do not have a lawyer by close of business today, I will get one for you." Several years later, Holloway, who became a good friend, told me of this encounter.

Reagan remained aloof from this political firestorm until it was clear that to save his presidency he needed real competence in the White House. Deputy Defense Secretary Frank C. Carlucci was given the responsibility to right the ship of state, as national security advisor. Carlucci plucked then lieutenant general Colin Powell from his command of V Corps in West Germany to be his deputy. After getting the NSC organization back on track, Carlucci went on to the Pentagon as secretary of defense, replacing his old boss, Cap Weinberger. Powell was then elevated to the top slot in NSC.

Reagan convened what was called the "Tower Commission" in late 1985, to investigate how Iran-Contra had gone adrift. John Tower, retired senator from Texas and former chairman of the Senate Armed Services Committee, was joined on the panel by retired lieutenant general Brent Scowcroft and Edmund Muskie, former Democratic senator from Maine. The report was scathing. Reagan apologized to the nation in a major speech, acknowledging that while his heart had told him he was not actually exchanging arms for hostages in Iraq or breaking the law in Nicaragua, his mind should have advised him otherwise. Due in large measure to his popularity, Reagan survived—barely.

The first real foreign-policy crisis for the administration was Argentina's seizure of Britain's Falkland Islands, located about three hundred miles southeast of South America's Patagonia coast, in early 1982. British prime minister Margaret Thatcher—a close confidante of Reagan's—sent a British task force on a mission code-named Operation Corporate to retake the islands. Washington was caught in the classic dilemma of having to choose between two allies warring with each other.

Clearly, the tilt was to Britain. The admirals in the Pentagon predicted that Britain's lack of airpower and numerical inferiority in ground forces would guarantee defeat, but those forecasts would prove dead wrong. Based on my time in the Royal Navy from late 1969 to 1971, serving in the frigate HMS *Bacchante* and then on the faculty of Royal Naval College Britannia, in Dartmouth, I was charged by the senior Pentagon leadership to put together a "red" team to provide the likely strategy the United Kingdom would employ to retake the Falklands. A "red" team is meant to offer contrarian analysis. I assumed the role of Rear Adm. John "Sandy" Woodward, Royal Navy, who oversaw the operation and would be later knighted and promoted to four-star rank.

We predicted, on an 80/20 percent basis, that the British would evict the Argentines from the Falklands and retake the islands. Argentina's airpower would be negated by the very long flying range to the Falklands and by the lack of tanker aircraft. Argentina had a very large advantage over the invading British force in total numbers of ground troops stationed on the Falklands. However, the Argentine force comprised ill-trained, ill-prepared draftees who would be no match for Britain's much less numerous but highly professional, capable, and aggressive Royal Marines and soldiers.

Virtually all the U.S. Navy admirals who were given this briefing strongly dissented, arguing that numerical inferiority of British ground forces and Argentina's airpower would turn Operation Corporate into a military disaster of the first order. Indeed, our predictions were not only rejected—some senior officers ridiculed the very idea of a British victory.

The team made one error in overestimating the effects of bad weather, concluding Britain would mount its amphibious assault far sooner than it did. Also underappreciated in projecting the outcome, ironically, was the heroism of the Argentinian pilots. In their determined attacks these pilots flew so low over the water to avoid heavy British antiaircraft fire that many of their bombs did not arm. Hitting their targets, they did not explode. Had the fuses been set differently, the skeptical American admirals could have been proven right. To repeat Clausewitz, luck counts.

In a Pentagon sensitive compartmented information facility (SCIF), fall 1982.

Navy captain (NC) heading CNO's Executive Panel (CEP): "What I am briefing you on is special access and one of CNO's most important projects."

HKU: "Why me?"

NC: "Admiral Watkins knows you have a Soviet background and wanted your reaction [handing me a briefing paper titled 'The Strategic Defense Initiative (SDI)']."

HKU, after scanning the paper: "CNO wants to make all Soviet intercontinental ballistic missiles 'impotent and obsolete,' by fielding space-based, high-technology sensors and interceptors, including lasers and high-energy weapons."

NC: "Yes, and he has the support of Edward Teller [nuclear physicist and so-called father of the H-bomb]."

HKU: "Do you want my honest reaction?"

NC: "Yes, of course."

HKU: "Put this program back in the box and never let it see the light of day. It will be hugely if not unaffordably expensive; I doubt the technology will ever work the way envisaged, because of the physics; and the Russians have too many countermeasures.

"They could easily launch killer satellites in peacetime to knock ours out. Even if Soviet ICBMs could be targeted, no system is 100 percent effective. Besides, Soviet submarines can fire low-trajectory missiles from close in to our coast. And the biggest hole is that we have no defense against cruise missiles or manned or unmanned bombers."

NC: "Um . . . "

HKU: "Um?"

NC: "Well, this brief is pretty well along. Reagan has been briefed on it, but in general terms. The full briefing is scheduled sometime after Thanksgiving, and a big speech is planned for early in 1983."

HKU: "I will draft a paper. However, it will be quite negative. And it also will be critical of the idea that we can force the Soviets into an arms race that will bankrupt them. Don't we know that much of their defense spending is a jobs program, as well as a way of pumping up foreign military sales?"

NC: "Anything positive to say?"

HKU: "Yes. This could be a brilliant bargaining ploy. Suppose Reagan met with Brezhnev and outlined the idea. Then he could argue that a better alternative would be substantial arms reductions, both at the theater and strategic levels. As a further inducement, if the Soviets cooperated, we could make the technology available to them to use against third parties. The PR value alone would be enormous.

"If the Soviets disagreed, we could make a modest start. But the last thing we want is to provoke an arms race. Their counters would be air-breathing bombers and cruise missiles. The latter are quite cheap and provide a huge cost-exchange benefit. Defenses will cost us billions and the Russians hundreds of millions. If I were Russia, I would increase conventional forces to threaten Europe and NATO. Then what would we do?"

On March 23, 1983, Reagan delivered his SDI speech, announcing the intent to make nuclear weapons "impotent and obsolete." The idea was mocked in much of the media as unworkable and unaffordable and was given the pejorative nickname of "Star Wars," after the movie. The only suggestion I made that survived—and Reagan may have done this regardless—was to offer the Soviets this technology. Reagan held SDI in such importance that he refused to negotiate it away at Reykjavik in 1986, when he and Gorbachev came close to eliminating virtually all of their respective nuclear inventories.

In June 1982, well prior to the SDI speech, Israel invaded southern Lebanon (with Reagan's tacit support) in Operation Galilee. That September, the president ordered Marines into Beirut, along with other peacekeepers. Both Weinberger and the new secretary of state, George Schultz, who replaced Alexander Haig, privately and strongly opposed the deployment as dangerous and destabilizing.

In April 1983, the U.S. embassy in Beirut was bombed, and 17 Americans were killed. On October 23, a large yellow Mercedes truck broke through a security barrier and crashed into the large building housing the Marines. Then the driver detonated several tons of explosives. The blast left 241 Marines, sailors, and soldiers dead. The nation was shocked by the carnage and death toll of our servicemen. The Reagan administration came under instant and intense criticism. The Marines were withdrawn and an investigation convened, headed by retired admiral Robert L. J. Long. The "Long Report" would be a devastating critique that condemned the entire chain of command, up to and including the White House, for failing to take even basic security precautions to defend against such attacks.

Two days after the bombing of the Marine barracks, on October 25, Operation Urgent Fury was unleashed on the Caribbean island of Grenada. Some argued that the Reagan administration was paranoid about "communist" expansion in the Western Hemisphere. If so, that article of faith would come to grief in Nicaragua, with the support of the Contras. Others argued that Grenada was a diversion from the Beirut tragedy—wrongly, because the invasion had been in planning before the bombing took place.

Grenada had won independence from Great Britain in 1974. Five years later the New Jewel Movement, led by Maurice Bishop, seized power. Then, in October 1983, a coup deposed Bishop; several days later, he was killed. The British governor general, Sir Paul Scoon, was placed under house arrest, and a strict curfew administered by the local military was imposed.

For a number of years, a long runway and airport expansion had been under construction by Cuban workers. The Reagan administration asserted that these facilities would be used by Soviet reconnaissance aircraft as a base, in collaboration with Cuba. With a coup in progress and more violence likely, the administration also concluded that 233 American students at the St. Georges Medical School were at great risk. Operation Urgent Fury was mounted to rescue the students and restore a government that would not allow Soviets access to the island. A task force of about 8,000 soldiers, Marines, and sailors was hastily organized under the command of the Second Fleet commander, Vice Adm. Joseph J. Metcalf III, a feisty, highly intelligent, cigar-smoking sailor. But the operation turned into tragicomedy.

The Navy SEALs, Army Delta Force, Rangers, 82nd Airborne Division soldiers, and Marines involved had never operated together before in such an operation. To keep the operation secret, maps of Grenada were not distributed in advance. The tides and currents were so underestimated that four SEALS died after being helo-dropped into the water for a seaborne entry. Metcalf was constantly harassed by the White House to expedite the rescue of the students. In frustration, Metcalf sent at the end of the first day an urgent message to the White House clearly and unequivocally stating that the students were in no danger. The White House seethed at the admiral's assessment. The primary reason for the invasion had been to rescue the students; now, the operational commander was repudiating that very rationale. Fortunately for the administration, that story never came out.

By the second day, the island had been virtually secured and about 680 Cuban "soldiers" taken prisoner. The White House hailed the operation as a great success, in part to deflect criticism over the Beirut disaster. The presence of these Cubans confirmed the White House belief that a Soviet-Cuban deal had been struck to build the 9,000-foot runway. However, had Reagan applied his famous "trust but verify" slogan to test this proposition, he would have reached a different conclusion.

Plessey PLC, a British defense firm then owned by the highly conservative and anticommunist Clark family, had won the contract

for a project originally envisaged in 1953 by Her Majesty's government to expand tourism in Grenada. The Clarks, being good busi-
nesspeople, had gone to the lowest-cost labor pool for the project.
Cuba had provided the laborers, with the proviso that loyal Cuban
paramilitary soldiers would accompany the workers to prevent
defections. This was not a Soviet-Cuban plot, and that could have
been confirmed with minimal effort. Such failure of intelligence and
the refusal to dig deeper would recur with disastrous consequences
nearly thirty years later, in the second Iraq War.

Worse, relations with Great Britain and Prime Minister Margaret Thatcher were badly strained. Grenada was part of the Com-
monwealth. Thatcher had asked Reagan not to invade. She had
sent Reagan a very strongly worded letter underscoring that as the
United States was at the time preparing to site nuclear cruise missiles in Britain to counter Russian systems, seizing Grenada would
anger much of her public, and it would not help her government
reverse the very sizable opposition to those deployments. On the
eve of the invasion, Thatcher called Reagan to ensure that the
rumored assault was not happening and would not. Reagan could
not bear to tell Thatcher the truth and denied to her that the operation was under way. Reagan later admitted, in his memoir, that
"there was little else I could say." As discussed earlier, twisting the
truth to suit his purposes would later almost cause Reagan's downfall over Iran-Contra.

The Grenada operation debacle contributed to legislative action
in 1986, in the form of the Goldwater-Nichols Act. This law mandated "jointness," by which the four military services were coerced
to operate "jointly" rather than independently, as had largely been
the case historically. This lack of jointness had been partly responsible for the 1980 Desert One failure. Over time, the services would
enthusiastically embrace jointness to prevent repeating the mistakes of Desert One and Grenada. Today, the concept of jointness
has been expanded into a "whole-of-government," or comprehensive, approach that recognizes that the other arms of government
must play significant roles if policy is to work and, to put it bluntly,
if conflicts of the twenty-first century are to be won or to succeed.

In 1985, terrorist attacks against airports in Rome and Vienna were attributed to Libya, whose leader, Col. Muammar Qaddafi, was very much an adversary of the West and of America. Qaddafi later laid claim to the entire Gulf of Sidra, adjacent to his coast, as territorial waters. By 1986, Libya was a growing burr under President Reagan's metaphorical saddle. To deal with Libya's illegal territorial claims and to teach Qaddafi a lesson, Reagan ordered the Mediterranean-based Sixth Fleet to deploy aircraft carriers into the Gulf of Sidra.

Libya made the foolhardy mistake of challenging the U.S. Navy. On March 23/24, Sixth Fleet units were threatened by several of Qaddafi's small naval units. The Sixth Fleet quickly sunk a Libyan corvette and several patrol boats, dispersing the very much outgunned enemy force. In retaliation, on April 5, Libyan agents bombed the La Belle disco in West Berlin, killing 229 people, including two American servicemen and an American civilian. Reagan was quick to retaliate again. After several days of coordinating with European and Arab allies, Reagan ordered air strikes against targets in Libya, in an operation code-named El Dorado Canyon. Addressing the nation on the night of April 14, Reagan stated, "Self-defense is not only our right, it is our duty. It is the purpose behind the mission . . . a mission fully consistent with Article 51 of the UN Charter." The operation was launched.

El Dorado Canyon was a further example of the lack before Goldwater-Nichols of unified and coordinated command planning. As in Vietnam, attacking U.S. Air Force, Navy, and Marine Corps aircraft were assigned separate targets to prevent confusion and blue-on-blue engagements. Because the French would not approve overflight rights for the strike, Air Force F-111 fighter-bombers based in Lakenheath, England, had to fly a long, circuitous route to their targets in Libya. Accuracy was abysmal. The French embassy in Tripoli was nearly hit—a foreshadowing of the 1999 Kosovo campaign, in which the United States was to bomb the Chinese embassy in Belgrade.

Qaddafi, shaken by the attack, nonetheless ordered further retaliation against America. Two years later, on December 21, 1988,

Pan American Flight 103 exploded over Lockerbie, Scotland, killing all 269 passengers and crew on board. Qaddafi's agents had planted explosives in the baggage of an unsuspecting passenger. But American reprisals were limited to sanctions and criminal prosecutions; the Reagan administration was about to leave office, and the newly arriving George H. W. Bush administration would be preoccupied with larger issues that would arise from the implosion of the Soviet Union and Saddam's assault into Kuwait.

Perhaps the most flagrant example of the Reagan administration's failure to apply sound strategic thinking was Afghanistan. That history is a long one, dating back to the Carter administration. In December 1979, to support a failing procommunist regime in Kabul, the Soviet Union intervened with about 15,000 troops. Furious at this invasion and flagrant violation of international law, the Carter administration drew up plans to support anti-Soviet elements in Afghanistan with weapons and CIA advisors. A year later, when Reagan entered office, the opportunity to strike back at the Soviet Union in Afghanistan was too tempting to ignore.

Reagan's support of the mujahedeen, or freedom fighters, was first reported nearly a quarter of a century later in a book by George Crile, which was made into the successful movie of the same title, *Charlie Wilson's War*. Charlie Wilson was a larger-than-life personality elected from Texas as a Democrat to the House of Representatives in 1972. After considerable debate and review, by the end of 1986 the Reagan administration had decided to ship Stinger surface-to-air missiles to the mujahedeen. But it was Wilson, on the House Defense Appropriations Subcommittee, who was the driving force behind funding this secret program, Operation Cyclone.

In his many trips to Afghanistan, Wilson fell into the company of Jalludin Haqqani and Golbidin Hekmatyar, leaders of two principal mujahedeen networks. Wilson established a bond with both. With Stingers and antitank and -vehicle weapons, the mujahedeen turned the tide of battle. The United States had been forced to retreat from Vietnam, and the same fate befell the Soviet Union in Afghanistan. But after the Soviets withdrew in 1990, the government in Kabul, headed by Mohammed Najibullah, was far from firmly in control; it collapsed in 1992. Wilson desperately tried to gain funding for the rebuilding of Afghanistan, fearing that Islamic extremists would fill the vacuum created by the Soviet exit. But Congress had no appetite for nation building. Afghanistan was a dead issue, especially with the collapse of the Soviet Union and later Saddam's occupation of Kuwait.

Four years later, the Taliban would be firmly in charge. Haqqani and Hekmatyar would find themselves atop the American most-wanted-terrorist list. Just as George W. Bush would never ask the "What next?" question in Iraq, so too the Reagan administration never inquired what would happen in Afghanistan once the Soviets left.

The lesson is clear. As a first assessment, paying any price and bearing any burden to blunt the Soviet Union seemed sound policy. Unfortunately, the "What next?" was never considered. The Reagan administration did consider the impact of providing Stinger missiles and whether those weapons might turn up in other locales to be used against us. Presumably, the weapons had some sort of safety devices installed to prevent that from happening. However, the question of what next for Afghanistan never shaped U.S. policy. Driving the Soviets out counted most.

The Reagan administration was courting Pakistan's president, Gen. Zia al-Haq, as part of the anti-Soviet campaign in Afghanistan. There too, the White House turned a blind eye, this time to Zia's Islamist preferences and the direction he was taking Pakistan. As it did in many other areas, cultural and societal ignorance persisted in the White House.

In broad brush, Zulfikar ali Bhutto, Pakistan's president from 1971 to 1973 and prime minister from 1973 to 1977 (and who would be executed by Zia, his former military assistant, in 1979 for treason), had nationalized and socialized what had been a well performing economy. Zia radicalized the country, creating thousands of madrassas, or religious schools, that teach the Koran from a highly conservative, even radical, point of view. Pakistan would never recover from these tectonic shifts. And its love-hate relationship with the United States, largely shaped by the war against terror and the thirty-five-year-old Afghan war, has, sadly, migrated to the adversarial side of the scale.

It would be unfair to relate directly the Reagan administration's largely uncritical support of the mujahedeen and the G. W. Bush administration's shift in 2002 away from Afghanistan to the invasion of Iraq. The reality is, however, that had the United States supported the government of Afghanistan, the Taliban and Islamist radicals would probably not have seized control of that country. Whether or not the attacks of September 11 might thereby have been averted, once again the United States failed to understand the conflict in which it was engaged or considered the longer-term consequences.

The first American serviceman was killed in Vietnam in 1959. Fifteen years later, the United States would finally withdraw. The Afghan war can be considered to have started for the United States in early 1980, and it is still ongoing. That makes a more than thirty-five-year war, and counting. It is doubtful that more than a handful of Americans are aware of that.

✦

One of Reagan's greatest legacies was the rebuilding of the U.S. military. No doubt the Reagan defense increases were vital to reestablishing a military that had deteriorated into a "hollow force." The term was invented by Gen. Edward C. "Shy" Meyer, who was appointed chief of staff of the Army by Jimmy Carter and served from 1979 to 1983.

Following the election of Jimmy Carter, defense had not been allotted the priority or money necessary to undo the damage done by Vietnam to the fiber, morale, and strength of the U.S. military. Meyer posited that a "hollow force" had resulted, a force that was incapable—ill prepared, unready, and ill equipped to carry out its missions. Meyer was absolutely correct. The phrase persists today as a warning of what could happen to the current military force.

While I was head of Navy Extended Planning from 1982 to 1983, we conducted an extensive analysis of the cost implications of the six-hundred-ship Navy. We concluded that while obtaining six hundred ships was indeed possible, unless drastic steps were taken to cut or eliminate costs and cost growth, a navy of that size was financially unsustainable. John Lehman was a formidable and dynamic Secretary of the Navy, perhaps the most effective since Teddy Roosevelt held the assistant secretary's job. Making this case of unaffordability would prove a Sisyphean labor, with about the same results.

Admiral Watkins was CNO and Gen. P. X. Kelley was Marine Corps commandant; both were highly supportive of our analysis and convinced of the need to make naval forces affordable. However, John Lehman was not. As a contemporary of mine (and someone I had known, though we had attended different graduate schools), Lehman was forthright with me about the analysis. "Harlan," he said, "my job was to get to six hundred ships. It will be someone else's to sustain that. I cannot do both."

Lehman was correct, regrettably. The Reagan administration had set six hundred ships as its goal (Kennedy had done the equivalent, in a different time, with strategic nuclear weapons), and no one would change course. As an alternative, my office resurrected Adm. Elmo "Bud" Zumwalt's landmark Project 60, done in 1970 when he became CNO. It had charted profound changes the Navy had to make to deal with the growing Soviet navy and the ravages of Vietnam.

Zumwalt had had two overwhelming worries as head of the Navy. First, he believed that the Soviet Union was rapidly overtaking an obsolete U.S. Navy. That navy may have numbered more than nine hundred ships, but most of those ships were World War II relics. Second, having just served as Commander, Naval Forces Vietnam, Zumwalt believed that the Navy was facing potential mutinies based on race. Zumwalt's conclusion was brilliantly simple. Einstein would have been pleased. First, Zumwalt cut the Navy almost in half, to save money and to recapitalize the remaining force. That money would be used to build modern ships, including two new aircraft carriers and more nuclear submarines.

Second, Zumwalt pushed technology. He invented the idea of exploiting space, establishing a program that became known as TENCAP (for "the exploitation of national capabilities"). Space-based detection and surveillance systems would provide the fleet unprecedented amounts of information and intelligence, on a virtual global basis. Zumwalt also sought to arm the fleet with modern weapons, including cruise missiles, newer antisubmarine torpedoes, and mobile mines.

Third, Zumwalt developed a concise and compelling four-point mission statement for the Navy: deterrence, sea control, power projection, and presence. Last, Zumwalt reformed personnel policies to avert the mutinies he so greatly feared. In sum, Project 60 was one of the most effective and far-reaching strategic planning exercises ever carried out in the Pentagon. My idea was to use a history of Project 60 to encourage the new CNO to take on the affordability of the six-hundred-ship Navy by a root-and-branch analysis of costs and of cost-avoidance and cost-reduction options.

Politics being what they were, John Lehman saw no need for an alternative to his plans for six hundred ships. Indeed, Lehman believed that even raising issues of affordability could redound against him and the case for six hundred ships. From the bureaucratic and political perspectives, Lehman was correct. However, the issue of affordability would return with a vengeance, and indeed today it could induce another "hollow force." Frustrated by the refusal of the Navy to address this matter, I knew that the idea for a new Project 60 had to find a home.

Army Chief of Staff's Office, the Pentagon, early 1983. Present are the former undersecretary of defense for policy, Ambassador Robert W. Komer (RWK); Gen. Edward Meyer (ECM), Army Chief of Staff; a few associated aides; and me.

RWK: "Shy, I have known Harlan since Vietnam days, when he was as much of a pain in the ass as he is today. He has a great idea. He did a study on how Bud Zumwalt's Project 60 revolutionized the Navy. He recommended that the Navy constitute a new version. But John [Lehman] wasn't interested. Harlan, please lay out the ideas."

HKU, summarizing the study: "General Meyer, you are in the process of modernizing the Army. My sense is that Zumwalt's format—the need for a four-part mission statement, to get rid of unnecessary force structure, to

exploit technology, and to put in better personnel policies—is applicable to each of the services today."

ECM: "I agree, and we are trying to do that. But I like
the approach. I am putting together a planning cell I am
calling a "continuity group" to prepare for the next chief
of staff, who will replace me later this year. This should
be a good guide.

"By the way, I am looking for a full-time head of this
group. Do you have any suggestions? The interim head
is my executive assistant, and I need him back."

HKU: "Yes, General, I do. And I think the timing is
correct."

ECM: "Who is that?"

HKU: "Brig. Gen. Colin Powell."

ECM: "Terrific idea. That's whom I was thinking about
anyway."

HKU to himself: "Why the hell ask me . . .?"

HKU: "Great choice, General."

◆

Colin Powell indeed got that assignment and, of course, went on to
the top U.S. military position, the chairmanship, in 1989. However,
the hollow force and the issue of unaffordability remained Damoclean swords, then and even today. While at the Center for Strategic and International Studies, we began in 1986 a study called "U.S.
Force Posture at a Crossroads," completed in 1987. A distinguished
panel of retired four-star officers, including Shy Meyer, concluded
that because of cost growth, likely budgets, and even with the Reagan defense-spending increases, we had about 25–30 percent too
much force structure. The implication was clear: another hollow
force lurked below the horizon.

In early 1988, I briefed the chairman of the Joint Chiefs of Staff,
then Adm. William J. Crowe, on the conclusions of the study. The

Reagan years were drawing to an end, and there was little the admiral could do. He recommended that we wait until the new president took office and then provide his team with the brief. That we did.

What turned out to be the saving grace was the end of the Soviet Union. That enabled Crowe's replacement, Colin Powell, to design the "Base Force," which was a 25 percent reduction in total numbers of active-duty forces. As will be noted, Powell's effort rivaled Zumwalt's Project 60 in impact, demonstrating how one individual with the right skills can move an otherwise immovable bureaucracy. Now, more than a quarter of a century later, the military's greatest threat remains uncontrollable internal cost growth.

When one reexamines the Reagan record of using military force or the threat of it, many of the misperceptions and miscalculations that doomed the Vietnam War reappear. Reagan actually believed that he did indeed have a strategic thought process, in terms of a vision for national security. He would have called it "peace through strength." His supporters would have insisted powerfully that the strategy of forcing the Soviets to compete in an arms race ultimately caused their self-destruction. SDI was part of that strategy, as well as Reagan's aspiration to make nuclear weapons "impotent and obsolete."

Yet, as with the decision to arm the mujahedeen, which would empower the Taliban to seize control of Afghanistan in coming years, and the mythology that took hold in the Vietnam years, like the discredited domino theory, causes and effects were not related. The Soviet Union collapsed of its own weight and of an irrational, unsustainable system. Even so, it took a visionary like Gorbachev to attempt the reforms that ultimately tore the system apart.

Similarly, the decisions to station Marines in Beirut, to occupy Grenada against a nonexistent Soviet-Cuban threat, to arm the mujahedeen, and support the Contras all proved to be failures, in that either the mission did not ultimately succeed or it was undertaken for the wrong reasons. The pinprick strikes against Qaddafi in Operation El Dorado Canyon of 1986 provoked predictable retaliation and did not have any remedial impact. It was only after Saddam had been ejected from Kuwait in 1991 that Qaddafi decided that it was time for him to come in from the cold. The reflagging of Kuwaiti tankers did indeed work.

Ironically, the Reagan administration did have a thoroughly viable process for strategic thinking. It was called the "Weinberger Doctrine" and later became the "Powell Doctrine." After the Beirut bombing in 1983, Secretary of Defense Caspar Weinberger announced the doctrine for using force that would bear his name. Had presidents abided by it, perhaps many defeats and setbacks would have been avoided. To excerpt the Weinberger Doctrine's key points:

- The United States should not commit forces to combat overseas unless the particular engagement or occasion is deemed vital to our national interest or that of our allies. . . .

- If we decide it is necessary to put combat troops into a given situation, we should do so wholeheartedly, and with the clear intention of winning. . . .

- If we do decide to commit forces to combat overseas, we should have clearly defined political and military objectives. . . .

- The relationship between our objectives and the forces we have committed—their size, composition and disposition—must be continually reassessed and adjusted if necessary. . . .

- Before the U.S. commits combat forces abroad, there must be some reasonable assurance we will have the support of the American people and their elected representatives in Congress. . . .

- The commitment of U.S. forces to combat should be a last resort.

Shortly before the start of the first Gulf war in 1990, General Powell laid out similar requirements for using force in what became known as the "Powell Doctrine." Originally, Powell called for the use of "overwhelming force"; that term was modified to the more benign "sufficient force," but the meaning was the same. Unfortunately, neither the Powell nor Weinberger Doctrine survived the change of administration. The three presidents immediately following George H. W. Bush chose not to heed this otherwise powerful advice concerning when to and when not to go to war.

Not all decisions to use military force involve making what can be termed "war." Since the end of World War II, military force had been employed hundreds of times, in ways varying from simple peacetime presence to retaliatory strikes and to interventions, some limited, others not. In many cases, the Weinberger-Powell Doctrine did not apply. It is in this large and often ambiguous realm between "war" and "peace" that a template for sound strategic thinking is sorely needed. Part of this vacuum speaks to the need for comprehensive, whole-of-government approaches to resolving national security problems and issues. The absence of follow-up in Afghanistan would pale in comparison to future missteps.

Finally, during the Reagan years, and despite Weinberger's doctrine, the errors and misjudgments of Kennedy-Johnson and Carter years were repeated. As we will see, failures for similar reasons would occur under future presidencies. Interestingly, the two presidencies that avoided many of these mistakes—Nixon's and that of the first Bush—ended in the resignation of the former and electoral defeat after only one term for the latter.

Five

George Herbert Walker Bush

Panama, Desert Storm, the End of the Soviet Union, Europe Whole and Free, and the Unintended Consequences of "the New World Order"

George Herbert Walker Bush was the most qualified presidential candidate to enter office since Richard Nixon. He would face the beginning of the most transformational period in international politics and national security since World War II. As will be argued, following the disastrous invasion of Iraq in 2003 by his son, the world has since entered into what is at least as tectonic a transformation—an era I term one of No World Order.

To his immense credit, George H. W. Bush would get the "big crises" right—namely, the integration of former Warsaw Pact states into a Europe that was whole, free, and at peace; and the first Gulf war, following Saddam Hussein's invasion and occupation of Kuwait in August 1990. But "the New World Order" he envisaged would also pose intractable, less visible, but nonetheless fundamental challenges to the international system.

The Soviet Union was withdrawing from Afghanistan and would shortly self-destruct as an entity. However, the forces that had helped drive the Soviet Union from Afghanistan would metastasize into the post–September 11 nightmare of radical and perverted Islamist violence, which today has global reach. Similarly, the dissolution of Yugoslavia would bring on the Balkan Wars, which would elude quick solution by the Bush and future administrations and their NATO allies.

Finally, the demise of the Soviet Union would allow the former members of the Warsaw Pact to democratize and to seek and gain membership into NATO. However, the issue of how to treat Russia for the long term would become an irreconcilable contradiction for Bush's successors. Indeed, that the end of the Soviet Union may have produced a Russia that is in collision with the West may, ironically, prove to be Lenin's last legacy.

The scion of two politically influential families, the Bushes and the Walkers, Bush graduated from Phillips Academy and after Pearl Harbor joined the Navy, where he became one the youngest torpedo pilots to win his wings. Piloting a Grumman TBM Avenger, he, with his crew of two, was shot down on September 2, 1944, during a mission to bomb the Japanese island of Chichi Jima. Bush and his surviving crewman were rescued by the submarine USS *Finback;* they were on board for a month.

After the war, decorated with a Distinguished Flying Cross and several Air Medals, Bush attended Yale on an accelerated program. Bush was Phi Beta Kappa and was elected captain of the baseball team. Graduating in 1948 and moving to Texas, Bush would become successful in the oil business.

In 1967, he was elected to the House of Representatives and served there until 1971, when he made an unsuccessful run for the Senate. Bush then held four consecutive senior appointments: ambassador to the UN, chairman of the Republican National Committee, envoy to China, and, from 1976 to 1977, Director of Central Intelligence. Ronald Reagan chose Bush as his vice president in 1980, and both served from 1981 to 1989. Bush won the presidency after handily defeating Democrat Michael Dukakis, former governor of Massachusetts, in the November 1988 election.

While Bush has been mocked for his "vision thing," "being a wimp," and his concept of "a thousand points of light," he brought an absolutely superb national security team with him. At State was James Baker, a veteran of the Reagan administration, both as treasury secretary and as chief of staff, and one of Bush's closest friends. Bush wanted as his secretary of defense John Tower, former senator from Texas and the highly autocratic chairman of the Senate Armed Services Committee.

The Tower confirmation was Bush's first setback. Senator Sam Nunn, who now chaired the Armed Services Committee, detested Tower for the way he had run the committee before retiring in 1984 to make a fortune in the private sector. Unedited FBI "notes" on Tower's drinking and womanizing were leaked. Also, Dick Cheney, Ford's second chief of staff and House minority leader, was not keen on the appointment. Faced with losing the confirmation vote, a very discouraged Bush allowed Tower to withdraw. Dick Cheney was offered the post and made secretary of defense. On September 30, 1989, Gen. Colin Powell replaced Adm. William J. Crowe as chairman of the Joint Chiefs of Staff.

Perhaps the most significant of Bush's national security appointees was Brent Scowcroft, a retired Air Force lieutenant general. Following a plane crash that ended his flying career soon after his commissioning, Scowcroft became the epitome of the brilliant staff officer. Seconded to the Nixon White House, Scowcroft became Henry Kissinger's trusted deputy. When Gerald Ford took office, he made Scowcroft his national security advisor. Scowcroft and Bush had become friendly during the Nixon administration.

Scowcroft's view of the role of the national security advisor was that of an objective interlocutor between and among the president's key cabinet advisors. Coordination was the aim, not usurpation of power or the control of the execution of policy that nearly destroyed the Reagan administration in Iran-Contra.

As noted, after Iran-Contra, Reagan appointed a three-person panel, the Tower Commission, to investigate. Scowcroft and Senators Tower and Muskie of Maine produced a blistering indictment of a failed NSC system. Scowcroft believed that the system had never adapted to the (too laid back) management style of the president and there had been no oversight or accountability. The panel report confirmed Scowcroft's convictions about the NSC and his ideas for correcting it.

When he became national security advisor, Scowcroft was to expand on the major changes to the NSC implemented by Frank Carlucci, who had become Reagan's national security advisor. When Colin Powell replaced Carlucci, Scowcroft felt strongly that Powell should have resigned his commission, as Scowcroft had done when he got the job from Ford. Powell obviously disagreed, and history was to support that view.

Despite appearing low-key and mild-mannered and remaining often in the background, Scowcroft possessed a first-rate intellect and was never reluctant to employ it. He could be steely eyed and ruthlessly decisive, qualities he preferred not to unveil until needed. Scowcroft believed that civility and teamwork were vital. So, much of the political infighting that had been ingrained in earlier NSCs went "missing in action." Collegiality—provided intellectual rigor was maintained—was Scowcroft's secret sauce. And that was powerful secret sauce!

The only surprise in Bush's choices for high office was that of Senator Dan Quayle as vice president. Quayle was an attractive, boyish-looking senator from Indiana, where his family had considerable influence (and in Arizona as well) through ownership of local newspapers. Elected to the House at twenty-nine, after two terms there he became the youngest Indianan to win a Senate seat, in 1981. He served eight years before becoming vice president.

In the Middle East, during the nearly ten-year Iran-Iraq War Saddam Hussein had become a (distasteful) de facto ally of the United States. Iran was vehemently hostile toward the West and Israel. As vice president, Bush had a front-row seat for the Gulf, the Middle East, and the tanker war. Bush had also witnessed the Beirut catastrophe, Grenada, Iran-Contra, and other uses of force under Reagan.

Bush had testified before the Tower Commission that he "was out of the loop." And however out of the loop the vice president may have been, Bush would have never approved the ludicrous scheme that became Iran-Contra. Bush was well aware of the shortcomings of the Reagan decision-making process and of the internecine war among cabinet officers. These tensions and battles were not necessarily much different from those of the Nixon White House. There Henry Kissinger had done his best to keep Secretary of State William Rogers on the sidelines and had contrived to get Secretary of Defense James Schlesinger fired—an allegation he strongly denied.

As president, Bush would face many challenges of extraordinary proportions. The most stunning and significant was the dissolution of the Soviet Union. Regarding military interventions and the use of force, Panama and Iraq were Bush's first major crises. The former Yugoslavia would disintegrate during his watch. Bush's New World Order would not produce quite the peace and stability the president may have wished. But his vision for a Europe whole and free was to be among his finest accomplishments.

Yugoslavia, like Afghanistan, would be deferred to Bush's successor. Meanwhile, the demise of the Soviet Union not only ended the Cold War but offered virtually unlimited opportunities for reshaping the world. One opportunity was to reshape and downsize the U.S. military for a future in which the Soviet Union, the enemy that had dominated the strategy of the Department of Defense and determined budgets, force levels, and weapons systems for more than four decades, no longer existed.

Five months after Bush took office, in June 1989, the Chinese government brutally and bloodily repressed student demonstrations in Beijing in what became known as the Tiananmen Square Massacre, for the site of these atrocities. As former envoy to China, Bush knew the Chinese leadership well and was indeed very bullish on the Middle Kingdom. Yet he would be limited in his immediate options for China by the massively negative political reactions provoked by these acts of brutality.

As will be discussed, on December 20, 1989, Bush ordered Operation Just Cause, to remove Panamanian dictator Manuel Noriega. Prior to this intervention, Bush's administration had been strongly criticized for not supporting the attempted coup in Panama, which had occurred two months before and had failed in part because the administration, informed in advance of the plot, declined to assist. Nor was Bush's handling of Afghanistan and Pakistan as deft as were his policies for Europe and Iraq.

At the end of Bush's first and only term, the humanitarian situation in Somalia and the Horn of Africa had deteriorated so badly that he felt compelled to act. That action would inadvertently set the stage for the Mogadishu shoot-out in the fall of 1993 between U.S. forces and thousands of attacking Somalis (as portrayed in the 2001 movie *Black Hawk Down*). Bush told the incoming Clinton administration that he would withdraw from Somalia if the new president so wanted. Clinton did not.

Less visible than the Somalia failure to Bush and his team at the time were the accelerating effects of the end of the Cold War, which were transforming the national security environment of the twentieth century. The second half of that century had been largely defined for the United States by the bipolar and binary rivalry with the Soviet Union. This interaction with the Soviet Union had been the most significant national security priority for every administration since FDR. The dominance of this relationship obscured what would become the bandwidth problem—that is the likelihood that the demands of simultaneous contingencies ("multicrises") would exceed the physical and intellectual capacity of any White House to respond effectively.

Adm. Jonathan Howe, U.S. Navy (Ret.), who had served in many senior positions, including deputy national security advisor, explained this phenomenon in his PhD dissertation and subsequent book on multicrises. Howe showed how secondary crises tended to be ignored when concurrent with major crises or overshadowed by the U.S.-Soviet confrontation. His most relevant example was the nearly simultaneous occurrence of the 1968 Tet Offensive in Vietnam and North Korea's highjacking of the unarmed Navy electronics ship USS *Pueblo* (AGER 2) in international waters off the Korean coast.

Given the fixation on reversing the Tet Offensive, there was little President Johnson could do to coerce or convince North Korea to return *Pueblo*, beyond the futile dispatch of two aircraft carriers into the Sea of Japan. In the twenty-first century, however, without a central foundation for national security and given a world that is instantly interconnected and interrelated, crises have become more complicated and more often simultaneous. Today, for example, President

Donald Trump faces a host of concurrent crises, from the Bay of Bengal to the western Mediterranean, each competing for attention.

Thus the bandwidth problem is now grave for the United States, characterized by some as the "indispensable power." While this shorthand is far from perfect, the United States is deeply engaged literally around the world in terms of business, trade, finance, security, alliances, and global stability. Without that presence, meaning with a return to a form of isolationism, the world would not be a better place.

Bush's priorities were, correctly, managing the emerging post-Soviet world and restoring relations with China. Members of his administration will agree that in this process Afghanistan, Pakistan, Yugoslavia, and other crisis regions did not receive the attention they otherwise deserved. But how does one organize any White House and administration for this bandwidth overload? This is another weakness that a brains-based approach to strategic thinking attempts to remedy.

Bush oversaw three principal uses of force: Just Cause, which removed Manuel Noriega in December 1989; Operations Desert Shield and Desert Storm in 1990–91; and humanitarian deployments in the form of Provide Comfort, in northern Iraq to help save the Kurds, and Restore Hope/Provide Relief, in the Horn of Africa in December 1992.

Just Cause, the incursion into Panama on December 20, was far from flawless. But the operation succeeded in removing Noriega and reinstalling Guillermo Endara, who had been elected president earlier that May in an election Noriega ruled null and void. Noriega had been indicted by the Reagan administration for drug trafficking. His partnering with the drug cartels, entangling himself in the Iran-Contra affair (in which he accepted large amounts of money from the CIA), and annulling Endara's election were amply sufficient reasons for regime change in Panama. The immediate catalysts were the unprovoked murder of an unarmed Marine lieutenant and one of his colleagues by the Panama Defense Force (PDF) and the beating of a Navy lieutenant and the threatened rape of his wife in Panama City. Bush was outraged.

On December 17, Bush authorized military action on these grounds:

- Safeguarding the lives of American citizens in Panama. Noriega had declared that a state of war existed between the United States and Panama and was threatening the lives of the approximately 35,000 American citizens living there.

- Combating drug trafficking and bringing Noriega to justice, he having been indicted in the United States for these and other crimes.

- Protecting the integrity of the Torrijos-Carter treaties, which had returned the Panama Canal to Panama but reserved the right of the United States to intervene militarily to protect the canal.

The actual military operation overwhelmed Noriega; it could not have failed. At 0100 on December 20, more than 27,000 Americans intervened in Panama. Just Cause was not, however, a military masterstroke. Twenty-three American servicemen were killed, several by friendly fire, and 325 were wounded. Somewhere between 500 and 1,000 Panamanians perished. Noriega, after seeking asylum in a church and being bombarded with intensely loud and bad music, surrendered on January 3, 1992. Endara was reseated as president, and by the end of January, American forces had been withdrawn from Panama.

The speed of the operation quelled any congressional opposition, as did the quick return home of American troops. The Organization of American States, however, was highly critical. The UN Security Council condemned the invasion (the resolution was vetoed by the United States). Several lawsuits were filed, and in 2015 Panama created a "truth commission" to identify Panamanians who deserved compensation for damages suffered during the brief invasion.

Goldwater-Nichols had surely improved the fighting capability of the American military by creating more "jointness" and interoperability among the services. However, it would take another conflict to restore fully the credibility and prowess of American forces. Saddam Hussein would provide that opportunity in August 1990.

In 1990, Iraq had complained loudly about Kuwait violating quotas established by OPEC (the Organization of Petroleum Exporting Countries) for exporting oil and thereby keeping prices low. Summoning Ambassador April Glaspie to his headquarters in late July before she left on home leave, Saddam asked about America's position vis-à-vis Kuwait and Iraqi border disputes with Kuwait. As reported in the *New York Times* on September 9, 1990, Glaspie replied,

> I know you need funds. We understand that and our opinion is that you should have the opportunity to rebuild your country. *But we have no opinion on the Arab-Arab conflicts, like your border disagreement with Kuwait. . . .* Frankly, we can only see that you have deployed massive troops in the south. Normally that would not be any of our business. But when this happens in the context of what you said on your national day, then when we read the details in the two letters of the Foreign Minister, then when we see the Iraqi point of view that the measures taken by the UAE and Kuwait is, in the final analysis, parallel to military aggression against Iraq, then it would be reasonable for me to be concerned.

Believing or liberally inferring that he had been given a free hand by the Americans and Ambassador Glaspie's comments (especially the sentence in italics above), on August 2, 1990, Saddam sent Iraq's army pouring into Kuwait. Local forces were overwhelmed in hours, and the ruling al Sabah family fled into exile. The West was shocked by this aggression. But what to do? After all, the Iraqi army was regarded as very combat experienced and able, having fought a long war against Iran. It numbered nearly one million troops. It was equipped with chemical weapons (which it had used against

Iran) and, many believed, biological weapons. It possessed Soviet Scud missiles, as well as other advanced Soviet- and French-made missiles, aircraft, and tanks. A French Exocet missile accidentally launched by Iraqi pilots had nearly sunk the frigate USS *Stark* in the Persian Gulf, reminding observers of the lethality of Saddam's weapon inventory.

Because Bush wanted a considered response to this invasion, he did not immediately react. On August 5, the president promised reporters that "this [invasion] will not stand, this aggression against Kuwait." Two days later, Bush authorized Operation Desert Shield, to protect Saudi Arabia in the event Saddam saw an opportunity to expand his growing empire into that kingdom. A small force was immediately dispatched to Saudi Arabia under the command of Lt. Gen. Charles "Chuck" Horner, U.S. Air Force. Horner regarded this force as merely a speed bump if Saddam chose to attack Saudi Arabia.

During the next few months, the Bush administration scrupulously, if not consciously, followed the Weinberger/Powell Doctrine in planning responses. Support was building, in the forms of nearly universal condemnation of the invasion and empowering UN resolutions, for ejecting Saddam from Kuwait if diplomacy and sanctions did not work. James Baker and Dick Cheney were actively building a broad international coalition, and the secretary of state was embarked on Operation Tin Cup to garner funds to pay for whatever military action might follow.

The history of Operations Desert Shield and Desert Storm has been well reported and can be summarized in terms of what went right and what did not. That analysis will point to conclusions that would support both the development and implementation of a brains-based approach to sound strategic thinking.

First, the Bush administration needed a full and complete understanding of conditions, not only in the region and globally but at home as well. Domestic opinion was at best divided, and the Democratically controlled 101st Congress was far from friendly. Tom Foley was the Speaker of the House, George Mitchell the Senate majority leader. Bush would have to work very hard to get a majority in Congress to support military action.

Second, while regional states voiced strong rhetorical support for action against Saddam, Saudi Arabia and the Gulf states would have to be convinced as to the urgency and necessity of stationing hundreds of thousands of American troops, as well as forces from other countries, inside their borders. A remarkable change in traditional and conservative Saudi policies that had long opposed such actions on religious and sovereignty grounds would have to take place. Kuwait itself was not particularly well regarded, because of its efforts to avoid the oil quotas, and the al Sabah family was neither well liked nor respected.

Third, Iraq had been a quasi-ally during its long war against Iran. Further, Ambassador Glaspie's comments to Saddam could have been (and were) interpreted as giving Saddam a green light. No strong case for a forceful intervention would be self-evident, especially given Kuwait's dubious reputation.

Fourth, what would it take to defeat the Iraqi army? Opinions of its ability varied, but for reasons listed above, it was likely to be a formidable adversary. For its part, the U.S. military had certainly been restored as a fighting force since the disaster of Vietnam, and very much organized against a Soviet-style threat like the Iraqi forces. But aside from Operation Urgent Fury, it had not been tested in a real war for nearly two decades. When the military had been used—in Desert One, Beirut, and Grenada—the outcomes had not been reassuring.

Fifth, and a subset of the above, how would an intervention force be organized, commanded, and resupplied? Would the Saudis tolerate a Westerner or American in command? Operations could be far more taxing in desert conditions than on the German plains. Heat, sand, and the absence of roads and infrastructure would not be easily overcome. Supplying a force that could number half a million troops or more with such basic items as water, fuel, ammunition, food, batteries, and medical support would require massive air- and sealift. That would tax even advanced countries in Europe. While Saudi Arabia had been building air and other bases for its largely American- and Western-purchased arms, that infrastructure would need to be greatly expanded.

Sixth, how quickly could this buildup be accomplished? Planning and preparation for the Normandy invasion had taken more than a year. The Bush administration knew that waiting a year would be unacceptable politically and operationally. If the assault were delayed to the spring or summer, the weather would be even more formidable an obstacle than it already was.

Seventh, what were the potential inadvertent or unexpected consequences—what Donald Rumsfeld would later call the "unknown unknowns"? And of course, aside from dozens of other unanswered and unanswerable questions, the crucial one remained: Could the United States ready and deploy a force of perhaps half a million troops, including coalition partners, four thousand miles to a hostile, logistically austere locale and be prepared to launch an assault to reoccupy Kuwait within six months if not sooner?

Eisenhower might have been daunted by the task. But Bush, Scowcroft, Cheney, and, most important, Powell were not. Powell had played a critical role in the rebuilding of the post-Vietnam U.S. Army. Having been V Corps commander in Europe, albeit for a short time, and then Commander, Army Forces Command, Powell, with his keen professional instincts, knew what the Army and the other services were capable of. Additionally, some of his key lieutenants—including Chuck Horner, who would command the air war, and John Yeosock, who would be the land component commander in Saudi Arabia—had been classmates and close friends at the National War College. Powell also knew well Norman Schwarzkopf, who as Central Command commander would lead Operation Desert Storm.

Pulling together this massively complicated operation, with all of its many moving parts, was a Sisyphean labor largely underappreciated by the public. Nor was waging this war always as straightforward as it may appear in retrospect. Congress was largely disposed against an assault into Kuwait, fearing that the Iraqi army, entrenched in the so-called Saddam line, would prove too formidable and impose too many American casualties. Memories of Desert One and Beirut lingered, and doubt about the American military's ability remained. And would Saddam use WMD—weapons of mass destruction?

One of Bush's unexpected allies on Capitol Hill turned out to be Democratic representative Les Aspin of Wisconsin, chairman of the powerful House Armed Services Committee. As a young House member in the 1970s, Aspin had been a long-standing critic of the Defense Department, a fierce enemy of the waste he believed abounded in the Pentagon. For years Aspin had campaigned to shut down the commissaries, which provided service members and families with lower-cost food and household goods. Aspin was heartily disliked by the military as a result of these and other criticisms, which found reflections in defense authorization bills approved by his committee.

But Aspin had matured. He readily understood what was at stake in Kuwait. When civilian analysts predicted that a war would cost the United States at least 50,000 casualties, Aspin held hearings to rebut those dire estimates. Ultimately, Aspin concluded that the coalition would suffer fewer than 2,500 casualties, an estimate that turned out to be, fortunately, greatly exaggerated. Aspin in fact became one of the strongest congressional proponents of ejecting Saddam from Kuwait. That was essential to the administration in neutralizing Democratic opposition. Sam Nunn, chairman of the Senate Armed Services Committee and the driving force in the rejection of John Tower's nomination as secretary of defense, was firmly set against war.

The decisive moment came on October 28, in a White House meeting of Bush's top advisors. Bush had just received a letter cosigned by Foley and Mitchell stating that unless Bush obtained congressional approval for any war against Saddam, impeachment could follow—quite a warning, just when the White House was deciding how far it would go if sanctions and diplomacy failed.

Powell was ambivalent on the question of a full-blown war. He held out the hope that sanctions, diplomacy, and the flow of U.S. forces to the region would bring Saddam to his senses. Knowing, however, that hope is never a strategy, Powell had to ensure that if as the last resort military action were undertaken, there would be absolutely no doubt about winning. Overwhelming force would have to be brought to bear. Saddam would need to be crushed, and crushed quickly. And American casualties needed to be minimal.

At this meeting, arguments for and against waiting or attacking flowed back and forth. It became clear that the president was not prepared to wait for an indefinite period, meaning that Desert Storm would be launched early in 1991. Bush turned to Powell and asked what it would take in terms of American forces. As he wrote in his memoir, *My American Journey*, Powell immediately responded, "About half a million troops."

According to both Powell's and later Scowcroft and Bush's joint memoir, Bush did not hesitate: "All right, then, that's what you will have," with the same determination he had shown in authorizing Just Cause in Panama. The decision was made. The Powell Doctrine had been fulfilled. Whatever Powell's reservations may have been, he had done his duty. The United States and the coalition would prevail. But few appreciated beforehand how dramatic and decisive that victory would be.

On November 29, 1990, UN Security Resolution 678 was passed, giving Iraq a deadline of January 15, 1991, by which it was to withdraw completely from Kuwait. On January 12, the Democratic-controlled House voted 250–183 to authorize the use of force, with the caveats that all other means had to be exhausted first and that if heavy casualties were taken, the United States would withdraw—both meaningless strictures once hostilities began. The Senate vote was much tighter: fifty-two to forty-seven. Several years later, Sam Nunn admitted that his vote opposing the invasion was one of the worst votes he ever cast. A demarche was delivered to Saddam Hussein. Saddam ignored the deadline. On January 17, Desert Storm began with an attack by F-117 stealth fighters on air defenses in Baghdad.

Powell was asked at a January 23 Pentagon press conference what his strategy was. He replied bluntly, "Our strategy for dealing with this army is very simple: First we're going to cut it off, then we're going to kill it." Few in the media were as confident as Powell. Memories of Vietnam still loomed. Iraq's military strength was still seen as formidable. Also, a war in which weapons of mass destruction could be used was a possibility.

Some argued that the United States would be bloodied badly. But the battle would not unfold that way—quite the opposite.

As Desert Storm got under way, General Schwarzkopf became an instant media celebrity, his almost daily briefings conveying a degree of confidence bordering on invincibility. Asked by a reporter about Saddam's generalship, Schwarzkopf could not have been more dismissive. And he could not have been more correct.

U.S. and coalition air forces pounded the virtually helpless Iraqi military for thirty-eight days. Saddam's only military response that had any effect was firing Scud missiles into Israel and Saudi Arabia, hoping to goad Israel into the war and thereby causing the Arab allies to desert the coalition. It was initially feared that the warheads might have been loaded with chemical weapons, such as those used during the Iranian conflict.

Fortunately, the Scuds contained conventional warheads, perhaps because Secretary of State James Baker had been blunt in warning and reminding Saddam that any use of WMD could trigger an American nuclear response. But the United States was slow in and not very effective at countertargeting Saddam's Scuds. This was one of the few instances where the mission exceeded the actual U.S. military capability. And Schwarzkopf was so preoccupied with the ground campaign that he failed to appreciate the political importance of neutralizing the Scuds to ensure Israel would stay out of the fight. Fortunately, Bush and Baker were able to keep Israel at bay, warning that if Israel entered the war by attacking Saddam, the Arab coalition would splinter.

On February 24, the land offensive began. Under the command of Gen. Walter E. Boomer, Marines quickly smashed through the "invincible" Saddam line on the southern border of Kuwait, remarkably without a single casualty. At the same time, the famous "left hook," an end-around through the Saudi desert to cut off the Iraqi army's retreat from Kuwait, was led by Lt. Gen. Frederick M. Franks, U.S. Army. Franks, who had lost a leg in Vietnam but had been allowed to remain on active duty, would soon receive a fourth star.

The Marine assault against the Saddam line succeeded so rapidly that the Iraqi army fled north before Frank's corps could trap it. The Saddam line had been manned mostly by underfed, under-trained recruits who cracked as soon as the Marine ground offensive started. These troops had been subjected to debilitating as well as frightening round-the-clock bombing and artillery fire. In the panic that now ensued, retreating Iraqi soldiers so overloaded the major road north that it became known as the "Highway of Death."

Indeed, the suddenness and thoroughness with which troops of the United States and some sixty coalition nations sliced through Saddam's defenses resulted in a slaughter of the retreating Iraqi soldiers. The war was so one-sided that the images of helpless Iraqis being killed now confronted the Bush administration with a crisis: Should the destruction of the helpless Iraqi army continue despite its seeming immorality, or should Desert Storm be halted?

The decision was not difficult. After 100 hours of operations, the coalition forces offered Saddam a truce, which was readily accepted. The war was over, and by March 10 nearly 540,000 U.S. troops would have started the long journey home. The United States had suffered 146 killed: 70 by friendly fire and accident, about two dozen when a Scud missile struck a barracks in Saudi Arabia. That about 50 Americans were killed in action in a war in which over half a million troops faced an army about double the size was extraordinary. Desert Storm was one of the most lopsided military campaigns in history.

After the war, some critics complained that the alliance should have marched to and occupied Baghdad. That would have been a colossal misjudgment. The Arab coalition would have collapsed. Saudi Arabia probably would have demanded the United States leave, meaning there would have been no infrastructure to support the advance into Iraq. Also, as Dick Cheney famously remarked at the time, the United States lacked the means to occupy Iraq and stay for decades. He was correct then, and the critics were profoundly wrong. Unfortunately, the attacks of September 11, 2001, were to change Cheney's mind, and as vice president he would summarily reject the good judgment he had shown as defense secretary.

No operation is perfect, although this one was close. The United States had not known how hollow the Iraqi military was before the war started. The Marines' frontal assault had been meant simply to hold the Iraqi army in place until Franks could envelope and then destroy it. But the assault was so devastating that Franks could not close the back door in time. Some were to argue that had the ground assault and "left hook" not been simultaneous and Franks had been given the lead in the offensive, perhaps the Iraqi army would have stood its ground and so been trapped. On the other hand, it is possible that had Franks begun the envelopment before the frontal attack into Kuwait, the Iraqi army could have cut and run anyway and thus more of it might have escaped.

Also, Franks, in his after-action report, would complain that because of weather and an absence of advanced reconnaissance assets, he often did not know what literally lay beyond the next sand berm. Occasionally U.S and Iraqi units would stumble into each other. The outcome was always fatal for Iraq.

The American technological advantage proved far greater than had been anticipated. Soviet T-72 tanks used by Iraq were supposed to be well armored and resistant to antitank weapons. In fact, quite the opposite was the case. American M-1 tanks reported getting kills firing through sand berms at ranges of almost a mile. On the other hand, desert weather and sand played havoc with much of the American equipment, and fighting in antichemical suits in blazing hot weather was always enervating.

At the truce talks at Safwan, Schwarzkopf gave permission for Iraq to use helicopters in no-fly zones, in which Iraq was prohibited from flying fixed-wing aircraft. Saddam exploited that permission to attack the helpless "Marsh Arabs" in the south who had revolted, convinced the United States would come to their aid. We did not.

But the larger dilemma of regime termination was raised by the air war commander. Chuck Horner was attempting to use airpower to collapse the regime. Saddam was targeted on several occasions but escaped. One bomb demolished a bunker filled with dozens of family members of the Iraqi leadership, killing many; the attack was strongly criticized as targeting innocents. But as Horner reported, he was unable to find a place "to stick the needle," to end the regime. His point was that even with the overwhelming U.S. military superiority, it still took a ground war to evict Saddam. Was it possible to end a war by ending the regime through other means?

Finally, as noted, Schwarzkopf did not immediately appreciate how politically vital countering the Scuds was for Israel and Saudi Arabia. Unlike in Vietnam, this time the "five-thousand-mile screwdriver" (control and influence by distant seniors) was important. Had Israel retaliated against the Scud attacks, as noted, the coalition could have splintered. This lesson is very applicable in the battle against Islamist extremism. The political optics are more important than the use of force itself. Today, sadly, the jihadis seem to understand this reality better than we do.

In any event, Bush's popularity soared. Victory parades lauded the military and erased the damning legacy of Vietnam. Generals Schwarzkopf and Powell were national heroes. The stunningly quick conclusion of the war, the lack of American casualties, and the stopping of aggression played very well with a public anxious for a military victory. In retrospect, however, perhaps Bush should have decided that the al Sabah family not be returned to power in Kuwait. The Kuwaiti people might have been given the right to decide who should lead them. Of course, the Saudi and Gulf state regimes would have been apoplectic, seeing themselves as excessively vulnerable to regime change.

The despicable treatment of the Kurds in northern Iraq led Secretary of State Baker to visit the region after the war. Seeing the deprivations of the Kurds and the continued attacks by Iraq, Baker quickly pressed Bush to authorize relief. Operation Provide Comfort did just that; it was a very effective humanitarian-relief effort. Since a no-fly zone was in force in the north of Iraq and U.S. forces threatened to return, Saddam posed no obstacle to this operation. Bush would repeat this move in Somalia, at the end of his term, with Operation Provide Relief.

The last strategic issue related to Desert Storm was the establishment of the "Base Force." When he became chairman in September 1989, Powell recognized that with the Soviet Union in a process of profound change, U.S military strategy and forces needed major adjustment. According to *The Military Balance*, produced by the International Institute for Strategic Studies, the U.S. Army had 18 active divisions; the Navy, 15 carriers and 550 ships; the Air

Force, 21 tactical fighter wings; the Marine Corps, 197,000 personnel, with a congressional mandate (Title X) of 3 active divisions and air wings and 1 each in reserve—a total active-duty force of about 2.1 million.

Powell began planning for a future force that would be based on "capability" and not "threat." Powell believed that under Goldwater-Nichols, the chairman could begin this planning on his own initiative. This was highly controversial, as the service chiefs and commanders in chief in the field had always been resistant to erosion—by anyone, in or out of uniform—of their authorities to affect force levels and budget allocations.

The budget debate was in full force in the summer of 1990 when Saddam invaded Kuwait. The Senate Armed Services Committee had cut the president's January request for $297 billion (in 1991 dollars, $520 billion in 2015 dollars) to $277 billion ($490 billion in 2015 dollars). So, while planning and executing Desert Shield and Desert Storm, Powell was likewise reshaping the nation's military posture for what would be the post–Cold War.

The Base Force was Powell's assessment of the floor below which U.S. forces should never descend. With the end of the Soviet threat, the United States no longer needed its then-current levels of forces and defense spending. Dick Cheney, as secretary of defense, and Paul Wolfowitz, his undersecretary for policy, disagreed with Powell on the continuing threat posed by residual Soviet (now Russian) military strength. However, Powell's arguments persisted and would carry the day with the president.

Finally, Powell pushed through his Base Force, by dint of personality, intellect, and forceful leadership. His prestige as the key architect of Desert Storm was enormous. In the end, budget realities made the Base Force the ceiling, not the floor. The military would be decreased by about 25 percent. The Army would have 12 active, 6 reserve, and 2 cadre divisions, a total of 510,000 active-duty personnel and 900,000 reservists.

Naval forces would consist of 12 aircraft carriers and a total of 450 ships, 15 active and 11 reserve fighter wings, and a Marine Corps of 170,000. The Air Force would move to 16 active and 12 reserve fighter wings. The total active-duty force would number just over 1.6 million. The best source for the evolution of the Base Force and how Powell succeeded against quite powerful (and understandable) bureaucratic opposition is *History of the Base Force 1989–92*, written in 1993 by Lorna S. Jaffee, of the Joint History Office of the Chairman of the Joint Chiefs of Staff.

It is in fact quite astounding that Powell was able to have this Base Force approved. Cheney and Wolfowitz were more than skeptical. The service chiefs, who were the guardians of force structure, were not entirely happy with the reductions. No service chief would be. Not all the major field commanders, who argued for force structure based on warfighting requirements, agreed with these reductions. However, as a strategic planning exercise and guidebook for the future, the Base Force is in the same category as Zumwalt's brilliant Project 60 of two decades earlier.

To recall the previous discussion about strategy/force-level budget mismatch, the Base Force addressed these concerns. However, a 25 percent cut in force levels did not translate to a 25 percent cut in budget needs. That mismatch continues today and if not addressed will produce a twenty-first-century version of the dreaded post-Vietnam "hollow force."

By mid-1992, despite his huge popularity and economic policies, which were about to produce significant economic growth, George H. W. Bush was trailing in the presidential polls. Governor Bill Clinton of Arkansas was a fresh and charismatic face, with ideas for a new Democratic Party of the center. Billionaire Ross Perot had entered the lists as an independent, arguing that unless correction of the federal deficit was the top domestic priority for the next president, the economy would crash.

> In former defense secretary James R. Schlesinger's (JRS) office at the Center for Strategic and International Studies, Washington, D.C., May 1992.

> **JRS:** "Harlan, you wanted to see me? You have something I need to know?"

HKU: "Yes, Jim. I know how close you and the Bushes are, going back to CIA days."

JRS: "Yes."

HKU: "And I think you agree with me that Bush is running behind in the polls and that Ross Perot could cost him the election."

JRS: "Yes, and I am stunned how Bill Clinton whose background is entirely opposite to Bush's, from avoiding the draft to his personal weaknesses, has used his charisma and charm to woo the public."

HKU: "What do you think could change that?"

JRS: "A miracle."

HKU: "I have a better idea."

JRS: "Go on."

HKU: "While you and I know there is more to Dan Quayle than the public appreciates, given his persona and reputation, he is a political liability."

JRS: "I agree. And?"

HKU: "Who is possibly the most popular American today?"

JRS: "Go on."

HKU: "Colin Powell."

JRS, collecting his thoughts: "That is a brilliant idea."

HKU: "There is one problem. Colin did not resign from the Army as national security advisor. He would have to do so if on the ticket, as he has another year left as chairman."

JRS: "I don't think that is a problem. If the president asks, who can refuse?"

In jest, Schlesinger told me that this idea was so secret we needed a code name. He selected "Black Magic"! We took it to the Bushes. Barbara was for it. George was circumspect. He later got back to Schlesinger thanking him for the thought but saying he was going to stay with Quayle. Who knows what would have happened if Powell had been on that ticket? Vice presidents usually do not sway elections, and Bush might still have lost.

◆

The George H. W. Bush administration deserves great credit for strategic thinking and for getting the biggest issues largely and fortunately right. Bush was instrumental in the reunification of Germany, one of the biggest gains post–Cold War. Here, Bush was ably assisted by National Security Advisor Brent Scowcroft. Bush also had excellent relations with Gorbachev (with whom we signed a strategic arms agreement) and then with Boris Yeltsin, who was elected Russia's president. Bush also provided several billions of dollars of aid to Russia when it was falling apart in 1992, a humanitarian act now lost in the mists of time.

One of Bush's biggest enemies was bandwidth. Afghanistan, Yugoslavia, and Somalia would be deferred to the next president, as well as no-fly zones and embargoes on Saddam and Iraq. The White House simply did not have the time or depth to deal with all these issues concurrently in an effective manner. Many of these lesser issues would later return with a vengeance. Of course, NATO expansion and Russia were the most critical issues, and they would assume even greater importance and priority in the coming decades.

On the other hand, Bill Clinton was lucky. He would inherit a growing economy, a dissolving Soviet Union, and an immense military victory in Iraq—all thanks to Bush, who would never receive all the credit he is due. In poker terms, Clinton was dealt a royal straight flush. Yet, some of the other cards in the pack were jokers, Somalia being the first to be turned up. Likewise, dealing with post-Soviet Russia would not be easy.

Six

William Jefferson Clinton, the Bottom-Up Force, Black Hawk Down, NATO Expansion, Yugoslavia, and the Rise of al Qaeda

W illiam Jefferson Clinton won the presidency with a plurality, not a majority, of votes. Independent Ross Perot took about 19 percent of the vote. While some polls showed that Perot had detracted equally from Clinton and Bush, the outgoing president believed otherwise. Nor could Bush, whose popularity immediately after the Gulf War had reached an unprecedented 90 percent, understand how he had been beaten by a man thought of by many, including most infamously by Maj. Gen. Harold N. Campbell of the Air Force, as a "pot-smoking, draft-dodging womanizer."

Yet it was Bill Clinton who took the oath of office on January 20, 1993. Clinton, as noted, was one of the luckiest presidents ever to assume office. The Cold War was over. The Bush administration had done admirably in transitioning the former Warsaw Pact's Eastern European states toward democracy. However, NATO and its expansion were far from settled issues. The fundamental contradiction was how to incorporate Russia with the West and not allow NATO expansion to become the grounds for future and unwanted rivalry between Moscow and Washington. This dilemma would haunt current and future administrations—and does, and will.

The extraordinary victory over Saddam Hussein had reestablished and burnished the reputation of the nation's military. American prestige and influence overseas had been greatly enhanced under Bush. As Clinton's future secretary of state, Madeleine Albright, would remark, this was a "unipolar moment." The economy was on track for a recovery; Bush had handed over to his successor economic growth and gains on which to build.

It would seem fate was on Clinton's side. Unfortunately, the Clinton administration would be severely tested by humanitarian crises across large swathes of Africa and the former Yugoslavia. Also, the metastasizing of Afghanistan into a base for Islamist terror was another smoldering crisis. And it would explode.

Clinton would also be the first of four successive presidents who collectively were perhaps the least prepared, least experienced, and least ready for the job since Calvin Coolidge. This inexperience became immediately apparent in how the new administration stumbled simply getting organized, as well as in Clinton's national security appointments. Representative Les Aspin was named secretary of defense.

Those who knew Aspin well understood that he could not manage himself, let alone the largest bureaucracy in the world. True, as an accomplished chairman of the House Armed Services Committee and twelve-term representative from Wisconsin, Aspin had an encyclopedic knowledge of defense. He was also a "middle of the roader," meaning that for a Democrat, he was on the conservative side. Aspin certainly had the right instincts, displayed in his support of Desert Storm. But given his undisciplined nature and distinctly unmilitary bearing, it was clear to some from the beginning that Aspin's days at the Pentagon were numbered. His being a defense intellectual and expert were excellent qualifications but far from sufficient for success in the job. And Aspin would have to deal with, in Colin Powell, arguably the most popular, successful, and politically skilled chairman of the Joint Chiefs of Staff the nation had had since General of the Army George Marshall and Admiral of the Fleet William Leahy were advising FDR.

Anthony Lake was named national security advisor. Lake had been a Foreign Service officer, assigned to Vietnam during the war and to the White House under Henry Kissinger. Lake had resigned in protest over the war and his discovery that Kissinger had been tapping his phones, suspecting him of leaking sensitive material. Despite his intellect, Lake would prove to be no Kissinger, Brzezinski, or Scowcroft.

For the CIA, R. James Woolsey was proposed as director. Woolsey, a conservative Democrat, had served as Undersecretary of the Navy under Carter and had been an arms control ambassador under Reagan. Woolsey, whose background was policy, later mused to me that he had known he was in trouble when White House press secretary Dee Dee Myers introduced him as "Admiral Woolsey." He, like Aspin, would have a truncated tenure.

Warren Christopher was the reliable old hand chosen to take the helm at State. An accomplished attorney, Christopher had served as deputy secretary of state under Carter. More an insider than a visible player, Christopher was a better tactician than strategist. Thus, Clinton did not have the formidable national security team he would need.

All new administrations, especially when a different party takes charge, are prone to rocky starts. Clinton's was particularly awkward. Naively, Clinton made it his first defense priority to permit homosexuals in the military to serve openly. Socially, the country and the military were far from ready to accept what was perceived as a radical change. Forced integration of homosexuals would not be easily accepted at that stage, if at all. Implementing this policy was complicated when Les Aspin was hospitalized in March 1993 with a heart attack, making Colin Powell the de facto center of power in the Pentagon. In the early years of the twenty-first century, American attitudes toward homosexuality would be completely reversed—it would be extraordinary and a credit to the nation. That had not happened yet in 1993.

Powell cautioned the president about this proposal, noting that it could only be accomplished after a lengthy period of, in military terms, "preparing the battlefield." The White House ignored this counsel. Realizing Clinton was making an unnecessary blunder that could compromise the White House in the eyes of the military, Powell gave an interview to *New York Times* defense reporter Michael Gordon. The headline read that the chairman might not wait until September to retire. The White House got the message instantaneously. The White House staff was furious with Powell for besting the president with this interview, but the chairman had done the right thing, both for Clinton and the military.

The compromise proposed by Senator Sam Nunn was "don't ask, don't tell." While this was at best a temporary measure, ultimately the Pentagon adapted. Now, the armed forces are facing another significant cultural change regarding women in combat, particularly in qualifying them for the Special Forces, long a male-only bastion.

Clinton also stumbled over his choice for attorney general, Zoe Baird, and of Kimba Wood for a judgeship. Neither was carefully enough vetted. It turned out that Baird had employed two illegal immigrants for household and nanny duties. Her nomination engulfed in what was termed "Nannygate," Baird had to withdraw. So did Wood, for a similar reason.

In February 1993, a bomb exploded under the World Trade Center in New York City—the first attempt by al Qaeda to attack America. The administration did not respond aggressively. This began the controversy over whether to treat terrorism as a law-enforcement or a national-security matter. Meanwhile, the president had put his wife in charge of health-care reform—a project Hillary Clinton would conduct in great secrecy, with disastrous results. Her recommendations were rejected out of hand. Each of these missteps underscored the lack of experience, insensitivity to the myriad of political and bureaucratic land mines inherent in governing, and overall unreadiness for arguably the toughest job on earth. More setbacks would follow.

Meanwhile, two legacy issues from the Bush administration were maturing into full-blown crises: Somalia and Yugoslavia. Haiti was also becoming a crisis—a lesser one but still bothersome. At the same time, Aspin had begun what he was calling the "Bottom-Up Defense Review." The new administration wanted to reexamine Powell's Base Force in light of the complete dissolution of the Soviet empire and the budget constraints mandated by an exceedingly large deficit that Clinton had promised to cut.

Defense would suffer its "fair share" of reductions. Clinton began this exercise by raising taxes, never popular. In 1994, as a result of that and other missteps, Republicans wrested control of both houses of Congress from the Democrats, in a stunning reversal of fortune for Clinton. Interestingly, Clinton and the new Speaker of the House, Newt Gingrich, would several years later become the oddest imaginable political couple, jointly managing to balance the budget. However, the Pentagon was grappling with the impact of smaller budgets and a still-changing international environment.

In the very early morning of July 26, 1993, I left the near-freezing temperatures of Ketchum, Idaho, nestled among the Sawtooth Mountains six thousand feet above sea level, to catch a plane to Dulles Airport and from there to Washington, D.C., which was about sixty degrees hotter. Secretary of Defense Aspin had been convening small groups of "experts" to discuss his plans for the Bottom-Up Review and to seek inputs. At 7 p.m. he was convening one of these meetings, with a few think-tank people he trusted, in his Pentagon office over dinner.

In those pre–September 11 days, getting into the Pentagon was easy. I drove up to the River Entrance, parked my car in an assigned spot, and showed my retired military ID to the gate guard inside the Pentagon's E Ring.

"Sorry, sir. I can't let you in. It's after 6 p.m."

"What do you mean?"

"You need a Pentagon pass."

Frustrated, I picked up the phone and dialed Aspin's office. No answer. Obviously, the secretary had adjourned to his dining room. How was I to get in? This guard showed no interest in helping me with my immediate problem. I saw General Powell's (unarmored) limo parked outside. Picking up the phone again, I dialed the chairman's number. Before I could tell his secretary, Nancy, what I wanted, she said, "I will put him right on."

No hello, just a "Where are you?"

"About fifty feet away. The guard won't let me in."

"I'll be right out."

Seconds later the large figure of Colin Powell emerged from his office by the River Entrance. The guard was clearly startled.

"Let him in. He's ok." Then, turning to me, Powell asked knowingly, "Where are you headed?"

"The third deck." That was shorthand for the secretary's office, 3E888.

"Let me know how it turns out," Powell asked, with full appreciation of where I was going.

Aspin was in his dining room. A few minutes later, the last of the invitees, about four or five of us in all, had assembled, and we sat down for dinner and discussion. Larry Smith, Aspin's chief aide, moderated the session. When it was my turn, I said to Les, "I have three points. First and most important, no matter what you decide, you can never, and I mean never, allow a hollow force to develop again. As you know better than anyone, the services will fight tooth and nail for force structure and platforms. I would always choose a smaller, well-equipped, highly ready, motivated, and capable force over a larger one that was not up to the task."

Aspin agreed.

"Second, and this is a lesson we should have learned from Vietnam, being prepared to fight a big war does not prepare you for smaller ones. You are wrestling with balancing forces for a major regional contingency, or MRC, meaning a big conventional war, with overseas presence, engagement, and crisis-management missions. Yugoslavia, Iraq, Somalia, Haiti are examples of these smaller crises, but ones that can have significant political consequences."

Aspin nodded.

"Before 1965, the Navy was out to sink the Soviet fleet. But the Vietcong and North Vietnamese did not have a navy. We trained, as you know, with the most advanced weapons systems—jet fighters, missiles, nuclear submarines, and space-based systems. But my weapons in Vietnam were 81-mm mortars, machine guns, hand grenades, and pistols that could have been used in

World War I. In fact, the Vietcong did use ammunition left over from World War II. Being ready for the big war is not the same as being ready for these peacetime tasks of lower-intensity conflict.

"Last, you have a bureaucratic nightmare facing you in acquisition. The Packard Commission [created by the Reagan administration after a series of so-called acquisition scandals involving $1,200 hammers and $600 toilet seats forced a complete review—I had been an informal advisor] didn't fix these problems. As you know, at the Center for Strategic and International Studies [former defense secretary] Jim Schlesinger and I cochaired a parallel study on acquisition. You will recall we briefed you and Larry Smith on the findings.

"The most important was to streamline and codify—or codify and streamline—the thousands of pages of defense-acquisition regulations. As an aside, several years ago, Honeywell Aerospace and Defense Company retained me to do a study on how much money could be saved in buying weapons systems. Honeywell made a cross section of weapons, from bullets to space systems. We engaged a wide spectrum of Honeywell's employees, soliciting ideas about how to cut or avoid costs. We showed that by taking commonsense steps, from reducing unnecessary oversight to simplifying regulations, savings of 25–30 percent could be made. The CEO then, Warde Wheaton, thought that number would not be credible. So we said 16–17 percent of the total contract value could be saved. Unfortunately, the Pentagon wasn't interested."

✦

Aspin would try his best. But in December 1993 he offered his resignation following the disastrous "Black Hawk down" crisis in Somalia that fall. However, the Bottom-Up Review (BUR) was completed. The BUR was a competent product, in an academic and intellectual sense. It also was a "top down" document, dictated by budget "top lines" rather than by strategic factors or, indeed, by the sound strategic thinking that should have shaped the BUR before any spending decisions were imposed.

The Clinton administration correctly reasoned that with the demise of the Soviet Union, the U.S. military would be needed to fill many less costly tasks short of a major conventional war. Engagement, crisis management, partnerships, and international participation to foster global stability would assume greater importance. This reshaping would occur concurrently and conveniently with defense budget cuts, to a level envisaged over five years to be about $112 billion (1995 dollars) lower than the Bush baseline.

The Bottom-Up Review started by aggregating the various missions the United States would have to undertake. The most taxing was a major regional contingency, or MRC, which would require a total of about half a million troops. The conflict would be fought in four phases (a definition that has lasted). The phases were "hold," "build up," "decisively defeat," and "assure peacetime stability."

The planning strategy for the review assumed that U.S. forces would need to be able to accomplish these objectives:

- Defeat aggressors in MRCs

- Maintain overseas presence to deter conflicts and provide regional stability

- Conduct smaller-scale intervention operations, such as peace enforcement, peacekeeping, humanitarian assistance, and disaster relief to further American interests and objectives

- Deter attacks with WMD against American territory, U.S. forces, or the territory and forces of allies.

Powell's Base Force would be reduced from 1.63 million active-duty personnel to about 1.5 million. As specified in the published and unclassified version of the BUR, the Army would have 10 active and 5 reserve divisions; the Air Force, 13 active and 7 reserve tactical fighter wings; the Navy 11 active carrier battle groups and 1 reserve; and the Marines, whose 3 active divisions and 1 reserve, and associated fighter wings, were specified in law, would be increased in total numbers to 179,000. Strategic nuclear forces would be defined by the strategic-arms treaties being negotiated with Russia.

In fact, the total number of active-duty forces would decline from 2 million in 1990 to 1.385 million a decade later. Defense spending would level out at about $270 billion in then-year dollars (about $445 billion today). The most significant legacy of the BUR was to lay the foundations for future defense planning within a smaller defense budget.

Adjusting the balance between preparations for the "big war," however unlikely, and the lesser tasks mandated by engagement, presence, enlargement, and crisis response, whether to acts of nature or man, remains critical in shaping the force structure. In 2017, the prospect of a "near-peer competitor," specifically Russia and China, has shifted (and will continue to shift) the balance back toward improving conventional war-fighting capabilities. This trend has emerged despite the ongoing battle against the Islamic State and Islamist-based terror and violence and the dominance of "capture-or-kill" missions largely conducted by small units.

Despite the impact of the Bottom-Up Review, some military thinkers and strategists sensed that certain conclusions from the stunning victory in the first Iraq war about a real revolution in using military force had been neglected or simply missed. In the 1980s, the concept of a "revolution in military affairs" became popular. The extraordinary increases in lethality made possible by the technology of precision targeting in war had been widely explored and debated among strategists. The Gulf war showed how a large enemy army could be annihilated through a combination of technology and military prowess made possible by a massive expenditure of money on advanced technologies, adequate training, and the costly all-volunteer force.

The unanswered and unaddressed question was whether military force now had the ability to achieve broader political and policy objectives, beyond disarming or defeating an enemy in battle. In late 1994, a small group was convened to address this question and determine how far military force might be used to influence political outcomes. Sponsored at first by the National Defense University, this team consisted of former senior military and civilian officials who had experienced war in Vietnam or Desert Storm (or both) and who had served at high levels in the Defense Department.

The initial team was made up of Gen. Frederick M. Franks, U.S. Army (Ret.), who had led the famous "left hook" through Saudi Arabia in Desert Storm; Adm. Leon A. "Bud" Edney, who had been Supreme Allied Commander Atlantic; Gen. Charles "Chuck" Horner, U.S. Air Force (Ret.), who had commanded the air war during Operations Desert Shield and Storm; Gen. Thomas Morgan, U.S. Marine Corps (Ret.), who had been assistant commandant of the Marine Corps; Dr. James P. Wade, who had held very senior Pentagon positions; and me.

Later additions to the group included retired admirals Jonathan Howe and Leighton "Snuffy" Smith, both of whom had commanded U.S. Naval Forces Europe. Howe had also served as the United Nations representative to the Somalia operation. Former and future secretary of defense Donald Rumsfeld was also a "rump" member. The team's final product was an idea that became known as "shock and awe."

The thesis of "shock and awe" (unlike how it was used as a sound bite in the first days of Operation Iraqi Freedom, the second Iraq war, which began in March 2003) centered on affecting, influencing, and even controlling the will and perceptions of an adversary in order to achieve policy and political outcomes set by leadership. Rumsfeld had a more concise explanation: to get people to do what we wanted and to stop doing things we did not want done. The idea was to use military force more imaginatively to achieve broader policy aims and goals than the traditional one of defeating an adversary's military. A hierarchy of inducements was devised, both positive and, of course, highly negative. For example, winning the lottery induces a positive form of "shock and awe."

The most controversial and probably misunderstood level was the "shock and awe" created by the dropping of two nuclear weapons on Japan in August 1945. The team's aim in that connection was not to laud the effectiveness or use of nuclear weapons—rather the opposite. Instead, the intent was to demonstrate that the will and perception of a society prepared to commit (or prefer) suicide in waging war and in refusing to surrender or capitulate could be profoundly and dramatically changed.

The group also believed that a military could be perceived as so dominant and overwhelming as to deter conflict, or win with minimum damage and casualties, preemptively, by defeating and eroding an adversary's will to resist. This thesis would become extremely relevant after September 11. Islamist radicals, seduced or deluded into believing martyrdom guaranteed entrance into an afterlife paradise, were not only prepared but in many cases willing to commit suicide in advancing a cause. Could their will and perception about martyrdom be directed into a different direction, as occurred in Japan that August 1945?

Unfortunately, so far, there has been no opportunity to test whether "shock and awe" can affect, influence, or control the will and perceptions of these violent extremists in ways that would defeat their aims.

> From 1996 to 1998, the "shock and awe" team briefed senior members of the Clinton administration, including then secretary of defense William Cohen. The following captures the key points about "shock and awe" made in these briefings.
>
> "Mr. Secretary, as you know, 'shock and awe' is aimed at affecting, influencing, and even controlling the will and perception of an adversary. Ideally, 'shock and awe' is meant to persuade, convince, coerce, or cajole an adversary to do what we want without the need to use—as opposed to threaten or imply—force.
>
> "'Shock and awe' begins with setting aims and objectives of policy that are to be achieved. In other words, 'shock and awe' is outcome generated and based. 'Shock and awe' has four elements.

"The first is to obtain as much knowledge and understanding as possible of the conditions and circumstances necessary to obtain the outcome we seek. We would like to call this perfect or near-perfect knowledge. Perfection is the goal we need to seek, realizing the difficulty of reaching this level.

"As you know, we failed dismally in Vietnam in terms of the knowledge or understanding we displayed in that war. Even in Desert Storm, our tactical knowledge, as General Franks admitted, was far from complete as to what was happening in real time on the battlefield.

"As General Horner complained, we just did not understand how we could have caused the collapse of the Iraqi will to resist without recourse to the ground assault. This was not an argument for an airpower-alone strategy. Yet, we never took the time to understand what more could have been done to force Saddam out of Kuwait through the more imaginative use of our military advantages.

"Second, brilliance in operations is vital. 'Good enough' no longer is sufficient. The operating environment in Desert Storm, with its nearly instantaneous media coverage, demanded that the operating standard be extraordinarily high. And brilliance is not beyond our ken.

"Third, rapidity is vital. The aim must be to operate far more rapidly than the adversary. When time is put to our advantage, it is much easier to anticipate and thwart an adversary's moves and countermoves.

"Finally, control of the environment must be a prerequisite. We must deny the adversary use of the environment, from the electronic and visual spectrum to physical operations. Disinformation, deception, and misdirection are inherent aspects of gaining control. As Sun Tzu argued, war is deception. And there are few better ways to affect will and perception than through these means.

"Last and perhaps most important, war is not only a contest of wills. It is the most extreme test of intellects. That means we need to realize that the brainpower of our people is the most important resource we have, transcending weapons and support equipment. The latter are, of course, important. But our defense must rest in the intellectual abilities of our troops and the fullest exploitation of this capacity."

✦

Secretary Cohen seemed receptive to the concept. However, the two hardest challenges for innovators are to persuade a large and resistant bureaucracy to accept new ideas and to shed old ones. "Shock and awe" may have impressed Bill Cohen. It did not move the Pentagon.

The Clinton administration would face three major challenges: Yugoslavia, culminating in the seventy-eight-day bombing campaign in 1999 to force Serbia to withdraw from Kosovo and end its campaign of ethnic cleansing, better described as genocide; the expansion of NATO; and the surfacing of Islamist terror, in the form of what became al Qaeda. In addition, humanitarian crises extended beyond Yugoslavia to Rwanda, where about 800,000 people perished in a brutal civil war. But in the first year in office, the Clinton administration's immediate crisis was in Somalia, a situation that had its roots in the prior Bush administration.

In January 1991, Somali president Mohammed Siad Barre was overthrown, and a civil war broke out among four factions: the United Somali Congress (USC), Somali Salvation Democratic Front (SSDF), Somali Patriotic Movement (SPM), and Somali Democratic Movement (SDM). That June a cease-fire failed to hold, and later a fifth faction, the Somali National Movement (SNM), declared independence in northwest Somalia.

In September 1991, severe fighting broke out in the capital, Mogadishu, producing over 20,000 casualties. The fighting destroyed much of Somalia's agriculture, leading to starvation across an already impoverished state. While the international community responded with assistance, the vast majority of food, water, and medical stuffs it supplied was stolen. For the next year, many more Somalis perished. In 1992, after another truce, the UN sent observers to preside over the distribution of food.

After visiting Somalia in 1992, President George H. W. Bush expanded Task Force Somalia to Operation Provide Relief, to support the UN's Operation Provide Hope. These efforts were overwhelmed by the tragedy. About half a million Somalis would die, and about 1.5 million would be displaced or become refuges. In response, in December 1992 the United States launched a massive coalition effort under UN Security Council Resolution (UNSCR) 794.

After Clinton assumed office, the American Somali operation was placed under UN control, with the aim of achieving national reconciliation as a first step in restoring an effective government and a safer environment for the Somali people. On March 15, 1993, a reconciliation conference held in Addis Ababa, Ethiopia, failed to reach agreement due to the opposition of warlord Mohammed Farrah Aidid and his faction. The situation deteriorated.

On June 5, a UN task force sent to shut down Aidid's insurgent radio station and, reportedly, to seize a weapons cache in Mogadishu was ambushed. Twenty-four Pakistani soldiers were killed and fifty-seven wounded, along with four Italian and American journalists injured. The next day the UN approved UNSCR 837, authorizing the arrest of those responsible for attacking the peacekeepers. American troops were ordered on a five-day campaign beginning June 12 to hunt down Aidid in Mogadishu. That mission failed. On June 17, retired admiral Jonathan Howe, who was the UN special envoy to Somalia (and a member of the "shock and awe" team), offered a $25,000 reward for information leading to Aidid's arrest. The United States continued its missions to find and detain him. None worked.

On July 12, a U.S.-led daylight operation was launched against a safe house in Mogadishu where Aidid was thought to be hiding. He was not. But during the seventeen-minute operation, U.S. forces fired thousands of rounds, killing about sixty people, including women and children. Four journalists covering the failed operation were attacked and killed by angry mobs.

Aidid's militia retaliated in August, killing a total of eleven American soldiers in two bomb attacks. In response, Clinton ordered Task Force Ranger, initially with about four hundred Special Forces soldiers and sixteen helicopters under the command of Maj. Gen. William F. Garrison, to Somalia to find and detain or kill Aidid. On September 21, Task Force Ranger captured Osman Ali Atto, Aidid's banker. Four days later, Aidid's forces shot down a Black Hawk helicopter with a rocket-propelled grenade (RPG), killing three crew members.

While this deployment was under way and prior to his retirement on September 30, Colin Powell recommended to Secretary Les Aspin that M-1 tanks, armored vehicles, and C-130 Spectre gunships be sent to Somalia to back up the U.S. forces in case conditions continued to worsen and they found themselves in extremis. Aspin declined. His argument was that a display of heavy weaponry would destabilize rather than defuse conditions on the ground. These forces were not sent.

On October 3, 1993, Task Force Ranger began a daylight operation to capture the leaders of Aidid's Habr Gidr clan in Mogadishu. The assault force consisted of 19 aircraft and helos, 12 vehicles (including 9 "Humvees"), and 160 men. The operation was to be completed in under an hour. Instead, the convoy was ambushed and pinned down by fierce local fighters armed with automatic weapons and RPGs.

An intense, lengthy, and bloody firefight broke out. Eighteen American soldiers were killed, and two Black Hawk helicopters were shot down. The body of one of the dead American pilots was paraded through the streets of Mogadishu. All of this was broadcast on television throughout much of the world. At least a thousand of Aidid's men were killed. That number is probably conservative. The surviving and trapped American soldiers ultimately made their way to safety when a relief column broke through.

The grim battle in Mogadishu stunned many Americans. The Clinton administration was subjected to stinging criticism for recklessly putting its soldiers in harm's way. The shootdown of the Black Hawks and videos of the dead American soldier dragged through the streets were politically devastating in the United States. The failure to provide heavy equipment and firepower for U.S. forces was often cited as incompetent and foolhardy. Also, it was pointed out, a daylight operation in a tightly packed urban environment carried very real risks, since surprise and the cover of darkness were lost.

Aspin loyally replied that the decision not to deploy these heavy weapons systems had been his alone. However, it is surprising that any secretary of defense would have taken such a decision without informing the White House—or without White House guidance. Aspin would submit his resignation in December and step down in February 1994, to be replaced by his deputy, William Perry.

The United States still maintains a large task force for the Horn of Africa, operating against al Qaeda and other Islamist groups. Aidid was elected president of Somalia in 1995 and died the next year from gunshot wounds. Somalia remains a region in conflict, underscoring the immense difficulty of dealing with humanitarian crises arising from failed and failing governments.

In an earlier book, *A Handful of Bullets: How the Murder of Archduke Franz Ferdinand Still Menaces the Peace* (Naval Institute Press, 2014), I argued that failed government is the greatest threat to society at large, whether in third- and fourth-world states, or even the most developed nations, such as the United States and in Europe. Events surely reinforce this conclusion, especially in an era of No World Order. Indeed, in Somalia, desperation has forced many to become pirates.

As badly as the battle in Mogadishu went for both sides, Yugoslavia was as complicated and even more deadly for its inhabitants. For a decade from 1991, a series of wars wracked and wrecked the former Yugoslavia:

War in Slovenia (1991)

Croatian war of independence (1991–95)

Bosnian-Herzegovina war (1992–95)

Kosovo war (1998–99), including the NATO bombing

Insurgency in the Preševo Valley (1999–2001)

Insurgency in the Republic of Macedonia (2001).

Both the UN and NATO were deeply engaged in these conflicts. Of particular relevance was the 1999 NATO intervention to halt the killing of ethnic Kosovars by the Serbs. However, the earlier wars set the precedent. Massacres and murders had become commonplace. Ultimately, a combination of NATO no-fly zones and air strikes throughout the early to mid-1990s produced the Dayton Accords of November 1995. Peace was obtained, more or less and temporarily, and an external peacekeeping force of 60,000 was ordered into the former Yugoslavia.

The year 1999 was not a good one for the Clintons. The House had passed articles of impeachment on December 19, 1998, citing perjury in Clinton's sworn testimony in the Monica Lewinski and Paula Jones scandals as "high crimes and misdemeanors." On February 12, the Senate voted not to convict Clinton on the two articles of impeachment. Meanwhile, a celebration of the fiftieth anniversary of the creation of NATO in 1949 and the signing of the Washington Treaty was being planned for a summit to be hosted by Clinton in Washington, D.C., on April 23–24.

But between the Senate vote and the NATO summit, action would have to be taken in Kosovo. "Ethnic cleansing," a euphemism for genocide, had grown out of hand and had to be stopped. The antecedents were as noted above, and a complete account of this episode must be left to the many pieces written on the war. But in brief, the prior year, on June 9, 1998, because of the brutal treatment Yugoslavia and Serbia were inflicting on Kosovars, Clinton had announced a "national emergency." On September 23, 1998, UNSCR 1199 had been approved in reaction to horrendous reports that over 230,000 Kosovars had been forced to flee by the excessive and indiscriminate use of force by the Serbian-dominated Yugoslav army. The resolution demanded an end to hostilities and an immediate cease-fire. The next day, NATO's North Atlantic Council (NAC), which consisted of senior representatives from each member state, issued an "activation warning" as a preparation for air operations to halt the forced dislocation and killing of the Kosovars.

Meanwhile, shuttle diplomacy was aimed at arranging a cease-fire. To empower that effort, on October 13 the NAC issued activation orders for a limited, phased air campaign in Yugoslavia aimed at stopping the genocide, to begin within four days. The threat worked, and Serbian withdrawal began at the end of October. But the cease-fire broke down in December; fighting resumed and increased over the new year. In the meantime, on February 6, 1999, talks for another cease-fire began in Rambouillet, outside Paris, France. Killings continued, including the Račak massacre, when forty-five Kosovar Albanian farmers were summarily executed by the Serbs.

On March 18, 1999, Albanian, American, and British delegations signed the Rambouillet Accords. However, the Yugoslav and Russian delegations refused. Events disintegrated rapidly. On March 22, the international monitors from the Organization for Security and Co-operation in Europe withdrew, as security was impossible to ensure and a NATO bombing campaign seemed inevitable. With negotiations stalemated, Yugoslavia announced a state of emergency, citing the imminent threat of war, and began mobilizing its military.

Late on March 23, 1999, NATO's secretary general, Javier Solana, directed the Supreme Allied Commander Europe, Gen. Wesley K. Clark, U.S. Army, to "initiate air operations in the Federal Republic of Yugoslavia." NATO's bombing campaign lasted seventy-eight days, from March 24 to June 11, 1999. Initially, the campaign was described as "pinprick," far from the massive air attacks of Desert Storm. Slobodan Milosevic, the Serbian president, refused to capitulate, and the campaign continued.

On the positive side, that (then) nineteen NATO members could unanimously agree on taking military action was commendable. The Balkan wars had plagued NATO and the European Union, atrocities occurring as it were in Europe's backyard. The Dayton Accords had been a stopgap. The former Yugoslav and Serbian governments were committing atrocities not seen in such numbers since Hitler's Nazis murdered millions. Europe finally had to act.

On the negative side, though NATO had the capacity to crush Serbia's military, it was practicing great restraint, believing that Milosevic would crack under the pressure of even limited air strikes and the threat of further escalation. But air strikes, once launched, have never worked without the threat or use of ground forces—although the warning order in 1995 had led to a cease-fire, however temporary. But the tragic events in Somalia and prior American failures in other military interventions understandably caused Clinton to fear being trapped in another land quagmire.

Further, the air attacks did not have the sanctions of a UN resolution, which undercut their legitimacy. This prompted dissent against NATO's air campaign to build outside the alliance. The length of the campaign, which should have been over in days, was a further political embarrassment, especially with the NATO summit soon convening in Washington. At the time, no one in NATO was certain how effective the strikes were or how long they would be needed to have effect.

NATO claimed destruction of a large proportion of the Serbian army's armored vehicles and artillery pieces. As it would turn out, these claims were greatly exaggerated. The Serbs had been clever in using dummy vehicles and artillery to deceive allied targeteers while hiding their actual heavy weapons from surveillance. This was one reason, perhaps, that Milosevic was able to resist for a comparatively long time.

The summit took place while bombs and missiles were falling on Serbia and Belgrade. On May 7, the Chinese embassy was hit by a missile. China furiously protested. NATO and the United States claimed it had been a horrible targeting error—the embassy was prominently featured on maps—and apologized. Cynics argued that given the tight control over every mission and virtually every weapon used, the attack could not have been an accident. Some suggested that this "mistake" was really a signal to China. Others believed that the embassy was hit purposely to discredit the bombing campaign in order to end it.

Throughout this campaign, General Clark argued for a more intensive air campaign and for at least the threat of ground forces.

His arguments were not well received in the White House. While Clark and Clinton had been fellow Rhodes scholars at Oxford, they had not known each other then. The White House was worried that Clark could be another Al Haig, with presidential ambitions, and hence a political liability. This clash would end with Clark's early retirement several months after the Kosovo campaign ended.

Finally, Milosevic relented. While it was probably continued threats of using ground forces and Russian pressure that carried the day, no specific reason for Milosevic's capitulation was self-evident. The conclusion is that an effective policy was limited by a reluctance to use whatever force was needed. The air attacks could have gone on for much longer than seventy-eight days.

U.S. Military Academy, West Point, New York, May 1999.

Every year, the West Point Social Sciences Department holds a Senior Seminar. The department is well-known throughout the Army as the intellectual home of many distinguished officers, including Lt. Gen. Brent Scowcroft and many, many others. In the May conference, Gen. Wesley Clark (WC), a department alumnus and Rhodes scholar, was addressing the small seminar by teleconference from his headquarters in Mons, Belgium. This was while the bombing campaign against Serbia and the former Yugoslavia was reaching a climax.

WC, concluding an update on the state of the campaign: "As we know, bombing alone rarely wins. I have argued with no success with both the chairman [Army general H. H. Shelton] and the White House that we need a substantial component on the ground. The threat alone will not work. It must be seen as deployable."

HKU (Clark could not see the participants, only hear them): "Wes, this is Harlan Ullman. We realize how difficult it is fighting a war when you need agreement among nineteen allies. And it is no secret that the White House is reluctant to deploy ground troops. Meanwhile, the press, as you know, is raising pretty profound questions as to why tiny Serbia is holding out against the combined forces of NATO.

"What do you think needs to be done to get the White House to listen to what it will take to force Milosevic to quit?"

WC: "That is a good question. I am doing my best. And if I have to break my pick, I will."

✦

At long last, the threat of ground forces was made. The Russians were siding with the Serbs and had opposed the bombing campaign in the first place. But Moscow wanted an end to the violence and reportedly warned Milosevic that if he did not accept NATO's demands, the use of ground forces would be inevitable. Milosevic finally capitulated.

Clark did indeed break his pick. As NATO commander, Clark was not in the American chain of command (although he was as Commander, U.S. Forces Europe). His exercise of that NATO authority did not go down well in the Pentagon. At a NATO conference after the campaign ended, Clark was informed that he would be retired early and before the normal three-year tour was over. Hard feelings, among other factors, added to Clark's pressure for ground forces, had forced the White House decision to retire him early.

Clinton assumed office at a time of enormous American power and influence, at levels second only to the end of World War II. The security crises that most affected his administration arose from humanitarian conflicts. Rwanda, Somalia, Afghanistan, and the former Yugoslavia were the most significant. Haiti was to be relatively easy.

The Yugoslav crisis was a legacy of the George H. W. Bush administration. The major, almost self-evident, lesson was that any intervention in the midst of a civil war or raging conflict was agonizing and filled with risk. If no intervention was made, as in the case of Rwanda in early 1994, hundreds of thousands would die. In the case of Somalia, intervention led to "Black Hawk Down." While the firefight that night was vastly uneven, the deaths of eighteen American servicemen and the wounding of nearly five dozen more made a heavy price for the United States to pay. Of course, Somalis did the bulk of the dying.

The Dayton Accords of 1995, followed by the 1999 bombing campaign to halt the genocide of ethnic Kosovars, demonstrated how elusive making peace was in the former Yugoslavia. To be sure, the bombing campaign demonstrated the shortcomings of minimal force. While that intervention did not fail, its goal should and could have been accomplished far more effectively—and it would have been, if ground forces had been put in place at the start. Because the Serbs had been cunning in using dummy equipment for the allies to bomb, the campaign was far less effective than NATO believed. The lesson here is that knowledge and accurate intelligence remain vital.

Haiti was a case where force and diplomacy worked. In October 1993, the landing ship tank USS *Harlan County* (LST 1169) was about to dock at Port au Prince carrying a number of peacekeepers. But crowds of Haitians threatened violence, and the ship was directed to back away to avoid perhaps something similar to what was transpiring in Somalia. The Clinton administration drew great criticism over the image of a U.S. Navy ship being forced to withdraw under threat of attack. It should be noted that *Harlan County* was designed to land Marines and equipment ashore and thus lacked the firepower of a major combatant. However, that distinction did not matter much.

In December 1994, following passage of a legitimizing UN resolution, Clinton decided to land the XVIII Corps, consisting of the 82nd and 101st Airborne Divisions, in Haiti to impose a peace if that became necessary. In a last-ditch diplomatic effort, Clinton sent a former president, Jimmy Carter, the former JCS chairman, Gen. Colin Powell, now retired, and Sam Nunn, former chairman of the Senate Armed Services Committee, to Haiti. Their task was to convince Haitian general Raul Cedras to step down and leave the country, allowing the duly elected president, Jean-Bertrande Aristide, to reassume power.

Powell's account of the trip in his autobiography, *My American Journey,* is compelling. After hours of negotiating, the three

Americans prevailed. Cedras backed down after hearing Powell's chilling description of the firepower the United States would bring to bear and his argument, to Cedras and his wife, that there was no honor in dying for a failed cause. Clearly, diplomacy backed by the intent to use force is a strong tool of influence.

While Clinton's record of using military force is modest and mixed, and world conditions were vexing, the expansion of NATO would prove to be his most controversial policy decision. There is no need for excruciating detail on NATO's expansion from the twelve original members who signed the Washington Treaty in April 1949 to twenty-nine (once Montenegro's accession was finally approved). Of the issues most relevant to Clinton's strategic thinking, the overarching dilemma was clearly how to deal with Russia as NATO moved its borders east.

George H. W. Bush had done well in assisting the transition of the former Warsaw Pact members to democratic states. At the 1990 London NATO summit, Hungary, Poland, Romania, Bulgaria, and Russia were invited to establish diplomatic links with NATO. In 1991, the North Atlantic Cooperation Council was formed; it in turn would become the Euro-Atlantic Partnership Council. Meanwhile, Bush had established good relationships with Presidents Gorbachev and Boris Yeltsin. Also, Bush had provided funds to Russia in 1992 when that nation was facing financial ruin. It was up to Clinton to carry on. NATO has had several expansions since its formation. By 1999, NATO had grown to nineteen members, with the additions of Poland, Hungary, and the Czech Republic.

One of the major achievements of the 1999 Washington summit was the approval of the Membership Action Plan (MAP) as guidelines for alliance review of the formal applications of aspiring members. Five criteria were set:

- Willingness to settle international, ethnic, or external territorial disputes by peaceful means, commitment to the rule of law and human rights, and democratic control of armed forces

- Ability to contribute to the organization's defense and missions

- Devotion of sufficient resources to armed forces to be able to meet the commitments of membership

- Security of sensitive information and safeguards ensuring its protection

- Compatibility of domestic legislation with NATO cooperation.

In 1997, the Founding Act was signed, and in 1999 the NATO-Russia Council was established. But, to repeat, the dilemma over how to deal with Russia had never been resolved. That dilemma is playing out today as Russia and NATO clearly are engaged in a military competition and a minibuildup of forces on both sides, following Moscow's incursion into Ukraine in early 2014 and its annexation of Crimea.

Throughout the 1990s the debate for and against NATO expansion was fierce (although not necessarily remembered today). The Clinton administration had adopted enlargement and engagement as means for expanding potential partners, in a process the White House believed would be beneficial for global security. Clinton and his administration were vocal champions of human rights—always a difficult balancing act, as interventions for humanitarian reasons are morally unarguable and hence justifiable even if not practical or achievable. In practice, the choices were never easy, and the risks were considerable.

As the Clinton presidency demonstrated, intervention in the midst of an insurgency or civil war is nasty and unpredictable. The "What next?" question was often unanswerable. In northern Iraq after Desert Storm and in Haiti, the security issues were less debilitating. That was not the case with Serbia and Somalia. Concern for human rights led to the strong support of democracies, which both Republicans, such as Reagan, and Democrats like Carter had reaffirmed. In the case of NATO expansion, arguments based on human rights and democratization played influential roles. Summarizing the key arguments for expansion will not do full justice to all. However, these were the main points.

First, collective defense remained imperative. A larger NATO membership would contribute much more to a Europe whole, free, and at peace. Second, joining would require and encourage strong democratic institutions, adherence to the rule of law, and greater respect for human rights. Third, membership would facilitate and foster willingness to resolve disputes among nations and thus contribute to stability across political, legal, and economic boundaries. Fourth, the cost of membership would be modest. While new members did not possess military capacity approaching that of the larger states, improvements on the margin would be useful. Besides, at the time, Russia was deemed a partner, not an adversary or competitor. Last, expansion would allow greater access to foreign bases if needed to project force "out of area"—the informal NATO slogan in the mid-1990s was "out of area or out of business," there being no threat in or to Europe.

The arguments against expansion were equally strong. They were encapsulated in a letter sent to President Clinton in June 1997 by a number of foreign-policy experts, including former senators Bill Bradley, Gary Hart, and Sam Nunn, as well as former secretary of defense Robert McNamara and ambassador to the USSR Jack Matlock. The letter warned that further expansion without consideration of how to deal with Russia would be "a policy error of historic proportion." While the record of Russia's reactions is ambiguous, both Gorbachev and Yeltsin complained bitterly that this expansion would not be welcomed by Russia over the long term.

The trenchant criticism today expressed by Vladimir Putin that NATO is surrounding Russia as it moves east echoes that of his predecessors. Gorbachev argued that the elder Bush had agreed to neither push enlargement nor station U.S. troops permanently in new accessions; officials in the George W. Bush administration disagreed. The compromise, if there was one, was that the United States would not deploy more than a brigade's worth of troops in eastern members. That too was contested by Moscow.

Beyond the failure to deal with the Russian dilemma, expanding NATO also expanded Article 5 guarantees. During the Cold War, if war broke out and went nuclear, many Americans had not been willing to exchange Bonn for Boston. Fortunately, the Cold War never went hot. Today, in the view of critics, the article's guarantee that new members with modest military power will come to the aid of the United States is not compelling, nor would it be sufficient compensation for America's risking war over the Balkans or the Baltics. That many troops from these new accessions have died fighting in Afghanistan over the past decade and a half (particularly from the Baltics nations and Romania, who proportionally took more casualties than the United States) did not mute the Article 5 concerns. As was pointed out emphatically in the 2016 presidential campaign, only five NATO states that year met the goal of spending at least 2 percent of gross domestic product on defense, and the United States is bearing an unfair burden underwriting the alliance.

The discussion of the current NATO-U.S.-Russia relationship will be found in the concluding chapter. But my view is that NATO's expansion, initiated by the first President Bush and greatly accelerated by Clinton, showed an absence of sound strategic thinking. Put another way, expansion responded much more to the attitudes of the administration and its aspirations to expand democracy and human rights than to a consideration of the longer-term geostrategic consequences.

Russia was never going to become a Western-style democracy, for well-understood social, historical, cultural, political, and ideological reasons. At some stage, the sense of Russian insecurity, which predated the tsars, would be triggered by revulsion to and an endemic fear of being surrounded by enemies. Gorbachev, Yeltsin, and Putin have all raised these concerns and fears. In a sense of goodwill, perhaps, and with malice toward none, the Clinton administration probably sensed a permanency in relations with Russia, that they would remain sound and amicable.

Those assumptions proved dead wrong. These flawed assumptions would be exacerbated by George W. Bush, in his abrogation of the ABM Treaty and the assaults into Afghanistan and Iraq, despite

Putin's strong warning about the latter. Barack Obama, his "reset button" withstanding, would hasten the decline in U.S.-Russian relations. Thus all three presidents hold some responsibility, as does Putin, for this deterioration.

Elsewhere, in two prior books, I argued for a different approach. The Partnership for Peace (PfP) seemed to be a better mechanism than NATO enlargement for coordinating and integrating new members. There would be no need for Article 5 guarantees. A quasi-military alliance among these new states to establish mutual interoperability seemed a more viable and less confrontational path. The EU should have been the principal candidate for expansion.

NATO was quite good with sixteen members. With twenty-nine members, reaching the required consensus, meaning unanimity, has been cumbersome and in some cases impossible. An arrangement organized with looser partnerships, characterized by military-to-military cooperation, integration, and interoperable standards, would have been sufficient. If an international coalition were needed, this structure would most likely have worked, given that the major powers in NATO would shoulder most of the responsibility.

Unfortunately, the failure to think strategically meant that potential long-term consequences were not fully understood and that the flaw in expansion—dealing with Russia—was not only ignored or dismissed but was allowed to worsen as the alliance took on new members. It meant the magnification of this profound contradiction, which is today the potentially fatal weakness in the NATO construct. And no remedy is in sight.

The Clinton administration struggled, understandably, in its interventions into humanitarian situations in which conflict was ongoing. In these cases, the choices were between bad and worse; no good or easy solutions were available. While strategic thinking was essential, no amount of cleverness could have alleviated the horrendous calamities posed by humanitarian crises.

Clinton also oversaw the Bottom-Up Review. That was an excellent academic exercise to define the future U.S. military. But the BUR was a failure, in that it was informed by budget caps and not sounder strategic thinking. As argued above, its greatest failure was in allowing the almost promiscuous expansion of NATO; no one grappled with the "What next?" question for Russia.

The bombing campaign against the former Yugoslavia that took so long likewise was a failure of strategic thinking, and even intelligence, as its effectiveness was vastly overestimated. As Clinton seems to have understood when he sent Carter, Nunn, and Powell to Haiti, diplomacy works best when force is credibly threatened. That did not happen in 1999. A bombing-only campaign was doomed. Clinton and his team should have realized that and agreed much earlier to make a credible threat to use ground forces.

The final aspect of Clinton's presidency regarding the uses of force pertains to al Qaeda, Iraq, and the nuclear aspirations of India and Pakistan. Al Qaeda had attempted the bombing of the Twin Towers in 1993. The CIA and FBI had closely followed the organization and the threat it posed to the United States. On August 7, 1998, al Qaeda orchestrated bombings against the U.S. embassies in Kenya and Tanzania, killing twelve Americans and about three hundred Africans.

After deliberating whether or not to deploy Special Forces to capture bin Laden in Afghanistan, the White House decided to retaliate instead with Tomahawk cruise missiles. On August 21, 1998, seventy-five missiles were launched against what was thought to be bin Laden's camp in Afghanistan and a suspected chemical weapons manufacturing site in Sudan, where bin Laden had lived after leaving Saudi Arabia. The missiles missed bin Laden. And the so-called chemical weapons site actually had been producing the equivalent of the antiweed agent Roundup.

In baseball terms, the raids accounted for no runs, no hits, and many errors. Their ineffectiveness probably emboldened al Qaeda, by affirming that the United States had no stomach for sending ground forces, a sign of weakness. But wary of repeating what had happened in Somalia, Clinton was reluctant to put U.S. forces unnecessarily in harm's way.

That was not the case with Iraq. By the very end of 1998, Saddam was preventing UN weapons inspectors from carrying out their responsibilities. The United Nations passed another

resolution of condemnation. The Clinton administration concluded that force was needed to punish Saddam and coerce com-
pliance with the UN resolutions.

Operation Desert Fox was carried out from December 16 to 19,
1998, with substantial air and missile strikes against Saddam's pal-
aces and other targets, including presumed WMD sites. At Central
Command, a tough, intellectually brilliant Marine general, Anthony
C. Zinni, believed that whatever WMD capacity Saddam may have
had, Desert Fox eliminated, and he judged the operation to have
been highly effective. That conclusion would be reaffirmed five
years later, when Iraq was occupied by the U.S.-led coalition and no
WMD were found.

> At the time, I was beginning as a contributor on Fox
> News. The prior May, I had been on with anchor Cather-
> ine Crier (CC) following India's test of nuclear weapons.
> The question was what Pakistan would do. The segment
> included the Pakistani minister of information. For some
> reason, it was cut short. I asked if the line to Islamabad
> could be kept open. It was, and I pushed the minister to
> comment about Pakistan's response. While not overtly
> declaring that Pakistan would test its own weapons, his
> hints were quite suggestive. The White House mean-
> while was pressuring Pakistan's prime minister, Nawaz
> Sharif, not to explode a bomb and remained optimistic
> that Pakistan would not. When I passed my input to a
> senior member of the NSC, it was rejected. A little more
> than a week later, on May 28, 1998, Pakistan conducted
> its first nuclear tests.

> In December 1998, Crier was quizzing me on Opera-
> tion Desert Fox, a name that evoked memories of Erwin
> Rommel, Germany's famed and highly respected com-
> mander during World War II, and thus was controversial.
> Why, it was asked, would the United States pay homage
> to a Nazi, no matter how much admired?

CC: "Well, what about Desert Fox? Did it achieve what it meant to, and what do you find most interesting or important about the operation?"

HKU: "Catherine, there is one aspect about the operation that is truly remarkable. How did Fox get General Zinni to name the operation after it?"

CC, unable to contain her laughter: "I think . . . we will . . . cut to . . . a commercial."

Seven

George Walker Bush and the Global War on Terror, Afghanistan, Iraq, and Russia

In one of the most contested presidential elections in American history, by a five-to-four vote the Supreme Court ended the Florida recount, making George W. Bush the next president of the United States. His opponent, Vice President Al Gore, had won, barely, the popular vote. However, as the Constitution specifies, the Electoral College decides the president. Florida put Bush above the necessary 270 electoral votes required. On January 20, 2001, George Bush became the forty-third president of the United States and the second son of a president to be elected.

Because of the contested election, Bush had a very truncated transition period. That the international and domestic scenes were relatively calm as Bush was preparing to assume office helped. Also, his national security team, on face value, was at least as strong as his father's, if not more so. It would have to be. The new president had no more experience than his predecessor, Bill Clinton. His judgment would soon be tested.

Vice President Dick Cheney had served in the White House as chief of staff, in the House of Representatives, and as secretary of defense, and he had been the chairman and CEO of the energy giant Halliburton. Colin Powell was secretary of state. Few had a better, or better-deserved reputation for competence, integrity, and experience. At Defense, Donald Rumsfeld had the distinction of being both the youngest and oldest secretary to serve, having held the post under President Ford. Condoleezza Rice became the national security advisor, groomed by Brent Scowcroft, also under G. H. W. Bush.

George Tenet, a Democrat, was held over at CIA. It was widely believed that "Bush junior" could and would rely on his father's wise counsel.

Unfortunately, this stellar team would not gel. Personalities clashed. Cheney, Rumsfeld, and Powell were very strong individuals, with powerful personalities and wills. Cheney had been a Rumsfeld protégé in the Nixon administration, and the two remained close.

Cheney and Powell had a history, going back to the first Bush administration at the Pentagon. Powell recalls tellingly in his autobiography that on Cheney's last day as secretary, the chairman went up to pay a farewell call. Cheney had left without a goodbye to his partner in winning the first Gulf war. As Powell wistfully writes, Cheney the cowboy from Wyoming had ridden off into the sunset.

Before the convention, Cheney had been chosen by Bush to find an appropriate vice president—little doubt as to how that would turn out. As for the national security advisor, someone confident and tough was essential to control this team of rivals. Condi Rice simply lacked the gravitas. Finally, Bush and Powell were not particularly close. This was possibly due in part to Powell's relationship with the elder Bush. Also, the general's reluctance to play a strong role in the campaign caused some disquiet among the Bush advisors, especially Karl Rove, who was most influential and would play a leading role in the administration.

The first crisis was the downing of a U.S. Navy P-3 antisubmarine aircraft after colliding with a Chinese F-8 fighter over Hainan Island on April 1. The crew was incarcerated. (The P-3 crew was released after eleven days in Chinese hands. Returning the aircraft took longer.) Powell took the lead in dealing with the Chinese, reportedly angering some of Bush's political advisors. Later, in a different context, Powell admitted in a CNN interview that he had leaned a bit too far forward "on his skis." During the summer, Deputy Secretary of State Richard Armitage observed that Powell (and State) had been put "in the refrigerator" by the White House until needed.

Bush's top priority was a massive $1.2 trillion tax cut designed to jump-start the economy. Unfortunately, the wars that began after September 11 and the resulting hikes in defense spending meant, combined with tax cuts, that the nation's debt would double during Bush's presidency. This continued accrual of debt would persist into future administrations and today approaches a staggering $20 trillion, about the same size as the nation's gross domestic product.

Regarding defense, Bush was determined to transform the U.S. military for the twenty-first century and promised to do it. Transformation topped his Pentagon agenda. But the key issue was, transforming to what? No specific plan had been created to that end. Transformation was simply a campaign promise that needed to be translated into action.

America's adversaries were not existential. Russia was friendly, and besides, NATO expansion would ensure stability in Europe. North Korea was a constant concern but had been deterred since the end of the Korean War in 1953, despite its nuclear ambitions. Iran was a regarded as the biggest state sponsor of terrorism, by virtue of its support for Hezbollah, Israel's archenemy. However, the Israeli military and its not-so-secret nuclear weapons overmatched Iran's.

The former Yugoslavia was largely stable. While the Taliban were ghastly and violently repressive rulers, and though the names "al Qaeda" and "Osama bin Laden," its leader, were not unknown to the intelligence communities, Afghanistan did not seem to pose a direct threat to America. But to the neoconservatives who had advised Bush during the campaign, the world did not appear so benign.

"Neocons" viewed Saddam Hussein as a clear and present danger and argued that regime change was the only way to end this threat. Congress had supported this ambition, passing legislation in the late 1990s calling for Saddam's ouster. North Korea was more than an irritant, especially since the 1994 agreement that was supposed to have prevented Pyongyang from acquiring nuclear weapons had been revealed as a fig leaf. Iran's hostility to the Great Satan, America, and its repeated calls for the destruction of the Zionist state of Israel were taken by the neocons as serious threats. To the neocons, a more muscular foreign policy matched with a stronger defense was the best and only way to ensure the security of America and its allies.

Thus, despite the relative stability of the international environment, Bush chose to run as JFK had in 1960, not on a nonexistent missile gap but rather on an urgent need to rebuild the American military. Transformation was aimed at this task.

Vice presidential candidate and former secretary of defense Dick Cheney brashly promised during the campaign that "help was on the way" for the U.S. military. The Department of Defense was not actually in the dire straits the Republican campaign warned. However, the rhetorical muscularity of the neocons meant that military strength would be fundamental to a successful Bush administration—rhetoric that ultimately would lead the president to cul-de-sacs in Afghanistan and Iraq.

Transformation posed a critical dilemma. It was marvelously unencumbered by specifics; no one offered a precise definition of what it meant or of where it was headed. There were only banalities: transformation was for strengthening joint operations, exploiting U.S. intelligence advantages, emphasizing concept development and experimentation, and developing transformational capabilities through greater reliance on technology and research and development, particularly intelligence. At the Pentagon, this absence of direction induced bitter reactions from a frustrated brass. Rumsfeld preferred to challenge his military subordinates to define transformation in programmatic and budgetary terms than provide them specific direction and guidance. Rumsfeld's aggressive and bullying management style generated resentment among the senior military that would soon become public.

The Bush team emphasized the priority of space and anti-ballistic-missile defense as deterrents and hedges against possible future North Korean and Iranian weapons capable of striking allies in Europe or, of course, the American mainland—a second cousin to Reagan's SDI. However, these ABM systems could not be pursued within the confines of the 1973 ABM Treaty between the United States and Russia. Bush elected to abrogate the ABM Treaty unilaterally and so notified Moscow. The evidence suggests that little analysis went into this decision and that the consequences were never fully considered.

President Putin was not happy with this decision. Nor was the Russian military. Russian military doctrine made no distinction in war between strategic and shorter-range tactical and theater nuclear-armed missiles. The Russians understood that a modest ABM system directed against Iranian or North Korean systems would have no impact on their own strategic missiles. However, ABM defense could be used against shorter-range Soviet missile systems. Russian military doctrine had moved to a variant of Eisenhower's strategic New Look, with greater reliance on nuclear weapons than on conventional forces.

The Russians fully understood that the United States and NATO had unmatched conventional superiority over Moscow; that was amply displayed in Desert Storm. Moreover, the Russian army maintained a largely drafted military force—and more than 80 percent of Russian youths were deemed physically unfit for service. The United States, arguing that its missile defenses posed no threat to Russia, failed to appreciate the Russian counterargument that the threat to the shorter-range, not long-range, missiles was the concern. Unfortunately, this dialogue became a monologue and served only to exacerbate already fraying relations. This friction continues today.

To guide military transformation, Bush chose Gen. Richard Myers of the Air Force as the next JCS chairman. Myers had commanded North American Defense and Aerospace Command and Space Command and was now serving as vice JCS chairman to Gen. Hugh Shelton, U.S. Army. Ironically, the administration was about to submit its military strategy and plans to Congress in the congressionally mandated Quadrennial Defense Review (QDR) when September 11 changed the world. It would also be unfortunate that Shelton, a Special Forces officer with great ground-warfare experience, which would be needed in the ensuing conflicts, would be replaced by a fighter pilot with skills in advanced technology and space.

Meanwhile, with Bush and Rumsfeld in office, transformation became the driving force in the Department of Defense. But specifics of how transformation would be translated into action and what that meant for the shape, size, and levels of future forces and for newer systems remained ambiguous. Vocal complaints by senior military leaders about Rumsfeld's brusque and abrasive style led to a flurry of press reports that Rumsfeld was not suited for the job. These stories peaked in press in the summer of 2001 over how badly Rumsfeld was doing at the Pentagon and that he was most likely to be the first cabinet officer fired.

All the while, the QDR was being written. Scheduled for release on September 30, the final draft was approved on September 10. The next day changed everything. The attacks on the Twin Towers in New York and the Pentagon in Washington, D.C., altered the course of history. And the attacks would transform the wounded Rumsfeld into a highly respected and seemingly invincible "minister of war."

Transformation would become the slogan for, if not the overriding vision of, how this new war declared against global terror would be waged. While the Twin Towers were still burning, the QDR was subjected to an immediate rewrite to take account of this tectonic event. The final version of the Quadrennial Defense Review released on September 30 did not get to transformation until page 16:

> Finally, the defense strategy calls for the transformation of the U.S. military and Defense establishment over time. Transformation is at the heart of this new strategic approach. The Department's leadership recognizes that continuing "business as usual" within the Department is not a viable option given the new strategic era and the internal and external challenges facing the U.S. military. Without change, the current defense program will only become more expensive to maintain over time, and it will forfeit many of the opportunities available to the United States today. Without transformation, the U.S. military will not be prepared to meet emerging challenges. At the same time, it would be imprudent to transform the entire force all at once. A balance must be struck between the need to meet current threats while transforming the force over time. Therefore, the Department is committed to undertaking a sustained process of transformation—based on clear goals—and strengthening the spirit of innovation in its people, while remaining prepared to deal with extant threats.

The reader can judge the clarity of this statement and how readily it could be translated into specific programs and actions.

George W. Bush was informed of the attacks on the World Trade Center by his chief of staff, Andrew Card, while reading to second graders at the Emma E. Booker Elementary School in Sarasota, Florida. TV images showed Bush understandably bewildered and dazed. The stunning nature of this audacious and vicious attack shocked Americans perhaps as much as Pearl Harbor had done sixty years earlier. The meltdown and collapse of the Twin Towers later that day, along with the loss of about three thousand lives, generated even more massive public outrage against the perpetrators and demands for retribution.

The attacks had extraordinary and what would prove to be catastrophic consequences beyond the physical damage in New York and Washington. The terrorist attacks focused Bush's sense of purpose as president. This new focus was so intense as to be an epiphany. The president himself suggested that when he spoke of answering to a "higher father." Before September 11, the Bush administration had not found its footing. While Bush personally enjoyed a measure of popularity, his administration appeared to be floundering, especially over foreign policy. Bush had needed a vision and purpose. Now that would come, in his "freedom agenda."

While not characterized as such by the neocons, this agenda was based on the proposition that democracies do not wage war against each other (Pakistan and India take note). The principal region that would preoccupy this agenda would be the Middle East—which, parenthetically, would guarantee the security of Israel. Bush came to believe fervently that democratization of autocratic states was the path to peace and stability. This agenda would be advanced through several speeches. Bush famously said that he intended "to alter the geostrategic framework of the Middle East" through his freedom agenda. He did. And future generations will deal with the consequences, which so far have proved disastrous.

The first target was Afghanistan. Shortly after the attacks, it became unarguable that Osama bin Laden and al Qaeda were responsible. On September 12, 2001, NATO's North Atlantic

Council—under the leadership of Secretary General, and former British defense minister, George Robertson (Baron Robertson of Port Ellen)—invoked for the first and only time Article 5 of the Washington Treaty: an attack against one was an attack against all.

The symbolism was important. That an alliance was engaged with the United States reinforced the legitimacy of military action. Still, Rumsfeld was not entirely pleased with this powerful invocation, perhaps because he had served as the U.S. permanent representative to NATO. He was aware that aside from Britain, France, and a few other members, the alliance's military capability was uneven. His concern was that NATO might hinder unilateral American action.

The Pentagon, under the outgoing chairman, General Shelton, was directed to develop various military options. The Pentagon already had dozens of contingency plans, but it had none for Afghanistan. The CIA was already way ahead of the Pentagon in producing the options for Afghanistan that Rumsfeld was demanding.

At 9:30 a.m. on September 13, Bush met with the NSC in the White House Situation Room. CIA director George Tenet began the briefing. The CIA had a long history operating in Afghanistan, predating Charlie Wilson's war during the Reagan administration. Cofer Black, head of the agency's Counterterrorism Center, followed with a highly theatrical summary of the CIA plans to capture bin Laden. It would use a combination of covert operatives, Special Forces, and the large ground forces of the Northern Alliance (which had been fighting against Taliban control and had been central to defeating Russia in the ten-year war). Black promised this plan would work. As reported in Bob Woodward's *Bush at War*, he then added dramatically, "You give us the mission. . . . [W]hen we are through with them, they will have flies walking on their eyeballs." Black also told the president that because al Qaeda and the Taliban were bound at the hip, both would be targets of this operation.

The previous day, in a speech to the nation, Bush had stated the basis of what would become the Bush Doctrine—the United States would make no distinction between terrorists who committed these acts and those who harbored them. This would give added emphasis to the global war on terror and expanded potential military action to not only the perpetrators but their supporters.

In late September, the Bush administration delivered two ultimatums to the Taliban, demanding that bin Laden be turned over to American custody. The Taliban offered first to have bin Laden tried by sharia law. The administration refused. The Taliban then proposed sending bin Laden to a third country. That offer too was rejected out of hand.

Bush addressed the nation on Afghanistan on September 20. On October 7, the first air and missile strikes against the Taliban began. CIA officers and Special Forces, fifty or so at first, joined with Northern Alliance troops, were suppored by massive U.S. air and missile power. Rumsfeld's view of transformation was encapsulated in the image of several Special Forces soldiers riding horseback on ancient Afghan saddles in full mujahedeen kit calling in B-52 strikes with their cell phones. This was the new way of making war.

The Taliban were quickly routed. Mazar-i-Sharif fell, then Kabul and Kandahar. More Special Forces and the 15th Marine Expeditionary Unit (MEU) and 26th Marine Regiment poured into Afghanistan in November, followed by other American, British, and other allied units. The "war" was over almost before it began.

During the earlier deliberations in September, both Vice President Cheney and Deputy Defense Secretary Paul Wolfowitz had raised the issue of Iraq. For the time being, dealing with Iraq was deferred. However, it was clear that the neocons had had Iraq in their sights since 1991, when George H. W. Bush had halted the "highway of death" slaughter and not pushed on to Baghdad. In early 2002, Iraq would come to the top of the agenda.

Following the rapid fall of the Taliban, the issue of what next for Afghanistan was pressing. Powell had assigned the seasoned diplomat James Dobbins as special envoy for Afghanistan. Ambassador Dobbins had been deeply engaged in the Balkans negotiations and was ideally suited for the Afghanistan talks. Also on the team was the future American ambassador to Afghanistan, Iraq, and the United Nations, Afghan-born Dr. Zalmay Khalilzad.

Under UN auspices, the Bonn Conference on Afghanistan was convened on November 28. Powell had instructed Dobbins to get an agreement quickly. Imposing a democratic agenda and nation building were not the main priorities. Establishing a government was. The Bonn Conference was a textbook case of successful international negotiations based on necessity and not aspiration. Iran was productively involved, and Powell had waived the strictures that prohibited meetings with Iranian officials. Dobbins had received assurances from Iran that Tehran was opposed to terrorism and would be supportive in Afghanistan. The Bush administration, however, rejected that support, as would become apparent. The Bonn Accords were signed on December 5, 2001. Hamid Karzai was appointed Afghanistan's leader, and the path for establishing the new government was specified. Bonn, at that moment, was a notable achievement. However, that moment would not be long-lived.

On January 29, 2002, Bush appeared before both houses of Congress and the American public to deliver his first State of the Union speech, which would be remembered for one phrase. Bush declared that an "axis of evil" existed between and among Iran, Iraq, and North Korea. This categorization had to be one of the greatest rhetorical blunders since Lyndon Johnson declared that "American boys were not going to die for Asian boys." The "axis of evil" speech cemented the accession of the neocons as influences on the president. Much has been made of Vice President Cheney's Svengali-like control over Bush. This is an overstatement. The neocons did not force positions on Bush. However, the neocons did greatly support and reinforce the president's convictions about the "freedom agenda" and his decision to impose democracy on Iraq. These two visions, those of Bush and of the neocons, worked in parallel to support the freedom agenda and apply it to the Middle East.

As quickly as the Taliban were defeated, Rumsfeld's prestige soared. He would be regarded for a time as "the minister of war" and his performance at Defense often characterized as brilliant. Of course, the initial planning had largely been the CIA's, if the Pentagon had provided the critical firepower the Northern Alliance needed to rout the Taliban. Less reported, however, were two other actions Rumsfeld undertook that were much needed.

Assisted by his very able senior military assistant Vice Adm. Edmund Giambastiani (who would later be promoted to lead Allied Command Transformation in Norfolk), Rumsfeld began a painstaking review of America's "war plans." Rumsfeld had not been popular when he renamed the various commanders in chief of the operational commands, or "CinCs," as they had been called for decades, "combatant commanders." War plans were the purview of the CinCs, and tensions between the civilians and uniformed military over those plans had existed going back to 1947 and the creation of the Department of Defense. Now, Rumsfeld spent part of every weekend grilling the CinCs and their staffs on the war plans, particularly the assumptions undergirding them. Such a review should be mandatory for every administration, concluding with a briefing for the president on the major war and contingency plans.

Second, Rumsfeld undertook a critical examination of the U.S. global force posture from the standpoint of transformation. Rumsfeld believed that the overseas basing structure needed to be modernized and, where appropriate, reduced. He was correct in that assessment. He insisted on a "lighter footprint" when deploying U.S. forces, meaning less "tail" and more "tooth." Meanwhile, Gen. Tommy Franks, commander of Central Command, was given the task of drawing up plans for an invasion of Iraq.

The history of the buildup for the second Iraq War is extensive and will not be recounted here. The question of sound strategic thinking is, however, vital. The success of Operation Enduring Freedom in Afghanistan was giving, wrongly, U.S. military power an aura of invincibility. The Bush administration also well remembered Desert Storm and the magnitude of the victory. Cheney and Powell had been architects of that war, and Wolfowitz and Armitage had also played key roles, while Condoleezza Rice had been a junior staffer on the NSC. Repeating that victory against an Iraqi army debilitated by arms embargoes and occasional air strikes would not be difficult, or so the neocons reasoned. "Cakewalk" was a term to describe coming hostilities.

Bush's vision was the driving force in intervening in Iraq; what he needed was a rationale for war. Saddam was an evil person. His regime did evil things. That had not stopped Reagan from dispatching Rumsfeld to Iraq to meet Saddam nearly twenty years before, nor the tacit U.S. alliance in the war against Iran. Saddam's simply being evil was not sufficient grounds for going to war. Where Saddam was most guilty was his defiance of UN resolutions and international law in preventing UN personnel from carrying out the agreed-upon inspections for weapons of mass destruction. The United States had mounted coercive strikes against Iraq to force adherence, but the neocons, in particular, were certain Saddam had hidden away substantial quantities of WMD. Few contested that assessment.

War would be premised on the conviction of Saddam's continuation of illegal WMD programs and his clear-cut disregard therein for international law. The various intelligence agencies were directed to find evidence to document this assumption. Interestingly, General Zinni, former Central Command (CentCom) commander, argued that whatever WMD Saddam might have had, Operation Desert Fox had eliminated in late 1998. Most foreign intelligence agencies too believed that Iraqi WMD had been largely destroyed, either by the inspectors or by military strikes. The Bush administration would not be so easily convinced. In fact, Cheney set up a separate operation dedicated to providing "smoking guns" to prove Saddam had WMD.

When the decision to go to war in Iraq was made is subject to debate. However, by August 2002 CentCom had been directed to plan actively for an invasion no later than early 2003. Colin Powell was skeptical at best. On August 5, 2002, Powell met privately with Bush in the White House living quarters. Condoleezza Rice joined them during what was a two-hour meeting. Powell brought with him a sheaf of long, yellow legal pages filled with questions and issues the president needed to consider in the context of electing to go to war with Iraq. As Powell would later comment, virtually all of the NSC meetings on Iraq had had to do with military options and consequences, not the fundamental geostrategic rationale for invading Iraq in the first place. The day before this meeting with Bush, Brent Scowcroft had solemnly warned on a Sunday-morning TV show that an attack on Iraq could turn the Middle East into "a cauldron and thus destroy the war on terrorism." The White House was not pleased, and this would not be the only time Scowcroft would find disfavor over his dissenting views on war with Iraq.

Powell was not close to Bush, and these meetings were meant to improve the relationship. In this meeting, Powell suggested to the president that in considering how to deal with Iraq, Bush needed to understand all the consequences—a basic, 101-level course in strategic thinking. Powell agreed with Scowcroft that "cauldron" was the right word. An invasion of Iraq would destabilize the region. Powell projected other consequences as well, from economic to the financial costs of occupying Iraq—all of which, tragically, would prove true, with a vengeance. Powell also added that an American general running an Arab country—a latter-day Douglas MacArthur in Baghdad instead of Japan—would be unacceptable to Iraqis. Unlike Desert Shield and Storm, access to the region was far from guaranteed by the local states. Nor was Baghdad proximate to the border, as Kuwait was to Saudi Arabia. Also, rallying a coalition equivalent to the one that defeated Saddam in 1991 would not be easy, if indeed possible.

Bob Woodward's *Bush at War* concludes that Powell was satisfied with his meeting with the president, having made all his key points. Powell, a reluctant warrior, believed he had laid out the most important consequences of a war, especially the difficulty, if not impossibility, of unilateral American military action. What Powell could not know was that by getting Bush to accept implicitly the absolute necessity for both UN and congressional resolutions to legitimize military action, he would ultimately become the administration's chief spokesman for the war, when he addressed the UN Security Council on February 5, 2003.

The buildup for the war began in earnest. On October 10 and 11, Congress voted decisively to approve the Joint Resolution Authorizing the Use of Military Force against Iraq. On November 8, the UN passed Resolution 1441, giving Iraq forty-five days to comply with prior UN resolutions or accept the consequences. Having exhausted his options to avert war, Powell told Bush that he believed another UN resolution was needed that would fully justify the use of force.

Bush did not quite ask Powell whether he was "with me or against me." But Bush was quite blunt, and Powell had no option.

> The Russell Office Building, U.S. Senate, late September 2002, my meeting with Senator John F. Kerry (JK).

JK: "Come in. What's on your mind, although I think I know?"

HKU: "I understand that you are going to vote for the war, and I know and understand why."

JK: "Yes. I voted against the first war in 1990 and was wrong. I am not comfortable with this vote, but I think it will give the president the leverage he needs to force Saddam into backing down. If that happens, then war will be averted. And the intelligence is fairly persuasive about Iraq's WMD, even if it is not conclusive."

HKU: "We got it wrong over the Tonkin Gulf. And what makes you think the CIA really believes Saddam still has WMD? Cheney and Wolfowitz have put together a team that I think is cherry-picking the information. And this character 'Curveball' has been repudiated by the German intelligence crowd that brought him in."

JK: "Curveball is very, very 'close hold.' How did you come by this info?"

HKU: "John, I think every reporter in town who is covering this stuff knows about Curveball. My source was a close contact high up in European intelligence. You can probably guess which country. I cannot say. However, if you spoke to Tony Zinni [the CentCom commander during Desert Fox] and other senior retired people, I am sure they would agree. If Saddam has any WMD, it is residual. And trust me, Curveball is not who he says he is. The White House wants a war, and that is what they will get. Speak privately with the secretary of state."

JK: "I appreciate that. My hope is that a strong vote will convince Saddam he has no choice. He cannot be that irrational. After all he knows what happened the last time. Why would he think he can bluff us this time?"

HKU: "You know that the reason the Soviet Union imploded was not Reagan or the military buildup. It was because the Soviet system was brittle, irrational, and would die of its own weight. Who knows what game Saddam is playing. Perhaps he thinks that if it turns out he does not have WMD, the big lie may topple him. So he is stuck. Fail to yield and face a war he will lose. Or allow inspectors and hope that the revelation that he does not have WMD will not bring him down."

✦

On February 5, 2003, with Director of National Intelligence (and Ambassador) John Negroponte and CIA director George Tenet seated directly behind him, Powell laid out the evidence that Saddam was harboring WMD. Powell and his deputy Rich Armitage had spent several long days at CIA Headquarters at Langley, Virginia, painstakingly reviewing the intelligence. Finally, Powell asked Tenet his view. Tenet had used the phrase "slam dunk" at the White House; he now told Powell that he had no doubts about Iraq possessing WMD and gave Powell his word as to the veracity of the intelligence.

Powell, again, had no choice. He could dismiss the CIA director's assurance. He could resign. Or he could go to the UN. Being the loyal soldier and not being able to reject categorically the CIA assessments, Powell presented a compelling case at the UN. Few watching the briefing had any doubt as to the presence of WMD in Iraq. Among the many pieces of evidence was an audio tape of Iraqi soldiers discussing the movement of WMD.

A few months later, when it became apparent there were no weapons of mass destruction, I asked a well-known expert on Iraq, Malcolm Nance, to listen to the tapes. Nance spoke fluent Iraqi Arabic. When he heard them he started laughing. "This is bullshit.

These guys are reading from a script. You can hear it in the tone of their voices."

"How is that?" I asked. Nance replied that many of the translators used at State and at Langley were Jordanian and did not speak the Iraqi dialect. One reason, he confided, was that we didn't trust Iraqi translators then. And no one thought that the Iraqi dialect was an issue.

As we know, the war started in earnest March 20. It was a repeat of the first Gulf war—on steroids. U.S. ground forces sliced through Iraqi divisions. Air and missile power eviscerated Iraqi armor, artillery, and troops. When a great sandstorm hit, critics carped that the offensive was stymied. None understood the all-weather capability of our surveillance and weapons systems, which easily detected unsuspecting Iraqi forces, who believed they were safely hidden by the weather. The storm was to our advantage.

By that time, I had been a Fox contributor for several years and had been retained by the *New York Post* to write three or four columns a week on the war. Before the war started, I had raised grave doubts about Saddam's WMD and had been one of the rare talking heads to warn that the chances were at least even that the WMD cupboard was bare. Iraq would be found not to have weapons of mass destruction. Only a tiny handful of other analysts had raised such doubts.

The one area where virtually all the reputable analysts agreed, on and off television, was the absolute need to prepare for the day after when Saddam had been defeated: the "What next?" question had become so commonplace as to be boring and repetitive. The administration assured the doubters that all was in hand. But all was not in hand, and this was negligence of criminal proportions. Yet the story would get worse.

When Zinni was commander of CentCom he had developed a campaign plan for a postwar Iraq called "Desert Crossing." After Zinni left, Franks completely dismissed the plan. Whether he did so because of Army/Marine rivalries or on the direction of higher authority is unclear. Powell at State also began a major examination of the "What next?" question in Iraq. That too was dismissed out of hand by the Bush administration. The White House knew better.

Ahmed Chalabi, the exiled leader of the Iraqi National Congress, would be given the keys to the kingdom, and the United States would leave Iraq in safe hands.

In January 2003, DoD established the Office for Reconstruction and Humanitarian Assistance (ORHA), headed by the formidable and highly experienced retired Army lieutenant general Jay Garner. Garner had overseen Operation Provide Comfort in northern Iraq after the first Gulf war. On April 21, the Coalition Provisional Authority, or CPA, was established, based on UN Resolution 1483, with the United States in charge.

Abruptly, Garner was replaced by former ambassador L. Paul "Jerry" Bremer, who had zero experience in the region or in Iraq. Bremer's nickname came from St. Jerome, who Bremer believed had saved his life as a very young child in a lightning storm. In his office in the "Green Zone" in Baghdad, two pictures stood on his desk—one of his wife Francine and the other of St. Jerome. Unlike Garner, who believed it was essential for Iraqis and not Americans to begin rebuilding, Bremer's first act was to impose de-Baathification laws that prohibited party members from government positions. With a stroke of the pen, the vast majority of bureaucrats essential to the functioning of government were dismissed. Then, on May 23, in a teleconference between himself and President Bush and the NSC, who were at Camp David, the decision was made to demobilize the Iraqi army. There was virtually no debate. Neither Powell nor Armitage attended.

Why Bremer was selected to head the CPA remains unclear. Cheney and the neocons favored Ahmed Chalabi to head a new government. Bremer, with his lack of experience, might have been easier to manipulate. Bremer was a devout Catholic, and that might have also influenced his selection, given Bush's born again Christianity. In any event, Bremer was poorly suited for the task. Whether a more experienced head might have made a difference, in view of the micromanagement of the White House and vice president's office, is unknowable.

The "What next?" question had never been fully addressed. Even though the CPA was supposed to report to Rumsfeld, Bremer often went directly to the White House. After Saddam's army was defeated and then dissolved, an insurgency broke out. Just as intelligence had failed about WMD, no one had predicted or knew about the so-called Saddam fedayeen. These were local troops deployed in towns and cities as storm troopers to ensure, through force of arms, loyalty to the Baathist regime. With the army gone, the fedayeen loyal to Saddam began insurgent operations against coalition forces.

The occupation disintegrated into a disaster, beginning with extensive looting once Baghdad fell. Rumsfeld responded to this looting offhandedly: "Stuff happens." Excesses in dealing with captured enemy combatants were laid bare in the exposure of "black sites" used for enhanced interrogation. The outrageous and illegal conduct of American military personnel at the infamous Abu Ghraib prison outside Baghdad sullied the American reputation for ethical behavior and greatly aided recruitment to the insurgency.

On June 28, 2004, the CPA was dissolved and government officially transferred back to Iraqi control. Of course, Saddam had by now been captured; he was later executed in a bizarrely bungled hanging that managed to decapitate the former despot instead of breaking his neck. As one more mark of the incompetence of this occupation, 363 tons of money, most of it in crisp hundred-dollar bills, was transported to Iraq, where much of it, as in Afghanistan, was stolen. Inexplicably, scrip—that is, currency printed for exclusive use in-country and not convertible, as had been done in World War II, Korea, and Vietnam—was not used.

Gen. Tommy Franks quickly departed Iraq after his victory to retire to the consolations of writing a book and giving a lecture tour that would make him a considerable amount of money. His operation plan—Operation Polo Step—is available in the George Washington University National Security Archives, and it is striking. CentCom had been preparing to withdraw most of the troops from Iraq by the end of 2003, leaving a small residual force.

What unfolded over the next several months was, to borrow from Tom Ricks' acclaimed book on the war, a fiasco. The insurgency was not a matter of "dead-enders," as Rumsfeld claimed. Nor were the WMD—of which Rumsfeld categorically stated, "We know where it is"—ever found. Saddam's WMD had, as some had fore-seen, been destroyed by a combination of coalition air strikes and UN inspectors.

Saddam had double-crossed himself. He had been most con-cerned with continuing the bluff. Not even Saddam's generals had known that his bluster over WMD was only that. Perhaps Saddam believed that if his generals knew the truth and reacted as he would have himself, the bluff might have led to a coup. Without Iraqi WMD, Israel might feel more emboldened. This lie preempted a war and, later, Saddam's execution. How many Iraqis would perish is unknowable. Figures range as high as more than a million.

Even to the most fervent neocons, by 2004 it was obvious that security conditions in Iraq were deteriorating. Advised by a former vice chief of staff of the Army, Gen. Jack Keane, and other retired generals, as well as one or two think tanks, Bush understood that a dramatic strategic change was imperative. The Iraq Study Group, convened in 2003 and cochaired by James Baker and Lee Hamilton, was finishing its recommendations. As highly critical as the report would be when it was published in December 2006, it was not crit-ical enough. Its recommendations not to increase forces until 2008 would be overtaken by the "surge."

By fall 2006, the Bush administration was facing political and geostrategic crises bordering on the humiliating. Favorability ratings plunged below 40 percent. On November 7, Democrats won a stun-ning electoral victory, taking control of the House with a majority of thirty-one, seating the first woman Speaker, Nancy Pelosi, and of the Senate, fifty-six to forty-four. The next day Rumsfeld resigned as secretary of defense. Cheney had made a desperate effort to retain his friend and onetime mentor. However, the president finally and fully understood that a major change was necessary not only in strat-egy but also at Defense. Former CIA director and national security advisor Robert Gates, a longtime friend and colleague of the Bush family, was persuaded to take the job.

Unlike President Johnson, who could not deal with the fail-ing war in Vietnam, Bush, to his credit, realized that conditions in Iraq could be reversed only by bold action. The result was the "surge"—also called, less dramatically, "the new way forward." The president announced the surge in a nationally televised address on January 7, 2007. It began with the deployment of five brigades, totaling more than 20,000 soldiers.

The bulk went into Baghdad to help Iraqis clear and secure local neighborhoods and protect people from the violence of the insurgency that was tearing the country apart. The president's objective, as noted on the White House media website, was to create a "unified, democratic federal Iraq that can govern itself, defend itself, and sustain itself, and is an ally in the War on Terror." The surge was to be commanded by Gen. David Petraeus, one of the most capable Army officers of his time and a protégé of Jack Keane's.

The surge succeeded in greatly reducing violence. However, it did not and could not resolve the political paradox that doomed Iraq to continuing violence. That paradox was the hatred between the majority Shia and the minority Sunni populations. Under Saddam, the Sunnis had repressed the Shia with unbridled cruelty. When the Shia took power under Prime Minister Nouri al Maliki, Shia repression of the Sunnis ran amuck. It was to be of this religious violence that the Islamic State would be born, the Frankensteinian legacy of America's assault into Iraq—a legacy that may confront and challenge many future administrations.

The Shia Iraqi government was not prepared to accept the continued presence of large numbers of American troops. Cheney's promise that Americans would be greeted as "liberators" proved as hollow a prediction as that WMD would be found. While the Obama administration was to be criticized for accelerating this drawdown after 2009, the Bush administration had signed an agreement mandating U.S. withdrawal. Unknowingly, the United States thereby consigned Iraq to becoming a failed state. Also, there would be very little America could do about it, especially with the Democratic candidate for president in 2008 campaigning to end that war.

Another policy contradiction also plagued the Bush administration. On October 9, 2006, North Korea exploded what it advertised as a nuclear weapon. The United States, which had intervened in Iraq to prevent Saddam from shrouding an American city in a "mushroom-shaped cloud," had no military options for North Korea. It was bogged down in Iraq and Afghanistan; in any case, a war in Korea would have caused hundreds of thousands of casualties on both sides, including the likely devastation of Seoul by North Korean artillery positioned just outside the demilitarized zone.

As for strategic thinking, the Bush administration was derelict, certainly throughout the first term and well into the second. Declaration of an "axis of evil" was rhetorical malpractice. No linkages between its supposed poles existed. Iran and Iraq had fought a decade-long war. Branding Iran a member of this "axis" immediately following the Bonn Conference guaranteed the alienation of a country vital to the future stability of Afghanistan. This was strategic incompetence of the highest order.

Part of the reason for this absence of strategic thinking rested in the president's personality and psyche. September 11 had solidified his vision and rationale for a freedom agenda. The three charter members of this axis of evil were the antitheses of democratic values and principles. The amazing military success in Afghanistan, expelling the Taliban with literally a handful of American forces in 2001, created a sense of invincibility. Also, regime change seemed the only reasonable way to alter the geostrategic landscape. Bush deeply believed that a free Iraq would spread democracy. Regional states, especially Saudi Arabia and Iran, would take note. Through democratization, the security of Israel would be made permanent.

Along a parallel track ran the thinking of Cheney, Wolfowitz, and other neocons in the administration. As early as the first NSC meetings following September 11, the question of what to do about Iraq was raised. That Saddam had tried to assassinate the president's father might have been a lesser reason for preemptive war. Perhaps recollections of failing to go to Baghdad in 1991 produced an overreaction. The neocons probably did not cause or convince Bush to attack Iraq. But certainly neoconservative views reinforced the decision to go to war in the Middle East.

The intelligence failure was colossal. Groupthink has been cited, most clearly in the final report of the September 11th Commission, as one reason. Bush obviously favored an invasion in Iraq.

The preferences of the commander in chief are never taken lightly. Maintaining objectivity in an environment as politically charged as the White House is exceedingly difficult.

Further, basic assumptions were not challenged. When Colin Powell met with President Bush in August 2002, the secretary raised all the key questions. But these concerns were not analyzed; instead, they were largely, if not entirely, ignored. Similarly, before the war Rumsfeld sent a long memorandum to Bush speculating on what could go wrong in attacking Iraq. These prospects too did not seem to challenge the administration's assumptions. The memo provided no answers to the questions or antidotes for the possible negative outcomes.

The fragility of the administration's assumptions, however, became too obvious when the chief of staff of the Army, Gen. Eric Shinseki, testified before the Senate Armed Services Committee just prior to the start of Iraqi Freedom. When pressed to answer how many troops would be needed to ensure stability in Iraq after the war ended, Shinseki reluctantly suggested that the number could be in the several hundreds of thousands. (In his own testimony before the House Budget Committee on February 27, 2003, Deputy Secretary of Defense Paul Wolfowitz would declare that this number was "wildly off the mark.") Perhaps in retaliation, Rumsfeld announced Shinseki's successor almost a year in advance, effectively destroying the chief's legitimacy. The successor was to have been General Keane, but he retired as vice chief and never took the position. Rumsfeld chose instead a retired general, Peter J. Schoomaker, which further angered the Army leadership. The Shinseki incident demonstrated that the administration would not tolerate any dissent, no matter how respectful.

Regarding understanding and knowledge, the administration was woefully unprepared. Before September 11, few Americans knew where Afghanistan was or anything about the more radical interpretations of Islam. Since the demise of the Soviet Union, Sovietologists had become an endangered species. This became apparent in 2008, if not earlier. Relations with Russia were becoming rockier, over both Iraq and NATO expansion.

At the NATO heads-of-government summit in Bucharest, Romania, in April 2008, George W. Bush proposed, as discussed in the preceding chapter, a Membership Action Plan (MAP) to Georgia and Ukraine. Other NATO members objected that this would be "an unnecessary offense" to Russia. In part to placate Ukraine and Georgia, Bush announced that both could become NATO members, that their MAP applications would be reviewed in December 2008. The Russian president, Vladimir Putin, who was in Bucharest for the summit, warned Bush that expansion of NATO to Russia's borders "would be taken in Russia as a direct threat to the security of our country." Bush's statement had been an "unforced" error with huge consequences.

Russia began planning for an incursion into Georgia, understanding that no country could be admitted to NATO if it had contested borders. That August, Putin set a trap for Georgia that its president, Mikheil Saakashvili, foolishly ignored. Saakashvili had become president in 2004 after the "Rose revolution" ousted Eduard Shevardnadze, a Georgian former Soviet foreign minister, from the office. Saakashvili was keen to regain territory in South Ossetia and Abkhazia that had been under de facto control of separatists wishing to remain with Moscow. Separatists now shelled a town in northern Georgia. Saakashvili, sensing an opportunity and not a trap, bit and bit hard, sending his army to punish the separatists. Moscow responded, citing the right to protect Russian citizens residing there. The Georgian army was quickly defeated. The border controversy meant membership for Georgia was out. Few in the West appreciated Putin's aims in Georgia. That summer Putin passed the presidency with Dmitri Medvedev and became prime minister. The seemingly mild-mannered Medvedev was more soothing to the West. Putin and Medvedev would later swap jobs again.

As Kennedy's ideological commitment to paying any price for liberty had led to Vietnam, Bush clung to his freedom agenda, forgetting that transferring democracy to other cultures was exceedingly difficult if not impossible. Bush never doubted: as the self-declared "decider," he was either arrogant or overconfident in his judgment. Humility is an often elusive virtue.

Bush looked into Putin's eyes and decided that, as Margaret Thatcher said of Gorbachev, this is someone with whom "we can do business." Bush never appreciated that beginning with the abrogation of the ABM Treaty and ending with the Bucharest summit, his actions helped turn Putin from a friend and possible ally into something else. U.S.-Russian relations would continue to deteriorate. The expansion of NATO was indeed a clear and present danger to Moscow, a reaction Washington could never understand.

Ironically, Bush having gone to war in Iraq over nuclear weapons that Saddam did not have, North Korea was too dangerous a place to risk military action even before it exploded what it called an atomic bomb in 2006. Sanctions were imposed. A decade later, Kim would announce that the North had exploded a thermonuclear weapon—a claim that is still in doubt. However, the North does have several nuclear weapons.

History allows no do-overs, as John McCain's top campaign advisor in 2008, Steve Schmidt, ruefully admitted after Obama had defeated his candidate. The shift to nation building in Afghanistan, one that was subtle at first, and the decision to remove Saddam seem in retrospect incomprehensible to rational thought. The same applied to Vietnam. Yet the parallels are virtually complete. There are pleas for listening and leading—but will anyone be learning? Sadly, the Obama administration was not and would not.

Eight

Barack Hussein Obama

Afghanistan, Pakistan, Iraq, Libya, Iran, Syria, and the Pivot East, and the First Days of Donald John Trump as President

Despite his inexperience but with huge promise for hope and change, on January 20, 2009, Barack Hussein Obama became the nation's forty-fourth president. Obama had been an attorney, community organizer, law professor, and state legislator before being elected U.S. senator from Illinois in 2004. At the Democratic Convention in Boston that summer, where John Kerry was nominated for president, Obama burst on the national scene with an inspiring and acclaimed keynote address.

Obama's decisive victory over Senator John McCain four years later made him America's first black president although, in fairness, he had a white mother. Not since Franklin Roosevelt had an incoming president inherited such a dire set of circumstances. The financial crisis of 2008 was far from over. Two wars were going badly. A third, what Bush had called the "global war on terror," would more than exacerbate the first two conflicts. And after Obama "led from behind" in the campaign that ousted Libya's Muammar Qaddafi in 2011, ultimately causing his death and the subsequent civil war, the Islamic State (IS) would find its way into that country.

Obama had promised to end the "bad" war of "choice" in Iraq and respond to the "good" war of "necessity" in Afghanistan. The phrase "wars of choice and of necessity" had been invented by Richard Haass, a senior official in both Bush administrations who had become president of the Council on Foreign Relations. Iraq, Haass argued, was a war of choice and Afghanistan one of necessity. But to those who start wars, every war is a necessity—win, lose, or draw.

When Obama took office the United States had, according to *The Military Balance*, approximately 300,000 U.S. military personnel deployed to the war zones: 240,000 to Operation Iraqi Freedom and about 50,000 to Enduring Freedom in Afghanistan. At least as many civilian contractors were also deployed with about 160,000 in Iraq. However, both military forces and contractors were being greatly reduced as George W. Bush was unable to negotiate a status of forces agreement and Baghdad remained adamant about Americans leaving. Another 55,000 U.S. forces were serving in the Persian Gulf; 38,000 in Afghanistan and about 17,000 afloat or nearby with a further 17,000 ground forces to be surged into the Afghan war.

Obama's national security team was, on paper, strong. Former senator Hillary Clinton was named secretary of state. Clinton had served eight years in the Senate, where she had gained favorable reviews as collegial, competent, and hard working. Her eight years as First Lady, obviously, had added important experience and understanding of many key issues and of how government operated.

Robert Gates, who had earned a well-deserved reputation as Bush 43's second secretary of defense, was kept on, demonstrating that the new administration wanted to maintain bipartisan cooperation. Gates had the experience of serving as national security advisor and of running the CIA. He had done well in overseeing the surge in Iraq and in bringing stability and a commonsense management style to the Pentagon, both sorely needed after Rumsfeld and his autocratic manner. Gates was respected by and popular with the generals. His straightforward and direct leadership was complemented by the ability to listen. A no-nonsense leader with a wry sense of humor, Gates harbored no political ambitions and was a thoroughly safe pair of hands at Defense.

As national security advisor Bush had chosen retired Marine Corps general James L. Jones. Jones had served as commandant of the Marine Corps and had moved to Europe as Supreme Allied Commander Europe (SacEur) in late 2003. Jones was sophisticated in manner and intellect, and his fluent French helped make him a very successful SacEur. He may have been seen as a closet Republican because he was close to Senators John McCain and William Cohen, but he would blot his copybook with Rumsfeld.

In Bob Woodward's *State of Denial*, Jones is quoted as telling the then chairman of the Joint Chiefs of Staff, Gen. Peter Pace, a fellow Marine, not "to be a parrot sitting on Rumsfeld's shoulder." Jones was referring to how Rumsfeld had run over General Myers and controlled Tommy Franks. Woodward passed the quote to Jones for his approval and got it. Interestingly, before the book came out, Rumsfeld asked Jones if he might consider the job of leading Central Command. The offer was not renewed once the book was published.

After Jones retired, he became chairman of the Atlantic Council in Washington, D.C. (I have been a senior advisor there for over a decade.) In early 2008, the council published a study on Afghanistan, *Afghanistan at a Crossroads*, signed by Jones that began "Make no mistake: NATO is losing in Afghanistan." (The line was later revised to read, "Make no mistake: the West is not winning in Afghanistan.") It was this paper that brought the general to the attention of then senator Obama.

Leon Panetta, the veteran House member from Monterey, California, became the director of the CIA. Panetta was liked and respected on the Hill. He had served as Bill Clinton's chief of staff and budget director. While personable, however, Panetta could become prickly and blunt. When he was later selected to replace Gates at Defense, David Petraeus became the CIA head.

Hillary Clinton and Gates had huge political advantages. Obama had wrested the nomination from Clinton and obviously wanted her as part of the administration. That tacit support gave the new secretary clear access and influence. Gates, as a holdover, had leverage as well. But, like that of George W. Bush, Obama's team would not coalesce. Hillary would surround herself with loyalists, who cut out much of the input from the State Department, isolating the new secretary.

Jones would not be allowed to choose his deputy. Tom Donilon, with long experience in Democratic politics, got that post; his loyalties were, understandably, with the president and not his immediate superior, General Jones.

Jones was further marginalized by Obama's chief of staff, former representative Rahm Emanuel, who controlled access to the new president. Other Obama confidants were assigned to the NSC staff. One, Mark Lippert, whom Obama later appointed ambassador to South Korea, consistently frustrated Jones by calling the president "Barry." Jones, a formalist when it came to the presidency, was unable to check Lippert, whom the president referred to as a "younger brother." Jones would leave, replaced by Donilon.

Other changes would take place. Susan Rice left her post as UN ambassador to become national security advisor. Denis McDonough would become Obama's chief of staff, replacing Emanuel. Deputy Secretary of Defense Ashton Carter took over from former senator Chuck Hagel, who had replaced Panetta and served only for about two years. Hagel's departure reflected his ongoing struggles with the White House. And in 2013, Senator John Kerry would assume the duties of secretary of state from Hillary Clinton.

Shortly after taking office, the Nobel Prize Committee bestowed its award for peace on the new president, who, aside from offering "hope and change" and winning the presidency had recorded no significant achievements. By that criterion, many earlier presidents should have been Nobel Prize winners too. Actually, however, the award recognized the optimism many had expressed about the new president and his administration, given the disasters under George W. Bush. Obama accepted the award in Oslo, Norway, on December 10, 2009, eleven months after taking office.

Obama would face grave tests in Afghanistan, Iraq, Libya, Pakistan, Syria, Yemen, and the Horn of Africa that would involve the extensive use of American force. He would be challenged by Russia's Putin in Europe and Ukraine and by China's President Xi Jinping, who was fortifying tiny islets in the South China Sea. He would also have to deal with the Islamic State, which he had once labeled the "junior varsity." And he would have to make the agonizing decision of whether or not to send Special Forces into Pakistan to capture or kill Osama bin Laden.

Regarding the head of al Qaeda, Obama did indeed, to his great credit, authorize Special Forces Command to send SEAL Team 6 on an early-morning raid on a house in Abbottabad, Pakistan, where evidence showed that bin Laden and his family were living. Obama had been advised that the odds of success were about fifty-fifty, meaning it was not certain bin Laden was in residence. A raid of this nature was inherently risky, putting Obama in an impossible situation. Had he not decided to approve the mission and word that bin Laden could have been targeted became public, Obama would have been politically crucified. If the raid failed, Obama would have his own Desert One debacle but on steroids.

The house was not far from Pakistan's equivalent of West Point. Abbottabad was an upscale city in which a significant number of military officers lived, many in retirement. With no advance warning of the raid to Pakistani leaders, for fear it would leak and Osama could be forewarned, American helicopters entered Pakistani territory on May 1, 2011. Despite a hard landing by one of the Black Hawks, the raid succeeded in killing bin Laden. His body was then shipped to an American aircraft carrier, where it received an Islamic burial at sea. All the SEALs returned safely, although one Black Hawk did not.

Justice had finally been meted out. The tragic events of September 11 had been to some degree avenged. Predictably, relations with Pakistan deteriorated badly. They had already been damaged by the Raymond Davis affair in February (discussed later); by a devastating U.S strike on Pakistani forces that had mistakenly opened fire on American units first; and by the so-called Memogate letter, in which the Pakistani ambassador to the United States, Dr. Hussain Haqqani, was falsely accused of plotting a coup against the Pakistani military leadership. It was difficult to see how much worse the relations could be.

Yet one of the grave failings of the Obama administration, and of its predecessors, was the inability to understand and have sufficient knowledge about the circumstances about which decisions to use force were made.

The following vignette is telling.

The White House, May 2009, the national security advisor's office.

James Jones (JJ): "Harlan, thanks for coming in. I am going ask two of our Pakistan analysts to join us. I know you were close to Benazir Bhutto and now to her husband, Asif Zardari, president of Pakistan."

HKU: "Yes, Benazir and I had known each other since I was at graduate school in Boston and she was at Radcliffe. When Benazir was making her political comeback here in the early 2000s, I was helpful. In 2006, her husband Asif was released from prison, and I got to know him well. After Benazir was murdered in December 2007 and Asif returned to Islamabad, I was asked to help him. Since, I have made a number of trips to Islamabad. As you know, he was elected president in September 2008."

JJ: "Let me bring in two of our Pakistan analysts."

First analyst: "We have real concerns about Zardari's physical and mental health."

HKU (restrained): "Go on."

Analyst: "We understand he has a bad heart condition. And when he came to the United States he retained a psychiatrist."

HKU: "Do you know of Dr. Asim Hussein?"

Analyst: "Who?"

HKU: "Zardari's doctor."

Analyst: "No."

HKU: "Do you know how Zardari got of prison?"

Analyst: "No."

HKU: "In Pakistan, jailing of opponents is, sadly, a modus operandi. Zardari was in jail for five or six years, although the conditions of his imprisonment are unclear. The ticket out was medical. Asim performed a minor surgery, placed a large band-aid over a small incision, and declared that Zardari needed treatment in Dubai. He was released."

Analyst: "Oh. . . . But what about his mental state? He had a New York shrink."

HKU: "Do you know the circumstances?"

Analyst: "No."

HKU, turning to Jones: "Jim, where do you find these people? 'Uninformed' is too polite. These two are dangerous in their ignorance." (Turns to the analysts.) "You know Zardari is called 'Mr. Ten Percent' on the grounds that this was his cut for doing business?"

Analysts: "Yes."

HKU: "As a result, Zardari has been sued multiple times. When he came to America, a lawsuit was pending in London for many millions of dollars. Zardari did not want to go to an English court. Do you know how that can be done?"

Analyst: "No."

HKU: "If a doctor certifies a patient is not fit to travel, he or she does not have to appear in a British court. If you pay a shrink, say, $25,000, you will get a letter excusing you. This is standard practice. I wish I were as sane as Zardari."

Sequel: Several years later I was dining in New York City with the CIA station chief. He informed me that the agency had the "goods" on the Pakistani ambassador to the UN. I asked what the "goods" were.

The station chief said the ambassador was "funny" in his sexual proclivities. I responded that everyone knew that, that he had diplomatic immunity, and his family had more money than the CIA. If you were to pursue this line of attack, the ambassador would be amused and file the largest lawsuit you ever saw. How can you be so naïve? This critique applies to more than the current Trump administration. How we continue to lack knowledge and understanding in these areas is incomprehensible.

✦

One of Obama's highest priorities was to reduce the threat of nuclear-weapons proliferation and do his best to cut the nuclear arsenals of Russia and the United States—very commendable intentions. Although it is impossible to prove, President Obama's most significant foreign policy accomplishment was preventing a grave escalation between the United States and Iran over the latter's nuclear ambitions. Despite denials by Iran's Supreme Leader, many in the United States were convinced that Iran was en route to developing nuclear weapons. The only options to avoid this outcome were preemptive military strikes to destroy Iran's facilities or an enforceable diplomatic solution.

Toward the last years of the Obama administration, momentum was building for the military option. This was not helped by congressional Republicans' unprecedented invitation to Israeli prime minister Benjamin Netanyahu to address a joint session on March 3, 2015. There, Netanyahu forcefully argued against negotiations, on the grounds that Iran could never be trusted to honor any agreement.

The Obama administration was rightly outraged at Netanyahu's address and the political tactics of congressional Republicans to impede negotiation with Iran, thereby leaving a military strike as the only option. Obama understood that any attack could defer Iran's nuclear ambitions only temporarily. It also would be dangerously escalatory, leaving Iran many options for retaliation. Fortunately, both the United States and Iran had many powerful reasons to reach an accommodation being negotiated by the permanent five members of the UN Security Council, plus Germany, with the EU as an observer.

Iran needed to have the economic sanctions lifted. Its leaders also wanted to rejoin the international community. Also, since the Supreme Leader had repeatedly called nuclear weapons immoral and against Islam, the need for them was not necessarily existential. Iran most likely wanted to develop a sufficient potential nuclear capability as an option if someday its national existence were threatened.

The result was the Joint Comprehensive Plan of Action, agreed to by all parties in late 2015 and signed in 2016. The JCPOA prevented Iran from developing nuclear weapons, certainly for at least a decade and a half, and likely permanently, although some critics disagree. Perhaps many critics of the JCPOA failed to read the document; their criticisms had nothing to do with the details, no matter how ironclad.

These critics argued that the JCPOA failed to address the broader issues of Iran's support for terrorism and its engagements in Iraq and Syria. Nor were the ballistic missile restrictions tight enough to preclude Iran from developing a long-range rocket capable of carrying a nuclear warhead. Critics also complained bitterly that in fifteen years, despite the permanent presence of inspectors from the International Atomic Energy Agency, Iran would be free to develop nuclear weapons.

Nor did these same critics fully appreciate the demands Iran accepted, demands that effectively ended the production of plutonium, reduced the number of centrifuges by about three-quarters, eliminated the vast bulk of Iran's enriched uranium, and permitted a very intrusive inspection regime. Iran could, it is true, at some future point reverse direction and opt for a nuclear weapon, even though the Supreme Leader has promised Iran would never build WMD of any type. However, without the JCPOA, preemptive strikes against Iran's nuclear facilities could never have been completely ruled out. Any preemptive attack could have provoked a regional war or worse.

Obama vigorously pursued the rest of his nonproliferation campaign. He signed and had approved a New START Treaty with Russia to limit strategic nuclear weapons. Obama presided over a number of nuclear security summits to advance his counter- and antiproliferation initiatives. Near the end of his administration, the

White House floated the idea of adopting a nuclear "no first use" policy. That idea was dead on arrival. Seventy years of reliance on nuclear deterrence and more recently the resurgence of Russia and China made the prospect infeasible.

Elsewhere, the administration took credit for moving Myanmar away from a highly repressive to a more open society. The recognition of Cuba, while long overdue, was a positive but not earth-shaking achievement. This and many other of its accomplishments, while effusively praised by proponents, were minor in impact when compared with the JCPOA—Obama's finest foreign-policy triumph.

For reasons of good or ill, Obama was unable to reverse or improve either the horrendous set of circumstances he had inherited or advance the position and leverage of the United States. His rhetoric often backfired. His Cairo speech in early 2009 was lauded as an opening to the Arab and Muslim worlds. But the United States did very little to advance the Arab Spring, which had been catalyzed by a desperate Tunisian fruit vendor lighting himself afire in protest of dire economic conditions. (The act was reminiscent of similar unsuccessful demonstrations by Vietnamese monks four and a half decades earlier.) Rhetoric would continue to get the president in trouble. When the Tahrir Square protests in Cairo threatened a coup in Egypt, the White House would abandon its long-term ally President Hosni Mubarak. Mubarak's legitimately elected replacement, Muslim Brotherhood leader Mohammed Morsi, was later overthrown in a coup by the army. The Obama administration now reversed course and supported Gen. (later Field Marshal and President) Abed Fattah al-Sisi.

In 2013, with the civil war in Syria raging and tens of thousands of innocents being slaughtered, Obama, like King Canute demanding that the seas recede, in 2013 ordered Syria's president, Bashar al-Assad, to leave office. Assad, of course, did not. When Syria employed chemical weapons against its people, Obama drew a "red line" against their use, which was ignored. In his September 10, 2013, address to the public, Obama announced two decisions.

First, he declared, the United States would carry out strikes against Syria to deter future uses of chemical weapons. Second, while he had the authority to order U.S. forces into action, he had decided to send the measure to Congress for approval. In fairness, Obama and British prime minister David Cameron had agreed to coordinate British and American punitive strikes against Syria. In a demonstration of political ineptitude, Cameron had recalled Parliament early from a long weekend at the end of August to vote on this decision. By a substantial majority, Parliament said no.

With the wars in Afghanistan and Iraq still raging and the fiasco of the Libyan strikes in 2011 fresh in mind, Congress was not prepared to authorize military action against Syria. If a vote had been taken, Congress would have mirrored Parliament. Obama was forced to back down. The United States took no action. American credibility was dealt a severe blow. Later, when Russia intervened and convinced Assad to forego his WMD, Obama argued that in the end, the United States had achieved the outcome it wanted. But this defense was hollow and not readily convincing. The "red line" and "Assad must go" became formidable ammunition for Obama's critics, who ridiculed both statements and condemned Obama for excessive caution and failure to act decisively.

In late 2011, Obama had announced a dramatic "strategic pivot to Asia," meant to recognize the growing strategic and economic importance of the Pacific. That declaration was a public-relations disaster. Allies in Europe, the Middle East, and Asia were very concerned, if not frightened, by this seemingly dramatic shift, made without much prior consultation. China was angered, regarding the "pivot" as a direct challenge to its sovereignty and standing.

The Pentagon tried to soften this shift, renaming it a "rebalance." However, as conditions in Afghanistan and the Middle East deteriorated and with Russia's 2014 intervention into Ukraine, the United States reinforced its military posture in both regions, further eroding the idea of a pivot eastward. Slogans had outstripped strategic thinking. A good sound bite was not a valid strategy. Ironically, while the "pivot" entailed increasing the percentage of the Navy in the Pacific to 60 percent, even that proportion, given budget cuts, meant fewer total warships serving in Asia.

As one of Obama's key foreign policy advisors, Derek Chollet, writes in his book *The Long Game*, the Obama administration did attempt to think strategically about future consequences. This mindset was described by Obama as "not doing stupid shit." However, while the future is unknowable, Chollet's interesting thesis appeared overly optimistic, especially in light of Obama's record. Worse, the seeming lack of understanding and of knowledge displayed by the White House was often striking. Pakistan and Afghanistan were, sadly, two examples of the absence of understanding or sound strategic thinking.

The Obama administration's first major strategic review was the Afghan-Pakistani Study, known as "AfPak." It was led by a former CIA officer and expert on Saudi Arabia and the region, Bruce Riedel. Riedel had served as Pakistan desk officer in the late 1990s and had experienced huge difficulty in dealing with Islamabad, including its nuclear tests. As a result, Riedel had developed certain understandable biases about Pakistan. These may have affected the nature of the AfPak review. That it was titled "Afghanistan-Pakistan" got the order of importance reversed and is perhaps the best critique of the study's shortcomings.

The review was completed in late March 2009. It is interesting that while General Jones, the national security advisor, had been Supreme Allied Commander Europe and thus in overall command of the International Security Assistance Force (ISAF) operation in Afghanistan until February 2007, his views were overridden by a less experienced president, who preferred a lower-key, minimalist approach. This preference would reflect the president's perception of a "long game" and his aversion to doing stupid stuff. Unfortunately, the solution was insufficient to correct the problems.

Obama announced the new strategy in a major speech from the White House in late March, stating the aim was "to disrupt, dismantle and defeat al Qaeda in Afghanistan and Pakistan, and to prevent their return to either country in the future." This was "not simply an American problem. It, instead, is an international security challenge of the highest order. Terrorist attacks in London and Bali were tied to al Qaeda and its allies in Pakistan, as were attacks in North Africa and the Middle East, in Islamabad and Kabul. If there is a major attack on an Asian, European, or African city, it, too, is likely to have ties to al Qaeda's leadership in Pakistan."

Regarding Afghanistan, the AfPak Study assumed that the security situation had become "increasingly perilous" since 2001, with insurgents controlling larger parts of Afghanistan and Pakistan. Further, the Afghan government might fall to the Taliban, and Afghanistan could again become a base for terrorists. Finally, Obama correctly argued that "Afghanistan has been denied the resources that it demands because of the war in Iraq. Now, [the United States] must make a commitment that can accomplish [its] goals [in Afghanistan]."

Regrettably, the AfPak strategy was flawed. In the first instance, Pakistan should have been the key focus. If Pakistan could seal its borders and restrain the Taliban, many of whom it directly or indirectly supported, progress in Afghanistan was probable. This was a difficult sell. The Pakistani army and its powerful Inter-Services Intelligence agency (ISI) relied on the Taliban both to influence the government in Kabul and to reduce Indian access and leverage in Afghanistan. Only through engaging the Pakistani army was stability likely to be achieved.

Second, NATO had divided up the various tasks of rebuilding the Afghan justice and legal systems, education, economy, police, counternarcotics, and infrastructure among its member states deployed in the country. That division led to uneven and often conflicting policies. As Vietnam had been an organizational disaster, Afghanistan was also, on an international level. This malorganization was obvious throughout the country.

For example, the provincial reconstruction teams (PRTs), of which there would be eighteen, were designed to help in nation building and reconstruction. However, there was no coordination between and among these teams, and their capacities differed. Nor did these teams learn much from the experience of their Soviet predecessors, who had been similarly organized and had failed. Because, as Obama understood, Afghanistan had been largely abandoned by the Bush administration in its zeal to attack Iraq, resources were marginalized.

Third, Afghanistan's social organization was tribal and local. Centralizing power in Kabul was never feasible. A subset was the economy's traditional agricultural focus. At an earlier point in its history, Afghanistan had been the agricultural center of South Asia with a crucial aqueduct system, built first by the Romans. What the Taliban did not destroy, the Soviets did. Inexplicably, this national irrigation system was never rebuilt during the NATO years, nor has it been since.

Fourth, the narcotics trade was the largest component of Afghan gross domestic product (GDP), excluding the dollars and euros that were pumped in from abroad. Only a healthy and lucrative agricultural sector could have competed.

Fifth, the West, especially the United States, imposed social and cultural changes on Afghanistan regarding the role of women and, of course, education. Given the highly conservative views of Afghan society regarding the place of women, this had to be done competently if it was to have effect. Too often, the metric of numbers of girls and women at school became the aim, not acclimatizing a society to the need for giving women greater roles and responsibilities.

Fifth, as in Iraq, insufficient attention was given to recruiting and training the police. Military forces were, of course, imperative. But in villages and small towns, police kept the peace. This was neglected.

Had we possessed a better understanding and knowledge of Afghanistan, could the outcome have been different? This question is largely unanswerable. However, it is hard to believe it would have been worse.

As the AfPak Study was in progress, 17,000 additional U.S. troops were already en route to Afghanistan. The White House directed that the general in command of ISAF, Stanley McChrystal, make a further assessment of troop needs and report back in the summer with his recommendation. When word leaked out that McChrystal would propose a "minimum risk" force—a militarily oxymoronic term—of about 80,000 more troops, Jones was dispatched to Kabul with what he called a "Whiskey Tango Foxtrot" message (referring to the well-known "WTF?"). On December 1, 2009, at the U.S. Military Academy at West Point, President Obama announced the second phase of his Afghan strategy and the surge of 30,000 troops.

Believing it to be the most effective means to pressure the Afghan government of Hamid Karzai to fulfill its commitments to expand its security forces, Obama would announce on June 22, 2011, the beginning of American withdrawal from Afghanistan. The plan was to turn all security responsibilities over to the Afghans by 2014. The declaration drew immediate criticism. Why tell the enemy your plans? The North Vietnamese had been able to wait out the United States; why would the Taliban not do the same?

Eventually, Obama would extend that withdrawal date and retain a larger U.S. force in Afghanistan, just under ten thousand. This constant changing of plans was a reflection far less of conditions on the ground in Afghanistan than of the absence of sound strategic thinking.

The same strategic flaws persisted in Iraq. Notwithstanding critics who later wrongly argued that Obama's Iraq withdrawal created the Islamic State—IS had arisen from the disastrous decisions of the Bush administration to disband the Iraqi army and fire from the government all who had been associated with the Ba'athist Party—the United States had no choice except to withdraw. The Shia government of Nouri al Maliki wanted the Americans out of its country. But acceding to these Iraqi demands meant that the benefits of the "surge" were lost. Obama would have to reevaluate conditions on the ground, and more American troops would be needed in the fight against al Qaeda and IS.

The one war that was more Obama's than Bush's was that against the Islamic State. While IS surely began during the Bush administration, it metastasized over the next few years into an ideological epidemic. Bush had mischaracterized the struggle against that epidemic as the "global war on terror." The strategic and semantic shortcomings in that title were demonstrated earlier.

Aside from the miscue of calling IS the "JV," Obama used his State of the Union Address on January 24, 2012, to present to the nation his foreign-policy and national-security achievements, if not outright victories:

> For the first time in nine years, there are no Americans fighting in Iraq. For the first time in two decades, Osama bin Laden is not a threat to this country.

But . . . with your help, because when we act together, there's nothing the United States of America can't achieve.

That's the lesson we've learned from our actions abroad over the last few years. Ending the Iraq war has allowed us to strike decisive blows against our enemies.

From Pakistan to Yemen, the Al Qaida operatives who remain are scrambling, knowing that they can't escape the reach of the United States of America.

From this position of strength, we've begun to wind down the war in Afghanistan. Ten thousand of our troops have come home. Twenty-three thousand more will leave by the end of this summer. This transition to Afghan lead will continue, and we will build an enduring partnership with Afghanistan, so that it is never again a source of attacks against America.

As the tide of war recedes, a wave of change has washed across the Middle East and North Africa, from Tunis to Cairo, from Sana'a to Tripoli.

A year ago, Gadhafi was one of the world's longest-serving dictators, a murderer with American blood on his hands. Today, he is gone.

And in Syria, I have no doubt that the Assad regime will soon discover that the forces of change cannot be reversed and that human dignity cannot be denied.

Five years later, the Obama record does not look quite so good. Indeed, no critique could be more powerful than a matching of the president's words (in this 2012 address and other speeches and press conferences) with the situation after his presidency and today, in mid-2017. Ambivalence seemed to be a common and recurring characteristic. The president was prepared "to talk tough" but not do stupid stuff. This dichotomy would not be able to turn his intentions into actions. Obama, too, was overly optimistic in his assessments. Also, his policies seemed derived far more from his cautious instincts than from a convincing strategic framework or thoughtful analyses and reason.

Finally recognizing that IS posed a mortal danger to the region, Obama took belated action. At the urging of Secretary of State John Kerry, in March 2014 Obama met with retired Marine Corps general John Allen. In 2006–8, Allen had served in Iraq, where he had been largely responsible for the "Anbar Awakening" of the Sunni tribes in fierce opposition to al Qaeda and the precursors of IS. He had gone on to command ISAF in Afghanistan, retiring from active duty in 2013.

Allen laid out for the president a comprehensive political-military-economic strategy for Iraq. For six months, as conditions continued to deteriorate, the White House sat on Allen's recommendations. Kerry had to intervene. Obama appointed Allen as his special envoy to the Global Coalition to Counter ISIL (ISIL was the White House's acronym for IS, standing for "Islamic State of Iraq and the Levant") in September. It was up to Allen to fashion the coalition.

The lost six months proved fatal. The Anbar sheiks Allen had so assiduously cultivated had either fled into exile or been killed. While I was lunching with Allen in December in a Pentagon City hotel, he excused himself for a minute to take a call. Returning, Allen looked physically ill. One of his closest comrades and friends, Sheik Lawrence Mutib Hazan—named for Lawrence of Arabia, with whom his great grandfather had once ridden against the Turks—had just been killed by an improvised explosive device, an IED.

Allen did his best. However, the coalition of initially sixty-two states that resulted was not a real alliance. Since the JCPOA, Saudi Arabia had seen America as abandoning it for Iran. Iran, the Saudis insisted, was the main enemy, not IS. While the Saudis sent troops to fight in Yemen, like the rest of the Gulf states, Riyadh was not prepared to send a ground force against IS.

Syria had become an impossible issue. Obama's "red lines" and demands that Assad go were empty threats that weakened American influence and prestige. Iraq was a Shia state, and hence the Sunni Arabs, underestimating the existential danger of IS, were reluctant to be fully supportive.

Allen was given virtually no support by the Department of Defense. The CentCom commander at the time, Army general

Lloyd Austin, warned Allen that coming out of retirement for this task had not been well advised. Austin of course oversaw Iraq.

That Obama promised to "disrupt and destroy" IS was taken as seriously as his other pronouncements. Disruption was feasible. Destruction seemed more a bridge far too far. The counter-IS effort became bogged down in Syria, which was the Islamic State's major refuge. While air and drone strikes piled up the body count, killing was not the way to victory. Training a handful of Syrian opposition soldiers at the cost of half a billion dollars was further devastating evidence of the obstacles and inefficiencies in fighting this kind of proxy war. While IS has been driven out of Ramadi and Fallujah, the test will come (at this writing) after Iraqi forces have taken Mosul, Iraq's second-largest city, from IS and as the city is governed after the liberation occurred.

Syria was indeed the conflict from hell. The regime was as merciless as the elder Assad had been in eliminating the opposition and killing innocent Syrians. After a series of "barrel bomb" and rumored chemical attacks in early 2013, Obama's senior advisors recommended crippling Assad's air force and air defenses as a powerful means to aid the opposition. He refused that advice.

Both members of his administration and critics called for "no-fly zones" and safe havens in Syria to protect innocents. However, safe zones would have required substantial ground forces for protection. No Arab or Muslim ally was prepared to send any ground troops. Neither was America. Also, no-fly zones, as we learned in Iraq after 1991, were quite complicated and expensive. When Putin intervened, as will be seen below, in September 2015, the danger of unwanted encounters with Russian aircraft made no-fly zones infeasible.

The Syrian tragedy is Exhibit A of the many that demonstrate how complicated and interrelated today's international security environment is. It is the antithesis of the twentieth century's largely binary world, in which two major blocs contested for power and influence. The United States and its Arab and Muslim allies are opposed to Assad. In particular, Turkey and Saudi Arabia are adamant about ending Assad's rule. But Turkey is paranoid about accepting Kurdish allies in this fight, because of the danger Ankara perceives from Kurdish nationalism and the PKK insurgency. Similarly, Iraq, a Shia state and former ally of Syria, opposes the Kurdish Pesh Merga, fearing Kurdistan could become a breakaway province. And as noted, Saudi Arabia worries that the United States has tilted toward its main adversary, Iran.

Russia and Iran are Syria's lifelines. Russia is not, however, committed to Assad's permanent rule. Russia is aware of what happened in Iraq and Libya. Nevertheless, driven by the prospect that instability will turn Syria into a worse disaster, spreading Islamist radicalism to Russia's significant Muslim minorities, Moscow has chosen to aid its long-term client. Likewise, Shia Iran has long aided Alawite Syria, in part to challenge Israel, one of America's closest allies. However, Iran has now signed the JCPOA with the West.

The civil war has displaced upward of ten million Syrians, large numbers fleeing to neighboring states hard-pressed to assimilate them. Several million have tried to escape to Europe, causing massive problems. With outbreaks of terrorist attacks—from *Charlie Hebdo* and restaurants and theaters in Paris to Cannes and airports and subways in Brussels—this massive emigration has imposed excruciating economic, social, cultural, legal, and political pressures on European societies. It may be impossible to fashion lasting solutions from outside. Tragically, as with civil wars elsewhere, the violence has to run its course before a measure of stability returns. Even temporary remedial actions are difficult.

Syria is illustrative of the foreign-policy nightmares facing any president. There may be no options other than "bad" or "worse" outcomes. This may be a fact of life. However, without sound strategic thinking and understanding, without knowledge of the circumstances and informed understanding of consequences, the worst is almost assured. Indeed, one assumption that should be challenged concerns exactly who is in control in Syria. There is evidence that Bashar al-Assad may be a figurehead. Those who know him well believe Assad lacks his father's ruthlessness. In fact, his elder brother was the chosen one until he died in an accident. The reason this understanding is important is that if his younger brother and one or two generals are indeed making decisions, focusing on Assad will not achieve any diminution in the violence.

Space precludes a comprehensive examination of the entire Obama presidency regarding its employment of military force. Consider, then, as representative of his administration's policies how it dealt specifically with NATO and Russia over Ukraine and with Pakistan, and the legacies of these events for American military capacity and capability.

In early 2009, Obama's secretary of state, Hillary Clinton, pushed the "reset" button with Russia, even giving the Russian foreign minister, Sergei Lavrov, a model button to commemorate the fact. Unfortunately, the Russian translation of "reset" on the model was incorrect, a precursor of things to come. The administration wrongly believed that Dmitri Medvedev, who as noted above had replaced Putin as president, would prove more flexible than his predecessor, who had reverted to the prime ministership. But Putin was still very much in charge.

Russia had strenuously and correctly warned George W. Bush of the folly of invading Iraq. Iraq had continued to deteriorate. The ill-advised NATO action in Libya had precipitated civil war and further instability. The emergence of IS and the establishment of a caliphate in Syria threatened the regime in Damascus and had exacerbated the civil war.

Russia had been crucial in redressing the inability of the Obama administration to remove Assad's chemical weapons, negotiating an agreement for their ultimate destruction or transfer elsewhere. America's support of the so-called Free Syrian Army seemed to Moscow a repeat of the Iraqi disaster. In September 2015, Russia intervened with a relatively modest military force to save the Assad regime and avoid a collapse of the Ba'athist government.

Meanwhile, Ukraine had become a flash point. Putin had warned about further NATO expansion. Ukraine had been negotiating an association agreement with the EU. On November 21, 2013, under great pressure from Moscow—worried about Ukraine drawing too close to the EU and out of the traditional Russian orbit—then president Viktor Yanukovych broke off negotiations with Brussels.

Mass protests followed, in what was called the "Euromaidan" revolt, centered in Kyiv.

Yanukovych was forced to flee Kyiv in late February 2014. A backlash in the largely pro-Russian and Russian-speaking eastern and southern regions of Ukraine erupted and grew in intensity over the forced and arguably illegal overthrow of an elected president. On March 18, Russia annexed Crimea. While Crimea was a virtual Russian province—it had been offhandedly ceded to Ukraine by Nikita Khrushchev in 1954 and was the site of a major military base housing some 20,000 Russian troops—the intervention created a crisis in the West. Western states rightly claimed Russia had violated the territory of a sovereign nation and thus challenged the post–Cold War order.

The crises escalated as "little green men" (Russian soldiers in combat gear without national insignia) infiltrated the Donetsk and Lubansk *oblasts*—called collectively the "Donbass"—in what was misnamed "hybrid war." That led to a conflict between Kyiv and the post-Yanukovych government against pro-Russian insurgents in the east supported by Moscow. Despite two attempts at arranging a cease-fire, known as Minsk I and II, that conflict continues.

NATO and the EU first responded with economic and financial sanctions against Russia. Meanwhile, Moscow denied that Russian troops had crossed into Ukraine. NATO's then Supreme Allied Commander Europe, Gen. Phillip Breedlove of the U.S. Air Force, maintained otherwise, supported by intelligence satellite photos and radio intercepts. Most interestingly, by using social media, including Facebook and Twitter, unimpeachable unclassified evidence of Russian military presence was collected.

How to respond became a heated debate. Many in Washington argued for the arming of the government in Kyiv. The White House demurred. The counter case was persuasive. Russia had interior lines of communications. Moscow would be at an advantage in reinforcing eastern Ukraine, given the distances support from the West would have to travel. Russia therefore could out-escalate the West.

Second, while a strong humanitarian argument could be made to provide Kyiv offensive weapons "to even" the fight, the reality was that escalation would have led to more casualties and the risk of a greater Russian intervention. Third, training the Ukrainian army to use these systems would take time, prove expensive, and put Western trainers at risk. Some defensive weaponry and logistics support, however, has been provided.

For unknowable reasons, hybrid war seemed to come as a surprise. "Hybrid" meant using more than conventional military forces. Propaganda, cyber, economic leverage, and political intimidation were part of these so-called new techniques. In fact, nothing here was new. In 1924, Lenin used similar tactics in trying to absorb Estonia. In those days, the telephone exchanges were the equivalent of the Internet and cyber. Lenin's coup failed.

Meanwhile, NATO, responding to the vociferous reactions of its easternmost members to Russia's incursion into and annexation of Crimea, debated what it should and could do. With the 2014 NATO heads-of-government summit, to be held in Wales, approaching, the opportunity for a major strategic redefinition of the alliance's purpose was present. But the White House was not in agreement.

Despite recommendations from the State Department and the Office of the U.S. Permanent Representative to NATO, the White House seemed indifferent. Perhaps the president believed that further confrontation with Russia was not useful. Cynically, allies in Europe preferred that the United States do the heavy lifting. Obama had set deadlines for withdrawal from Afghanistan in part to force the Afghans to assume responsibility for their security. The same line of reasoning could apply to Europe: force Europe to spend more on defense rather than always depend on the United States to come to the rescue.

Regardless, it was through the initiative of SacEur that the agenda for Wales contained very specific recommendations. Most important was a Readiness Action Plan (RAP). The plan dealt with increasing deployments of military forces to Europe and with training exercises designed to reassure allies and impress Russia, thus building on the concept of deterrence. The allies also agreed to commit at least 2 percent of GDP to defense. (Only five of twenty-nine members have met this criterion.) The RAP was expanded at the

2016 summit in Warsaw. A total of four additional battalions—from the United States (two), the United Kingdom, and Canada—would be deployed to Poland and the Baltics. A series of exercises in the eastern Mediterranean, Black Sea, and Baltic Sea were scheduled.

Russia had meanwhile reacted to the NATO measures and, of course, the sanctions. A series of "snap" military exercises showed Russian capacity to react at no notice. Propaganda and cyber activities against the West were increased. Russian aviation and naval units often recklessly approached NATO units in international waters and airspace. The beginnings of a new "cold war" seemed imminent.

NATO and the United States had predictably responded in twentieth-century terms. Instead of seeking alternative means of checking Russia, NATO resorted to conventional forces and means. Reassurance was important, and small-scale deployments were helpful. However, four battalions would hardly be even "speed bumps" if Russia chose a major conventional attack—which it would not, because the risks were too great.

A fundamental change in strategy would have been a good start. Providing the Baltic and Black Sea NATO members with a "porcupine" defense, one that would badly bloody any attack, would have been a much more cost-effective strategy than massive reinforcements. This defense would rely on antiair Stinger missiles and antivehicle systems, such as Javelin, along with other weapons to stop or kill "little green men" at the border. NATO would also employ its capacity for countering propaganda, intimidation, and cyber, along with the other aspects of hybrid war. The Finnish-Soviet Winter War of 1939 would be the model for preventing any incursion—cyber or otherwise.

The West also has the powerful leverage of sanctions. Why has the West not negotiated with Russia over Ukraine on the basis of sanctions relief? Instead, it has allowed Putin to steal a march in innovative and imaginative offsetting strategies. The Russian intervention into Syria has been limited to five or six thousand troops—a contrast to the hundreds of thousands of coalition personnel who fought in Iraq and Afghanistan. That small force has saved the despicable Assad regime. Firing Kalibr cruise missiles from gunboats in the Caspian Sea against opposition targets in Syria, while a demonstration rather than a serious tactical move, was a public-relations victory.

It was also a good advertisement for Russian weapons, even though the U.S. Tomahawk cruise missiles were far more effective and had been deployed for decades. In late August 2016, Russian Tu-22 bombers, antiques left over from the Cold War, flew from bases in Iran to strike targets in Syria. Russia heavy-handedly made these flights public; Iran then demanded that Russia leave.

The audacity of the Russians in operating from Iran, even for a short time, sent a powerful political message to the region and to Europe. Putin was following Churchill's stricture that having run out of money, one needs to think one's way clear of danger. Putin, or someone in Moscow, is clearly doing that, running strategic circles around the West and Washington.

> Moscow, Ministry of Defense (MoD), May 2016, a meeting between the Russian deputy minister of defense, Gen. Anatoly Antonov (AA), and HKU. Antonov had a PhD and had been transferred from the diplomatic corps of the Foreign Office, where he had served as an ambassador, to the MoD, as senior deputy minister, since 2011. This meeting took place just after the Fifth Moscow International Security Conference, which I had attended as one of the few Americans present, military-to-military talks having been suspended.

> **HKU:** "General, what can be done to improve U.S.-Russian relations? We have common interests in deescalating the conflict in Ukraine, defeating the Islamic State, and helping reduce the humanitarian crisis in Syria. Yet we are becoming more adversarial. Russian fighters have buzzed U.S. and NATO warships. A single mishap could create a crisis. Suppose one of your planes collided with one of our ships or aircraft? Or suppose one of your fighters was mistakenly evaluated as making an attack and was shot down? This happened in Turkey, and of course,

there was the tragic shootdown of an Iranian Airbus in 1988 by a U.S. cruiser in the Persian Gulf."

AA: "Those are good questions. And, by the way, our planes are unarmed . . ."

HKU, interrupting: "Does our side know that?"

AA: "I am not sure. I think we have told them. But the larger problem is that the United States and NATO have cut off most communications with us. We need to talk."

HKU: "Anatoly, General Dunford, the JCS chairman, told me that he tried to contact your chief of staff, General Gerasimov, and got no response."

AA: "Maybe he should try again. Look, Russia considers the expansion of NATO so far east as a direct threat. You have just commissioned an Aegis missile-defense site ashore in Romania and have broken ground for one in Poland. You know this is a violation of the Intermediate Nuclear Forces agreement. You also know that we are worried by these systems not because they can threaten our Strategic Rocket Forces but because they can be used against our shorter-range tactical missiles." [The Russians are correct, in that this is a potential technical violation. The United States has assured Moscow it would not violate INF by upgrading the system. Washington also argues that Moscow has already violated INF with its own testing.]

HKU: "We are talking past each other. Why don't we convene a major U.S.-Russian conference on INF, on incidents at sea to prevent an unwanted or unprovoked crisis, on Syria and Ukraine to see if or where there are points of common interest and agreement?"

AA: "Both we at the MoD and Putin have already proposed this. The United States refuses to respond. In fact, the same is true at NATO. We invited the secretary general to our major conference this year and did not get a response."

HKU: "As Reagan said, trust but verify. I am off to NATO next, and let me check. I find it hard to believe that you are not getting any responses." [Antonov proved correct.]

AA: "We are having a dialogue of the deaf. We are not without blame. However, our arguments, cautions, and most importantly, our interests, go unheeded."

HKU: "Yes, but Lavrov and Kerry have a good relationship . . ."

AA: "They are not the issue. The White House and Pentagon are hostile. Susan Rice [the national security advisor] and Carter [defense secretary] are taking tough lines. I think Kerry has been cut out. We will have to wait for the next administration, but quite frankly, neither candidate seems to have a better understanding of Russia."

HKU: "That is not a promising outlook."

AA: "That is why we are pursuing this foreign policy of finding new allies to counter what is happening. In fairness, we cannot trust the United States to do the right thing. Wherever you have gone—Iraq, Afghanistan, and Libya—conditions now are worse. We have a far larger Muslim population than you, and we fought a war in Chechnya against fundamentalism. You remember the attacks at the Moscow Opera and Beslan School."

HKU: "Let me urge you to seek some sort of military-to-military dialogue or 'Track II' [nongovernmental, unofficial diplomacy between influential elites]. It is in neither of our interests, nor anyone else's, that a new form of cold war take hold."

AA: "I agree."

Alas, in the ensuing year, relations between East and West continued to deteriorate. The Sixth Moscow International Security Conference, held in April 2017, was far more somber and sobering. It is discussed below.

◆

Pakistan would return as a major issue well after the bin Laden raid. Administrations going back to Eisenhower's have had difficulty in dealing with Pakistan. An important Cold War ally against the Soviet Union, Pakistan became a vital partner in Bush's global war on terror and was designated a "major non-NATO ally." The infamous U-2 plane, in which Francis Gary Powers was shot down over Siberia in May 1960, had been flown from Miram Shah, a base in Pakistan. Unfortunately, Pakistan still suffers from three significant political forces.

First, Pakistan is still largely feudal, ruled by three and a half families. The army "family" has run the country for nearly half of the nation's life since it was partitioned from India in 1948. The Bhutto-Zardari and the Sharif families constitute the other two and the Chouddrys the "half." Zulfikar Bhutto was both president and prime minister until he was convicted of treason by his former military secretary, Gen. (and by then President) Zia al-Haq and executed in 1979. His daughter Benazir was twice prime minister and would have won a third term had she not been assassinated in December 2007. Her husband, Asif Ali Zardari, was elected president in 2008. His civilian government was the first to serve a full term. The Chouddrys, for their part, have been influential in politics and the law.

Second, Bhutto nationalized the economy in the 1970s, effectively consigning Pakistan to second-class status. The economy never recovered from his decision. Third, President Zia radicalized the country, moving it toward a more fundamentalist form of Islam. Zia also increased the number of madrassas (religious schools), where radicalism has flourished. Attempts to reform these institutions—the only places where millions of impoverished Pakistani men and boys can receive food and shelter, along with radical religious indoctrination—have failed. Nearly 20,000 still exist, and fundamentalism prospers.

Too often, American administrations have failed to understand the basic forces affecting Pakistan—and Pakistani officials in turn have been effective in manipulating U.S. governments. The AfPak Study failed to recognize or acknowledge fully these basic political facts of Pakistani life. Relations between the United States and Pakistan have been rocky at times and while improving (as of this writing) are still not good.

One incident is instructive. In January 2011, an American, Raymond Davis, reportedly working for the American consulate in Lahore, stopped his car and shot and killed two Pakistanis who had been following him, presumably for the ISI. Assistance was dispatched from the consulate. Rushing to the incident, the consulate's SUV drove the wrong way down a one-way street to avoid traffic and struck and killed an innocent bicyclist. Because of the ongoing war on terror, the conflict in Afghanistan, and drone strikes that were perceived as killing innocent Muslims, Pakistani public opinion, manipulated by propaganda, had become violently and explosively anti-American. Outrage spread throughout Pakistan over this incident. Davis was arrested and imprisoned. The United States began a diplomatic effort to free him, arguing that he had diplomatic immunity, as did the driver of the consulate's SUV.

Since the mid-2000s, I had been advising Benazir Bhutto, a close friend of long standing. Her husband, Asif Ali Zardari, had become a friend after he was finally released from a long prison sentence (fortunately avoiding the fate of his late father-in-law). I had been a frequent visitor to Pakistan and had become acquainted with the top civilian and military leadership, including the army chief of staff and the then director of the ISI.

When the Davis case erupted, I received a call from the Office of the Chairman of the Joint Chiefs asking for help in freeing him. The office assured me that Davis was "one of ours," presumably meaning that he had been working for Joint Special Operations Command, JSOC. I conferred with President Zardari, who accepted the argument that Davis had diplomatic immunity. But Pakistani media are among the freest in the world, and to say that there was public fury would be an understatement. The public was demanding a trial and a death penalty for Davis. Zardari's argument for immunity was undercut by Pakistan's foreign minister, Shah Mahmoud Quereshi. Quereshi, who sensed a political opportunity, declared that Davis was not entitled to diplomatic immunity. But that created a new political firestorm for President Zardari, now challenged by his foreign minister. Quereshi was forced to resign.

> May 2011, the Georgetown home of Senator John Kerry (JK). Also present were Pakistan's able ambassador to the United States, Dr. Husain Haqqani (HH), and me. Kerry was on two cell phones, one with President Obama and the other with Secretary of State Clinton. Haqqani likewise was speaking on two cells, with President Zardari and the ISI chief, Lt. Gen. Ahmed Shuja Pasha.

> **JK:** "Mr. President, it appears that we may have an alternative means of freeing Davis. Ambassador Haqqani is on the phone with President Zardari and General Pasha. The idea is to use what is called *diyya*, or a payment to the family in compensation. In return, all charges might be dropped."

> **JK, in response to a question from either the president or secretary of state:** "Yes, that can also be called 'blood money.'"

> **HH, on the phone to Pasha:** "General, how might this work?" [After receiving an answer, Haqqani told Kerry that the ISI would be the intermediary with the family to make the deal and transfer funds.]

> **HKU:** "In any event, are we sure that Davis was not a CIA employee? If he is, and not an employee of the consulate or JSOC, the blowback will be enormous. Zardari's position will be weakened. The army may be forced to continue denying us use of our Predator bases in Pakistan as well as the land route to Afghanistan through the Khyber Pass."

JK, holding the cell phones next to his chest to mute them: "The president's priority is getting Davis back, no matter what."

HKU: "Understood. But at what price? Davis ought to be tried and held accountable."

HH: "It would be useful if the United States promised to investigate these murders, at the least."

JK: "I agree, but this will not fly. We can try to investigate here. But I doubt the White House would follow up. The case for adhering to international law and diplomatic immunity is seen as overriding."

Relations with Pakistan during the Davis release could hardly have been worse (although the May 1 raid that killed bin Laden did in fact worsen them). It turned out that Davis was indeed a CIA contract employee and did not enjoy diplomatic immunity. Later that year, Davis would be arrested in a Colorado mall for assaulting a fifty-year-old man in an altercation over a parking space. Had the White House been fully informed on the Davis case, and perhaps it was, there might have been a different outcome. If the reverse happened here, and a Pakistani employed by the ISI and so lacking immunity killed two American citizens working for the government, it is doubtful that the person would have been released.

◆

The conclusions to be drawn reinforce the observation that our most recent presidents have been far too inexperienced for the demands of the office when assuming it; that strategic thinking has been rare in their administrations; and that understanding and knowledge of important issues and conditions are lacking. Obama's ambivalence was evident in his changes of policy direction. Likewise, his rhetoric was not matched by action.

As Bush got Iraq wrong, Obama also made serious mistakes, albeit none quite as catastrophic—or none have proved so yet. In fairness, the demands of the presidency are often overwhelming. In the twenty-first century, it may well be that no one, no matter how qualified and experienced, is equipped to deal with all of these demands in ways that lead to outcomes successful from an American perspective. And a broken government, paralyzed by toxic partisanship, compounds the exquisitely excruciating demands thrust on the Oval Office.

In terms of military force, the Obama administration left three legacy crises for its successors. The first is the pursuit of "immaculate war" to minimize collateral damage. The second is a changed operational character of American forces because of the new focus on counterterrorist missions. The third, guaranteed by a government riven with partisanship, is a variant of the post-Vietnam "hollow force," a situation that unless addressed now will affect the future strength, capacity, and capability of our armed forces, for the worse.

Obama aggressively pursued Islamic terrorists with tactics and methods that minimized the risks to the U.S. military and, ideally, of collateral damage. Drones are the most obvious of these methods. However, "capture-or-kill" missions became central to the global war on terror and how American forces operated in Afghanistan, Iraq, Libya, and Syria.

Obama, preferring the phrase "violent religious extremism," did not wish to suggest a direct link with Islam. Unfortunately, this reasonable approach provoked extreme criticism from those Americans who believed that inherent flaws in Islam were responsible for this radicalism. Instead of the mature and civil debate that should have followed, partisan politics unnecessarily made this single word a cause célèbre.

Wanting to end the costly wars in Afghanistan and Iraq, Obama saw in America's technological superiority in surveillance and drones a relatively immaculate option. Enemy combatants would be targeted and attacked largely by unmanned systems. This placed fewer Americans at risk, as the drones were operated at safely distant locations, particularly Creech Air Force Base in the Nevada desert. Targets would only be attacked if properly identified and if collateral damage could be kept to an absolute minimum.

Complementing this standoff capability was the enhanced use of Special Forces. Under George W. Bush and during the "surge,"

Gen. Stanley McChrystal had run the JSOC in Iraq. As a part of what McChrystal saw as a "network of networks" to roll up the insurgents, "capture-or-kill" missions became the stock in trade of both special and regular U.S. forces. The bin Laden raid in Abbottabad was a prime example of this tactic.

The consequence of this emphasis on intelligence, surveillance, and small-unit counterinsurgency tactics produced the second legacy, a shifting of the focus of the U.S. military away from "big wars" to smaller ones. This has been going on for at least a decade. Hence, the more aggressive actions on the part of Russia and China and the increased capabilities of their conventional forces raised understandable concern, especially as the American drawdowns in Iraq and Afghanistan continued.

During the George W. Bush administration, Gen. George Casey, when he became Army chief of staff, originally argued that preparation for fighting a "big war" would carry over to smaller ones. To his credit, Casey realized during his tenure that this assessment was wrong. Big and little wars require different skill sets. Training for one is not sufficient for fighting the other. This contradiction remains for the new president to resolve.

Meanwhile, ground forces in particular have trained for "capture-or-kill" and other small-unit operations. This training produced a huge cadre of junior officers and enlisted men with exceptional war-fighting skills along these lines. The cost, however, was diminished capability to fight the big war. As General Casey would come to admit, preparations for the big war do not subsume those needed for lesser forms of conflict—in fact, the reverse is true. Experience in small-unit, counterinsurgent, and terrorist operations, no matter how extensive, is not sufficient for fighting the big war against like forces.

With the emergence of so-called peer competitors—Russia and China—the military will have to change its focus. It took decades for the post-Vietnam military to readjust; no one can predict how long it will take to return to conventional forms of war. If this is to happen, the third legacy will have to be overcome. This is the most threatening of the three, and I would argue that it is potentially more dangerous to the security of the United States than any outside adversary—a new hollow force.

The most obvious factor that will lead to a hollow force is uncontrolled internal defense-cost growth, currently some 5 to 7 percent annually. The components are soaring personnel, medical, retirement, weapons systems, logistics, and overhead costs. At an annual increase of 7 percent, costs double in ten years. Many studies, especially those conducted by the Defense Business Board, confirm these estimates.

Funding for readiness, modernization, and training will shrink. How those cuts are taken raises a set of impossible choices. To sustain an active-duty military force of about 1.2 million at high levels of readiness, modernization, and capability, the current budget for fiscal year 2017 of over $600 billion is not adequate. That budget is, in real terms, more than it was at the height of Reagan's defense buildup. The military services are arguing, not without reason, that given the operational tempo and the "four plus one" threat scenario (discussed later) that Secretary of Defense Ashton Carter set, higher force levels are essential.

Compounding this cost crisis, broken government precludes and stymies sensible defense planning and management. The Budget Control Act and "sequestration" mandate automatic cuts equally across all defense programs. How can one buy 10 percent less of a fighter aircraft, warship, or bullet? This ludicrous, wasteful, and inefficient requirement adds to the reasons why a hollow force is almost certain to occur.

The Obama-era national security and national military strategies, which at this writing remain in force, are aspirational. In fact, the Pentagon's major strategy publication, *DoD Contributions to National Security*, is a rejection of strategy and strategic thinking. Further, instead of setting guidance for contingency planning, the Obama White House preferred asking the Pentagon and operational planners for "options," which are often deferred or dismissed as not up to the task, leaving strategy in limbo.

Because U.S. military capability is dependent on highly expensive all-volunteer professional forces and technological solutions to operational issues, DoD is losing the cost-exchange-ratio battle with far less expensive adversaries. Combatting IEDs is an example. The department has spent in excess of $70 billion countering relatively low-technology and cheap mines, booby traps, and suicide vests. Suppose adversaries in Iraq and Afghanistan and the Islamic State have spent only seven million dollars on IEDs, which is very conservative. The cost-exchange ratio is ten thousand to one against us. If $70 million were spent, it is a thousand to one against us. The same logic applies to the larger global war on terror. How much is the nation spending, and is that cost-effective?

When the costs of the associated command, control, intelligence, and other supporting systems are included in addition to the weapons, drone strikes are not cheap. As for manned aviation, the helmet for an F-35 pilot costs about half a million dollars. It is part of the combat system, and each pilot has two. If the United States buys two thousand F-35s, helmets alone will cost two billion dollars. Unless or until this cost-exchange equation is profoundly altered, it is clear where the United States is headed.

The present consequence is a force that is from a quarter to a third larger than current or likely future budgets can sustain. Spending our way clear is, short of another war, not an option. Slashing force structure enough to achieve huge savings is required, along with other cost-avoidance efficiencies, to constrain this explosive growth.

A fourth legacy may be emerging: the dominance of planning for near-peer adversaries. Former secretary of defense Ashton Carter laid out a "four plus one" matrix for force planning. The four main contingencies dealt with Russia, China, North Korea, and Iran. The aim was to be able to deter and if necessary defeat each in conflict, not all at the same time. The "one" in this matrix is disruption and destruction of violent religious extremism, aka radical Islam.

Such a matrix is profoundly flawed. Is the United States at such a stage that it seriously needs to deter and defeat Russia and China in a war? Of course, the interwar "Rainbow" war plans contained contingencies for conflict with Britain well into the 1930s. But publicly declaring the need to deter and defeat major states that are not now enemies is dangerous if not foolish. To be sure, field commanders have to have a range of contingency plans. That none was available post–September 11 for Afghanistan was a deficiency of a kind that must be corrected. However, contingency planning must be kept at very high classification levels.

Additionally, nowhere does the "four plus one" matrix explicitly state what it takes to deter or defeat Russia, China, North Korea, or Iran. It simply gives the services good reason to call for larger force structures at a time when the budget cannot sustain those already existing.

Evaluation of any presidency is subjective. No doubt Presidents Bush and Obama deserve great credit for dealing with the financial crisis of 2008. The U.S. and global economies did not implode. While the recovery has been neither robust nor even, there was no meltdown.

The overarching foreign-policy and security achievement of the Obama administration was the JCPOA. The future will determine its significance and effectiveness. Arguably, however, Iraq and Afghanistan are both more unstable and problematic in 2017 than either was in 2009. Libya is embroiled in a civil war resulting from the attacks in 2011 that overthrew the Qaddafi regime. Relations with Russia and China are worse. Such relations should not be a zero-sum game. The Obama team believed that Russian interests could be expected to fit American policy interests, such as that Assad must go or red lines against the use of chemical weapons—examples of the downsides of substituting sound bites for strategy. The pivot to Asia and its rollout clearly provoked China.

While the tactical battle against the Islamic State is certainly killing many tens of thousands of enemy combatants and IS has been forced to retreat and give up territory it once occupied, the fight is far from over. Terrorism inspired by violent Islam has spread. While nothing has approached September 11, the frequency and number of Islamist-inspired attacks is on the rise, particularly in Europe.

Ironically, having preferred caution and minimal use of force, the Obama administration's legacies have had the opposite effect, leaving the Trump administration to deal with each situation and deciding how much force is needed and how, where, and why that force will be used.

✦

On January 20, 2017, Donald J. Trump took the oath of office. After an election that was as surprising and controversial as that of George W. Bush in 2000, when the Supreme Court awarded him the presidency, Trump lost by nearly 3,000,000 votes but won the Electoral College—an unprecedented event in American presidential annals giving the size of popular vote for the loser. Trump ran on a platform that would "make America great again," put America first, build a wall on the southern border and make Mexico pay for it, repeal and replace the Affordable Care Act ("Obamacare"), grow the economy by 4 percent a year, create millions of jobs, reform the tax code and regulatory system, reject the Transpacific Partnership Pact (TPP), renegotiate the North American Free Trade Agreement (NAFTA), rely on bilateral vice multilateral trade agreements, rebuild America's military with very substantial spending increases, and other promises.

Given the time a book must be in the printer's hands—this one will appear in the fall of 2017—a studied analysis of the Trump administration is impossible. Indeed, given the president's often-instant reversals on policy promises and statements, informed analysis has a half-life of a few hours, or a day or two. However, the president's intent to carry out his campaign promises and his almost daily use of Twitter to signal his policies and views to the public give rise to several observations. These are in the context of the failure of administrations to think strategically or have sufficient understanding and knowledge of the issues on which they must act.

Unfortunately, Trump's first hundred plus days in office provoked far more chaos and controversy than clarity and steadiness. With a barrage of executive orders, Trump immediately began to put in place his campaign promises. Yet any fledgling administration needs a great deal of time to organize itself and nominate and get confirmed the thousand-plus officials needed to lead the government. That has not happened to date.

Regarding national security, Trump appointed and had confirmed (overwhelmingly) retired Marine general Jim Mattis as secretary of defense. Former chairman of Exxon Mobile Rex Tillerson was made secretary of state, and a second Marine general, John Kelly, served briefly as secretary of homeland security before taking over as White House chief of staff in July 2017.

The initial choice for national security advisor, Lt. Gen. Michael Flynn, U.S. Army (Ret.), lasted just over three weeks. He was forced to resign after lying to Vice President Mike Pence about conversations he had had with the Russian ambassador to the United States, Sergey Kislyak. In his stead, Trump selected Lt. Gen. H. R. McMaster, a battle-tested tank officer both in Iraq and Afghanistan, as well as a scholar and author of the book *Dereliction of Duty: Lyndon Johnson, Robert McNamara, the Joint Chiefs of Staff, and the Lies that Led to Vietnam*, which was a stinging indictment of senior U.S. military officers who were simply not candid with the American people or Congress in their assessments and predictions about that war. Indeed, McMaster accused the chiefs of either lying or covering up for the falsehoods of the Johnson administration about the real state of the Vietnam War. Given the only occasional intersection of President Trump and the truth, McMaster will be tested to ensure he does not fall prey to the same pressures that led the generals and admirals who served during that conflict into the expedients that earned his searing critique.

Trump has been criticized for relying so heavily on four generals, and certainly Flynn was not a good choice. Yet Barack Obama also had three flag officers in senior roles: as noted, General Jones was national security advisor, Gen. Eric Shinseki was secretary of veteran affairs, and Adm. Dennis Blair was Director of National Intelligence. All were gone in two years.

This book argues that the last four presidents to enter office were (grossly) lacking in experience and preparation for the job. But none had less government experience than President Trump. And while all presidents generally have a very difficult first year, none has done more self-imposed damage than the forty-fifth has thus far. He fired Flynn. He fired Acting Attorney General Sally Yates for refusing to carry out an immigration ban that she believed to be illegal. And he fired the director of the FBI, James Comey, the day before he met with Foreign Minister Lavrov and Ambassador Kislyak in the Oval Office. It was clearly a jovial encounter and came just as the brouhaha over alleged Russian interference in the U.S. elections as well as collusion with the Trump campaign was at a boiling point.

The president has, wisely, reversed his position on many issues. He called NATO obsolete; now it is important. He promised to punish China as a currency manipulator; President Xi Jinping is now a good friend for the moment. Having promised to put America first and reduce foreign entanglements, Trump has threatened North Korea with an overwhelming response if it does not denuclearize and has fired sixty Tomahawk cruise missiles against a Syrian air base as punishment for using sarin gas (fifty-eight hit their targets). His proposed defense increases have been whittled down. He is arming the YPG—our Kurdish allies—for the assault on Raqqa in Syria in defiance of Turkish president Erdogan's warning not to and appears ready to increase U.S. forces in Afghanistan by from three to five thousand personnel.

The current confirmation process is an abomination. That said, the Trump administration has been especially slow in nominating candidates for senior positions. In the Pentagon, while one service secretary has been confirmed, at least three have withdrawn because of potential conflicts. The State Department's cupboard of senior officials is bare. Meanwhile, General McMaster is quietly rebuilding the NSC staff after the disastrous but thankfully short tenure of his predecessor.

In a word, the administration is in chaos, not helped by the president's tweets, his lack of knowledge of issues, and his almost cavalier view of the duties of his office. He may, in time, learn. Or he may not.

If the president has a broad strategic view, so far it is not evident. Sound strategic thinking seems to have been overwhelmed by campaign promises and visceral judgments not always informed by fact. It seems that rapid and constant action to disrupt the system, rather than thoughtful execution of a well-planned agenda, will be the order of the day. The lack of understanding and of knowledge of issues—problems every new administration counters—has been apparent in virtually every decision made so far. While the expectation is that Messrs. Mattis and McMaster may bring common sense back into play, administrations are run by the president, not his advisors, no matter how good the latter may be. George W. Bush had on paper one of the finest national security teams ever. That did not prevent the administration from committing arguably the worst strategic miscalculation in the nation's history since the Civil War in invading Iraq in 2003. In any case, a public accounting will occur in the 2018 by-elections for Congress. Some on both sides of the aisle with long memories recall that the year after Republicans shut down Congress in 1995, the Democrats took back both houses of Congress and Bill Clinton won a second term.

In an era of No World Order, competent and informed leadership in and by the United States is essential. It is by no means clear it will be forthcoming. As history does repeat in some fashion, the first year or two of all presidents' tenures are bumpy at best, with disaster and catastrophe never far away. The best advice is to buckle up. As time progresses, readers might make their own assessments of how well or poorly the Trump administration is doing with respect to sound strategic thinking and understanding of the profound nature of the issues at stake.

A Postscript

I attended the sixth annual Moscow International Security Conference (MISC) and a second one sponsored by ISKRAN (the Institute for the USA and Canadian Studies, in Moscow), Carnegie and the Gorchakov Foundations during the last week in April 2017. The public and private discussions concerning the West, the United States, and Russia were more somber and sobering and in many ways the most inflexible I have witnessed since the end of the Cold War. All the senior Russians had virtually the same message: the United States was actively hostile to Russia and the primary source of the crises today, from the Middle East to NATO, that have sent relations

An earlier version of these remarks originally appeared in "U.S.-Russian relations: At least do no more harm," published May 15, 2017, by UPI.

to a "catastrophic" low, according to Russian chief of defense staff, Gen. Valery Gerasimov.

These charges are not new. But compared with last year's conference, the tone and substance of Russia's alleged grievances were far more negative. Even with close Russian colleagues, reaching some accommodation or grounds for rebuilding confidence and reducing tensions seemed almost as impossible or distant as Democrats and Republicans establishing a detente (or cease-fire) in Congress.

The responses to the following two challenges uniformly reflected a combination of denial and disbelief. First, if there were irrefutable evidence of Syria employing (and still keeping supplies of) sarin gas, would that change your thinking and Russian policy? Second, if there were irrefutable evidence of Russian interference in U.S. and other elections and political processes, would that change Russian thinking? Hell *nyet* was the stinging answer.

Much of General Gerasimov's unclassified briefing to the MISC on Russian military strategy was as alarming. Gerasimov blamed NATO and the United States for precipitating tensions with Moscow. Further, the general greatly exaggerated NATO's military capability and argued that what NATO considered modest increases in military presence and a more robust series of military exercises were direct threats against Russia. He also wrongly implied that Supreme Allied Commander had the authority to deploy forces and hence start a war. And he perceived U.S. Cyber Command as directed solely against Russia.

This is not, however, just Russian paranoia. Current U.S. military strategy is based on the "four plus one" matrix and the requirement to deter—and if war comes, defeat—Russia or China or Iraq or North Korea while battling the Islamic State and other jihadi groups. It is understandable that the Russian military would take this American declaration of intent with the utmost seriousness. That said, Gerasimov's talk ended on a very positive and optimistic note.

The general was not necessarily pleading for, but was surely very intent on reestablishing, a military-to-military dialogue with the United States and the West on common interests, such as defeating terror and preserving arms-control agreements. Whether this call for dialogue will be heard in Washington is another matter. Only a small number of the nearly eight hundred attendees were Americans, and each of those was a private citizen. While the U.S. embassy in Moscow had a few "observers" present, the absence of senior American government officials was not helpful to prospects of improving relations.

The second conference, attended by very senior Russian officials and four former (as well as the current) U.S. ambassadors to Russia, did not evoke a great many positive ideas. Regarding the forthcoming July summit between presidents, the debate was between taking small steps in a low-risk, low-outcome meeting or seeking a broader and grander bargain, which would be high-risk, high-payoff. It was also clear that despite the competence of the Trump administration's national security team, none of its members had any experience with arms control or security issues directly regarding Russia. One wag drove this point home by comparing the last American secretary of energy (an eminent nuclear physicist with huge experience in these areas) and the current secretary.

Obviously, reestablishing dialogue or finding new confidence-building measures is essential. Yet virtually all members of Congress see Russia as an adversary, if not an enemy; could any administration overcome this domestic reality and advance relations with Moscow? Perhaps then, the best that can be achieved is to do no more harm. More likely, the relationship will worsen.

The costs will be that opportunities where our interests are in common will go unexploited. The tensions and differences could spread, if not like cancer, certainly like a bad case of the flu, to infect the healthier or less contentious issues—a grim but sadly objective conclusion drawn from attendance at these conferences.

Nine

How to Win

History Counts

T he great coach Vince Lombardi, whose Green Bay Packers dominated football throughout much of the 1960s, maintained, "Winning isn't everything. It is the only thing." Future presidents need to remember Lombardi's dictum each and every time a decision is made whether or not to use military force. Will the use of force work? What are the consequences of success or, as important, of failure? These are the crucial questions to be asked and answered. Yet, for whatever reasons, this commonsense idea has too often been missing in action.

In the cases examined to this point, the lack of sound strategic thinking has been a root cause of failure. It is not that administrations have not attempted to apply sound strategic thinking. But too often they did it badly. Adding to this chronic problem is lack of understanding and knowledge of the circumstances where force may or may not be employed. Reluctance or refusal to challenge ruthlessly the most basic assumptions underlying decisions to go to war or to use force is likewise a significant contributor to failure.

The alternative is a brains-based approach to sound strategic thinking. It consists of three parts: complete knowledge and full understanding of all aspects of the problem set and solutions; a mindset that is based on the realities of this, the twenty-first, century and not the last one; and a focus on affecting, influencing, and controlling the wills and perceptions of real and potential enemies.

✦

History has repeatedly shown that no matter who is president and no matter how able, competent, wise, well intentioned, and experienced that person may be, success has been, at the least, elusive. Serving as president is tough and sometimes seemingly impossible. This daunting task is not helped by a political system that is currently dysfunctional at best, and more likely profoundly broken. Perhaps one principle should be to fashion policies and strategies that above all, as physicians are trained, "do no harm."

The American system of checks and balances was purposely designed to limit the power, authority, and reach of each branch of government. This structure is inherently inefficient unless one party controls both houses of Congress (and sixty votes in the Senate) as well as the White House or a truly frightening threat forces consensus. But even FDR did not always get his way with an overwhelmingly Democrat-controlled Congress.

Today, in a divided government further riven by divisiveness, the inherent inefficiency arising from separation of powers has led to political paralysis. This failure to govern has been accelerated, in part caused, by the increasing politicization of both parties toward the extremes of left and right. In this downward spiral, compromise and civility have become casualties, and without them checks and balances cannot work. The result is gridlock or worse in even the most crucial issues, as well as the least. The furor created in the first months of the Trump administration, including the difficulty of obtaining Senate confirmation of senior nominees, was symptomatic of the septic nature of American politics. Democrats are now retaliating against the GOP for past actions that were themselves in large part based on how the Republicans believe Democrats treated them in prior administrations. This vicious cycle is simply growing worse.

More than a decade and a half ago, the original congressional "authorization to use military force" (AUMF) was approved against the perpetrators of September 11. The Bush administration drew on the AUMF and a further congressional resolution to invade Iraq in

2003. In 2017, the United States is still waging these conflicts, and on the basis of these authorizations. How can the United States justify using military force against IS (an enemy that did not exist in 2001), taking Qaddafi down in 2011, or launching strikes in Syria and Yemen against enemies never specified in the AUMF?

It cannot. And Congress is unable and unwilling to renew or update that authorization. This failure is a striking and depressing indictment of a government incapable of performing its most basic duties and content to wage wars without legally constituted authority.

Around-the-clock, ubiquitous media coverage has put White Houses on a 24/7 response mode, stretching the capacity of even the most able officials to react intelligently and effectively all, or even most, of the time. The interrelated and interconnected nature of the twenty-first-century world has made for increasingly complex dangers and challenges, some of them intractable and impervious to reconciliation. The binary nature of World War II and the Cold War, in which two major blocs dominated global politics, has long since been superseded by what George H. W. Bush called "the New World Order," and that in turn has now devolved into an era of No World Order.

Beyond all this, one observation remains stunningly and regrettably unarguable—that since the latter half of the twentieth century, America has lost wars it started or provoked and has failed in military interventions for the same reasons. The fundamental source of these failures can be found in the overall absence of sound strategic thinking and judgment and in a lack of sufficient knowledge or understanding of the circumstances.

Throughout this record of failure are presidential decisions to go to war or use force predicated on what turn out to be false or mistaken assumptions. The lack of accurate and comprehensive understanding of the situations in question exacerbates the negative consequences of these decisions. In short, failure becomes predictable when administrations neglect, disregard, distort, or simply do not apply sound strategic thinking and judgment.

The absolute necessity for sound strategic thinking is something that every president and administration should keenly understand. Unfortunately, no warning has been chiseled into the fireplace in the Oval Office or made part of a permanent presidential turnover file for required reading. In whatever time incoming and outgoing presidents choose to spend together, rarely if ever has the successor been alerted and warned to predicate his decisions on sound strategic thinking.

Why does this weakness persist? Why do successive administrations so often fail to apply sound strategic thinking? Every administration seeks the "best and brightest" of its generation in its councils. No administration intends to fail. Nor should White Houses be accused of having anything less than the best of intentions for the nation. As Clausewitz observed, war is filled with fog and friction; in any case, human error is always present. The choices of nations for war or peace are inherently susceptible to misperceptions, mistakes (honest or otherwise), and misjudgments. The challenge is to minimize these negatives—no easy task.

One wonders if this pattern suggests broader systemic shortcomings in the nation's strategic culture and its DNA. Successive White Houses have failed to recognize that we have been waging wars in Afghanistan and Iraq for more than thirty years. We intervened in Afghanistan in 1980, to check the Soviet invasion; thirty-seven years later, Afghanistan remains at war, and the American military still plays a crucial role there. Likewise, the relationship with Iraq goes back to the Iran-Iraq War of 1980–88 and America's de facto support of Saddam. These histories have been ignored or forgotten. The lessons of Vietnam and of unsuccessful military interventions since have been largely relegated to history books and college courses. Presidents and advisors are surely not purposely ignorant of the past. But successive administrations forget this history or are overwhelmed by the press of daily events, crises, and issues.

Studying the pathology of these failures leads to specific reasons why we have not succeeded in war or the use of force. First, as noted repeatedly, because of its importance, the history of what worked and what did not is overlooked or not considered even by senior officials who had played key roles in prior administrations. To take the saddest example, several of George W. Bush's most senior advisors ignored the past and overrode the very few who knew better and dissented.

Second, too often, administrations have aspirations and objectives that are unachievable. LBJ wanted to win Vietnamese "hearts and minds." Richard Nixon had a "secret plan" to end that war. George W. Bush wanted to "transform the geostrategic landscape of the Middle East." Barack Obama wanted to "disrupt and destroy" the Islamic State. Whatever the nobility (or superficiality) of these aspirations, none succeeded: each proved unrealistic, too expensive, and thus impossible to achieve. In large measure, these aspirations arose from flawed ideology: unconstrained belief in American exceptionalism and moral superiority and in the ability of the U.S. military to resolve complex political, socioeconomic, religious, and cultural divides and conflicts. Such distortions helped guarantee the setting of goals that could never be met. The present legacy of nation building—of transporting democracy to Afghanistan, Iraq, and elsewhere—is a stark reminder of how noble but naïve aspirations go awry.

Third, insufficient knowledge and understanding of situations and of first-, second-, and third-order consequences have likewise denied success. Kennedy's best and brightest never understood the complicated and interconnected conflicts consuming Vietnam. Before September 11, 2001, few Americans were familiar with the terms "Sunni" and "Shia," let alone the differences between them. The United States still has not been able to define exactly who the enemy is in the war on terror, beyond the broad descriptors like "al Qaeda," "Islamic State," and "Da'esh" (an Arabic acronym for one of the names by which the latter is known).

A fourth contributor to failure is "groupthink." Groupthink eliminates the rigorous challenging of assumptions and arguments, by generating a wide consensus to support and trust implicitly the judgment of the commander in chief. Reagan famously said, "Trust but verify." "Verify" we did not always do well. Iraq's nonexistent weapons of mass destruction constitute a devastating example of the pernicious effects of groupthink. By August 2002, the decision to invade Iraq and overthrow Saddam Hussein had been made. The presumed existence of Iraqi WMD was taken as the major rationale for this decision. It proved wrong, and there had been an alternative. Had the evidence not seemed so conclusive—groupthink at work—Bush might have instead called for a preemptive attack to prevent Saddam from *ever* fielding such weapons.

Fifth, politicization of almost every issue, including the most vital ones of war and peace, has played an outsized role. As George W. Bush put it, "You are either with us or against us." Iraq became a "Republican" war. When Obama ordered troop withdrawals from Afghanistan, that became a "Democratic" war. Each political party sought to savage the other, without restraint, on grounds often specious, even invented. Without persistent bipartisan cooperation, failure is the most likely outcome.

The propensity, based on these factors, for failure and misunderstanding is in turn greatly intensified by a twenty-first-century environment that is profoundly different from that of the twentieth century. This global environment is so interrelated and instantaneously interconnected that it creates, as noted, a huge bandwidth problem—too many simultaneous issues requiring extensive understanding and knowledge. Any relatively small bureaucracy, even a National Security Council staff numbering between six hundred and eight hundred, is simply overwhelmed.

No president can delegate responsibility for making crucial or life-and-death decisions. And no presidential advisors and staffers are fully knowledgeable on every issue. Bureaucracies, no matter the intent to integrate them and coordinate between them, are inherently isolated from each other. The reasons are human. Rivalries, distrust, sensitivity of access and information, political ambitions of senior appointees, cognitive dissonance, and other such factors can never be entirely eliminated from the decision-making process. The bandwidth issue, therefore, must be resolved. A new organizational model that ensures that expertise across the spectrum of challenges and issues will be engaged is proposed below.

One other reason for continuing failure rests in the lack of experience and the weakness, inevitably, of judgment in those elected to the Oval Office. The four men elected president in the

quarter-century from 1993 to 2017 entered office lacking most qualifications for the position or experience of its rigors. Of course,
nowhere does the Constitution specify judgment or experience as
a prerequisite. On the basis of their resumes, it is doubtful that any
of them (with the exception of Donald Trump, who is also the least
experienced in elective office) would have been elevated to very
senior positions in the private sector or, for other than political reasons, to the cabinet. Each, however, became commander in chief and
the nation's chief executive.

Inexperience is usually dangerous. However, it is clear that three
of these chief executives suffered from inexperience that surely contributed to failure. The fourth seems to be joining that category, if
the first months in office are representative. Clinton was the luckiest
of the three, taking office at a golden time; the first President Bush
had put in place the means for economic recovery, presided over the
demise of the Soviet Union, and had defeated Saddam's army.

The decade of the 1990s was indeed very good for Americans
and America. The one that followed was not. Obama, when his turn
came, was clearly the unluckiest president since FDR, inheriting two
failing wars and the worst economic and financial meltdown since
1929. However, his inexperience certainly hobbled him in coping
with these wars and limited the degree to which these dire domestic conditions could have been improved. And in many ways, President Donald Trump is the least prepared, least experienced, least
ready person to enter the Oval Office in the modern age. Overall,
then, none of the last four candidates elected president were even
nearly qualified or prepared for the job. The profound dilemma is
that there is no way to avoid that, to guarantee that future presidents
will be sufficiently qualified and experienced to hold office.

As background for a new approach, one of sound strategic thinking, understanding why and how the United States has been successful in war and in the use of force is important. The United States
won (or helped win) the three most important wars of the last century: two world wars and the Cold War.

America shifted the balance of World War I in favor of the allies,
was indispensable to victory in World War II, and won the Cold War,

for many reasons. The attack on Pearl Harbor on December 7, 1941, rallied Americans into united action that would force the enemy to accept "unconditional surrender." The nation mobilized for that war, bringing to bear the potential of its nearly unlimited resources, which had been in a state of suspended animation since the stock market collapse of 1929 and the Great Depression. Indeed, it took World War II to end the effects of that depression and generate an economic recovery.

In that war the United States had allies. British tenacity—personified by that greatest of all English bulldogs, Winston Churchill—enabled that island nation to stand alone against Hitler and the Nazis, who had conquered Western Europe. In the East, and as much as we despised Stalin's ruthlessness and murderousness, Russia bled the Wehrmacht white—at the cost of its own blood and treasure. While dissension and debate over strategy, as well as interservice and intra-alliance rivalries, persisted throughout the war, the overall aim—winning first in Europe and then in the Pacific—was agreed. The chain of command was fairly direct, if at times convoluted—as in the Pacific, where Adm. Chester Nimitz and Gen. Douglas MacArthur were commanders in chief of adjacent areas.

For their parts, the service chiefs then had great authority, uncomplicated by the excessive rules, regulations, and oversight common today. That does not mean oversight was, or is, unnecessary. It is vital. But too much oversight is crippling. Today's redundant and overlapping congressional oversight jurisdictions; the need for legal approval of many military operations, especially "capture-or-kill" missions (because of what is called "lawfare," the manipulation by adversaries of international law); and choking super-regulation—all these lead to failure, beyond the waste and inefficiency inherent in large bureaucracies.

Given the combined power of the Alliance fighting them and the unprecedented scale of its arsenal, Nazi Germany and fascist Japan had virtually no chance of winning, once the disastrous effects of Pearl Harbor and the occupation of Europe had been absorbed. The Allies did not fail to ask and answer the "What next?" question of how to treat the enemy after the war was won and unconditional surrender imposed. Planning for the occupations of Germany and Japan had begun as early as 1943. The success of that planning and of the accompanying Marshall Plan was extraordinary. Germany, Italy, and Japan became liberal, functional, and very successful democracies, with strong and open economies. Also, the United States still has substantial forces stationed in those states, as well as in South Korea, to maintain stability and reassure allies.

The Cold War was won largely because the relatively free and open markets of liberal democracies proved far more flexible and sustainable than command economies. The closed and authoritarian Soviet system was incapable of reconciling basic societal contradictions. It craved legitimacy that could only come from denying reality. This denial ultimately broke the brittle Soviet system. There is a sentiment that Ronald Reagan bankrupted the Soviet Union into collapse. But the fact is that the Soviets did it to themselves. Reaganites attribute the implosion of the Soviet Union to the arms buildup, but it was Mikhail Gorbachev's perestroika and glasnost initiatives that ended the communist system. At some point, the Soviet system had to implode or seek an alternative path. War in the thermonuclear age was not an option.

Thermonuclear war was too destructive to be a plausible policy choice. Fortunately, both the "irrational" Soviet and "rational" American leadership understood that catastrophic prospect. There were close calls. The Cuban Missile Crisis was perhaps the most dangerous. However, the reason why in that instance Khrushchev attempted to outflank America's strategic nuclear superiority, despite Kennedy's alarm about an alleged "missile gap," was to offset the American military advantage, minimize Soviet defense spending, and reach some kind of accommodation with the United States.

For its part, from Truman to the first Bush, American strategy rested on containment and deterrence—which worked as long as the adversary was basically compliant or had no intention of breaking certain rules of the game. Tactical shifts occurred, such as the doctrinal change from massive retaliation to flexible response. But in general, and ironically, the Cold War was made safer and more stable by self-imposed constraints of both sides to avoid and prevent a third world war.

As in World War II, the United States in the Cold War relied on allies, surrounding the Soviet Union with alliances. NATO was the most formidable and effective. Following the Korean War, the United States used its overwhelming economic advantages and plentiful resources to maintain a large and technologically driven military that emphasized its military superiority until the Soviets caught up. Despite many setbacks—losing in Vietnam, the hollow force that followed, and the Soviet Union's attempts to close the military-technology gap—the military balance between East and West was maintained.

Of course, many mistakes were made. Above all, the United States failed to conclude, as it should have, that the profound weakness of the Soviet Union was that the communist political system was not sustainable over time. Eisenhower allowed the CIA to dabble in too many places, from Latin America to Africa to the Persian Gulf, fomenting regime change. Opposition to the Soviet Union became the criterion for U.S. interests and actions. Autocrats and despots were recruited to the American side however unsavory, irrespective of democratic values, the rule of law, or social justice, provided they would join against the larger threat from the East.

Insufficient understanding of the Soviet Union and, later, of Russia precipitated arms races and interventions in the misguided hope of halting the spread of communism "there, not here." Kennedy's invented missile gap, the Vietnam disaster, Reagan's "evil empire," and the second Iraq war demonstrate this colossal lack of sound strategic thinking and understanding. Despite the extraordinary efforts of Secretary of State John Kerry, the failure of President Obama to pursue forcefully long-term negotiations with Moscow toward ending or mitigating standoffs likewise suggests that long-range strategic thinking was never undertaken seriously after Putin invaded eastern Ukraine and annexed Crimea in 2014.

The common absence of strategic thinking was (as it is today) reinforced by vagueness as to what deterrence meant and the role in it of assured destruction. During the Cold War, the United States had no definitive idea of what it took to deter the Soviet Union or to defeat it in war. Secretary of Defense Robert McNamara arbitrarily defined assured destruction so as to limit further procurement of nuclear systems.

Because we have entered a different era, one of No World Order, concepts of the last century must be revised and redefined. Deterrence and containment top the list. During the Cold War, the United States used both as foundations for the policies and strategy to deal with the Soviet Union. Both concepts worked during the latter decades of the twentieth century. But the twenty-first century is far different. Globalization and the diffusion of power, accelerated by the information revolution, have empowered individuals and nonstate actors at the expense of states and of the nearly four-century-old Westphalian system of state-centric politics. While in absolute terms the United States is more powerful militarily and economically than any other state or indeed some combination, its relative advantages are declining.

As the world becomes more interconnected, what happens in any part of the globe can easily affect the rest of the world. The Ebola epidemic in West Africa could have become a global pandemic. The Syrian civil war has displaced so many people as to create crises in Europe and the United States on how to deal with this mass migration, overladen with the potential for terrorists to use these flows of humanity to enter other nations. Unless or until valid and applicable strategic concepts are created for today, failure will be, if not inevitable, surely more likely. This is another reason why sound strategic thinking is vital. Without it, do not expect future results to be very different from those of the past.

In the twenty-first century, no one knows what it takes to deter. Consider China, Russia, Iran, North Korea, and the Islamic State. What does it take to deter each, and from what? If there is no intention to go to war, does deterrence have any meaning? Regarding IS, deterrence is automatically moot. If people are prepared to commit suicide to advance a set of beliefs, can they be deterred?

During World War II, the Japanese employed kamikaze aircraft and banzai charges in suicide attacks. Civilians killed themselves in large numbers in Saipan and Okinawa rather than be captured by

Americans. While the fire-bombings of its cities and the blockade of its shipping brought near famine to the country by late 1944, Japan fought on. Projections of Allied casualties in an invasion of the Japanese home islands ran into the hundreds of thousands. Japanese casualties could have been in the millions. It took two atomic bombs to force the Japanese war cabinet to vote on ending the war.

Even then it deadlocked, until Emperor Hirohito intervened; the cabinet then voted to surrender—by a single vote. The reason it finally did so was that the destructive impact of nuclear weapons overcame the cultural power of hara-kiri. The Japanese were aware that thousand-plane fire-bombing raids by B-29s could kill more citizens in a long night of attacks over Tokyo or Haruna than perished at Hiroshima and Nagasaki. But most, especially the military leaders, could not comprehend how a single bomb had such destructive power. "Shock and awe" turned suicidal behavior into surrender.

No one is suggesting that nuclear weapons will have the same effect on IS. However, the jihadi ideology can be shaped and redirected to delegitimize suicide if—and this is a huge if—ayatollahs and mullahs of traditional Islam can be mobilized to make that case and a majority of the Muslim world rejects this perverted interpretation of its religion. That is, a twenty-first-century concept of deterrence must be created for this new danger. But no one seems interested in pursuing this important objective. A simple Google search on "new thinking on deterrence" produces a nearly null set.

A new definition of deterrence must also be fashioned for so-called peer competitors. In 2016, Secretary of Defense Ashton Carter announced his "four plus one" threat matrix. The four main contingencies for which the Pentagon was to be prepared concerned (a resurgent) Russia, China, North Korea, and Iran. The "one" refers to IS. Given this planning guidance, it followed that the services would attempt to identify what it would take to deter and if necessary to defeat such an adversary if war were to come.

In my mind, this amounted to a clear-cut case of inadequate and flawed strategic thinking. Planners were asked in this past case to employ mind-sets and concepts of the twentieth century to deal with twenty-first-century issues. This, as happened in Vietnam, would prove unsuccessful. Neither Russia nor China has the intent to attack its neighbors, especially those allied with the United States. Thus, the question of what it takes to deter war with either is meaningless.

Similarly, what it would take to defeat Russia or China in a war that could become nuclear is a question that should be addressed only in the deepest and most secret compartments of government. As former secretary of defense Robert Gates warned, any American president engaging in a land war in Asia needs his or her head examined. Of course, it is true that the United States still regarded Britain as a potential adversary in its Rainbow War Plans until the early 1930s. But the twenty-first century needs different means to deal with states that are competitors and rivals but not military enemies.

Korea is different. Here, the South Korean military and other regional states should be given the bulk of responsibility for blunting an attack from the North. The United States can support it, and its nuclear arsenal could be a counter to North Korea's. However, a new version of the old Nixon Doctrine described earlier is the best way to cope with contingencies on the Korean Peninsula.

As for IS, the Pentagon can plan as much as it wishes. However, only a whole-of-government approach can succeed, one in which, as in the case of Korea, regional states must assume far more responsibility for regional security and in dealing with IS. Unfortunately, while the Obama administration created an anti-IS coalition of some sixty-plus states, the reality is that only a few of the members provide the lion's share of the capabilities. Unless or until the regional states understand the existential nature of the IS threat to themselves and respond with real action and not rhetoric, "this will be," as a former secretary of defense, Donald Rumsfeld, cautioned, "a long, hard slog."

Similarly, the Cold War specter of thermonuclear Armageddon—called "MAD," or Mutual Assured Destruction—has been replaced in the twenty-first century with a new MAD. This MAD is Mutual Assured *Disruption*. Disruption, whether from acts of man or of nature, is the danger. When bin Laden collapsed the Twin Towers in New York, perhaps even he never anticipated the extent of disruption this attack would cause. Trillions of dollars in stock-market value instantly disappeared. For the rest of our lives, we air-line passengers will be subjected to the indignity of invasive security searches at airports—searches that perhaps violate the Constitution but do not ensure the safety and security of passengers, as too many tests of the system have amply demonstrated.

Cyber attacks are disruptive rather than destructive, although the Stuxnet virus surely made many of Iran's centrifuges inoperable. As anyone who has been hacked or whose identity has been stolen knows, the effect is one of disruption. Climate change, extreme weather conditions, and global warming are twenty-first-century examples of natural disruption, threats that if unchecked obviously have hugely destructive potential, possibly more threatening than nuclear war.

Violence by disturbed individuals and radical jihadists obviously kills and harms people. The larger consequence is the way that they disrupt ordinary lives. Nearly a decade ago, two snipers held Washington, D.C., and its Maryland and northern Virginia suburbs in a mini "reign of terror." People were afraid that to show themselves was to risk being shot. This is not a new phenomenon. In terms of historical comparisons, the decades between the 1880s and 1920s were far more rife with terrorist attacks, including the assassination of kings, tsars, prime ministers, and presidents. Past successes against them surely are helpful in dealing with the future. Adjusting the old Nixon Doctrine into a new one for the twenty-first century is one example. In addition to practicing "triangular politics"—playing and balancing China and the Soviet Union against each other—Nixon also created a doctrine. Its thrust was to encourage and engage regional and local states to assume greater responsibility for security while the United States would be the enabler, assisting and providing the strategic context for stability.

Presidents have tried to do this, with limited or marginal success. This effort must continue and be central to future American policy. That effort should begin with the rejuvenation of NATO as the building block for future American, Western, and even global security, a view that President Trump, at long last, seems to understand.

The United States must make more effective use of friends and allies, focusing on enhancing mutual interests. The explosive costs of national security are exceeded by unbalanced liabilities for entitlement and retirement programs. When interest rates return to higher levels, debt service becomes more expensive. The self-evident consequence is less money for national security.

Meanwhile, if Russia and China are perceived to be growing threats, the United States cannot be solely responsible for providing counters and safeguards. As was true in World War II, the United States cannot operate unilaterally. Withdrawal and retreat are incompatible with a global economy and with the instantaneous interconnectivity and interrelationships that mark this century.

All this does not mean that past administrations did not employ the best intellects and means to derive strategies and policies for using force. The criticism is that too often they failed, and what we did was not successful. The issue is how best to ensure success in a future that will be unpredictable, unsettled, and far more complicated and complex than what we have dealt with in the past.

Ten

The Way Forward

A Brains-Based Approach to Sound Strategic Thinking

S ince the earliest days of the Republic, in waging war and defending the nation's interests and security, presidents and administrations of all parties have been accused of having no strategy,
the wrong strategy, or a strategy unconnected to resources. Underscoring this criticism, over the past sixty years, every war the United
States started it lost, and every time it used force for flawed reasons
it failed. Today, however, the greatest threat to the United States
is not the Islamic State, a recrudescent Russia, an assertive China,
a nuclear North Korea, or even Iran. Instead, the greatest threat is a
badly broken government, torn apart by the fiercest partisan differences that have metastasized since the end of the Cold War. There
is little expectation of this condition repairing itself in the short term
or absent an existential crisis.

Translated to the U.S. military, the greatest danger is, similarly,
not from abroad. It is at home. The issue is uncontrolled internal cost
growth, which if not contained will do more damage to the U.S. military than did the wars in Iraq and Afghanistan.

On the current trajectory, uncontrolled internal cost growth for
people, health care, retirees, overhead and administration, operations, and weapons systems will produce a "hollow force," a military
unready and underequipped to carry out its duties even at current levels of defense spending. And current spending, in constant

dollars, exceeds the largest defense budgets of the Reagan buildup, for an active force nearly a million stronger in numbers.

Few now fully appreciate the Damoclean fiscal sword, believing instead that lifting sequestration and other marginal actions will avert this crisis for the Pentagon and American military power. This failure to understand and recognize the impact of exploding cost growth will inevitably produce a hollow force, a condition no one ever hopes to witness again.

Regarding strategy, we must ask: "Why is it that, given the historical realities of the past seven decades, the United States and its presidents too often did so poorly? Why did they not make better strategic calculations in committing the nation to major military interventions?" Of course, the West won the Cold War. But that war never went hot. The wars that did go hot have plagued us the most. One reason is that in those cases brains and intellect were never fully applied, leading to misjudgments, mistakes, and misperceptions that ultimately created failure. Brains and intellect alone have been insufficient to inform and educate the elected leadership, to inculcate in its members a complete understanding of the grim fiscal realities and the current dangers to the U.S. military of uncontrolled internal cost growth.

Obviously, no sensible person would advocate rejecting the use of brains and intellect, especially not in the tortuous problems affecting vital national security issues. The key question is how best to *apply* brains and intellect. Too often, other factors have taken precedence: domestic political pressures, appointment of civilian officials to key positions whose success in winning elections was not matched by the ability to govern, ideological convictions, flawed assumptions, narrow bureaucratic or parochial interests, disregard of budget realities, the use of money as an alternative or palliative, normal human frailty, and intellectual laziness. All these have negated or overridden the need for a rigorous, relevant, and above all objective intellectual framework. Such a framework would be a "brains-based approach," working from a mind-set appropriate for the twenty-first century.

For example, despite the experience of the senior members of George W. Bush's cabinet, no one seriously asked or answered the

"What next?" question about Iraq during the buildup to that war in 2002 and 2003. No one considered what needed to be done once Saddam had been dethroned.

The Obama administration was made to look impotent by drawing "red lines" against Bashar al-Assad's conduct in Syria and demanding his ouster without the means or a plan to make good on that threat. Regardless of the arguments for or against a strategic pivot to Asia, the manner in which the strategy was announced scared allies and friends and provoked China. In any case, the situation in the Greater Middle East soon deteriorated, and the pivot was eclipsed by the need to "rebalance" forces to that theater.

What is needed first is a model, a foundation, to show how such a strategic approach could be applied. Recall World War II's Manhattan Project, which built the first three atomic bombs. One factor made that work: $E = mc^2$. What is missing today in our search for an effective national-security strategy is the geostrategic equivalent of $E = mc^2$.

I will argue that a brains-based approach is that equivalent, or at least a vital step in creating such a model. This argument for a brains-based approach is made at length in my last book, *A Handful of Bullets: How the Murder of Archduke Franz Ferdinand Still Menaces the Peace.*

A brains-based approach to strategy can be characterized as having three elements. First, it must be knowledge based, to facilitate as complete an understanding as possible of all aspects of strategy. These range from basic aims to intimate analysis of the adversary, various courses of actions and assumptions underlying each, the consequences (including the resource implications), costs, and the objective calculation of affordability measured in blood and treasure.

Second, this approach must have a twenty-first-century mindset. It must be based on an understanding of current conditions, especially the challenges and changes to the Westphalian system of state-centric politics caused by the empowerment of individuals (Edward Snowden, Julian Assange, Osama bin Laden), transnational organizations (the EU, UN, International Court of Justice), international agreements, and such nonstate groups as al Qaeda and the Islamic State. Understanding must include the realization that the strategic slogan of Mutual Assured Destruction is flawed, that it reflected the Cold War and the thermonuclear stand-off between East and West. A twenty-first-century view encompasses the transition to a strategy of Mutual Assured Disruption, against the destabilization of the international order envisioned by terror, cyber, environmental catastrophe, and other dangers to safety and security.

Third, the policy aim must be to affect, influence, and control the will and perception of the "others" so as to allow our brains to beat their brains, in part by greater innovation, ingenuity, and inventiveness—often called "out of the box thinking." This approach would abandon all boxes.

The basis for sound strategic thinking must be understanding of the fundamental forces that are in play and are changing international politics. Driving these changes is the assault on the Westphalian system manifest in three overarching realities that, being largely invisible, have been ignored or dismissed.

- First, the most powerful armies, navies, and air forces in the world are hard-pressed to, and usually will not, defeat a determined adversary who, lacking those forces' capabilities, chooses to wage war with what Clausewitz called "other means" and with great resolve and tenacity. IS is the most relevant example.

- Second, while we use the term "asymmetrical" as promiscuously as we do "hybrid warfare," the reality is that adversaries in such conflicts are beating us badly in terms of cost-exchange ratios and, particularly, political and propaganda narratives. The Islamic State is ahead in both areas, and Russia's Putin is sweeping the public-relations battlefield.

- Third, and most important, the strategic linkages between and among many disparate conflicts must form the foundations for responses in this post-Westphalian world, in a context of Mutual Assured Disruption.

Regarding the first two challenges, the United States spent around $70 billion to counter IEDs that cost the other side pennies, by comparison. Today, we are in the ludicrous position of spending millions of dollars to destroy *our* Humvees and other equipment captured by the enemy, gear that cost them nothing! Likewise, to be brutally frank, suicide bombers are cheap. Also, tragically, despite all the money spent on counter-IEDs, those weapons still inflict about two-thirds of our casualties.

An expectation persists that sufficient money will be available, either through congressional largesse or such financial sleight of hand as the extra-budgetary "overseas contingency operations" (OCO) account (which has added billions to defense spending to offset the effects of surging internal cost growth). Sequestration is the current target for budgetary relief. Certainly, mandating proportionate cuts across all defense programs is bureaucratic lunacy. But absent a crisis of existential proportions, the United States no longer has the option of spending its way clear of danger.

Magnifying any advantages an adversary may possess, U.S. strategies too often are reactive, oversensitive to political pressures, unresponsive to the Clausewitzian view that war is a conflict of wills with an admixture of policy, and prone to address the symptoms, not causes, of violence. Of course, having a single overarching or existential state-based threat, such as Nazi Germany or the Soviet Union, throughout the 350 years of the Westphalian world made strategizing easier. Nevertheless, unifying linkages among today's many disparate threats, dangers, and challenges do exist. Globalization and the diffusion of power have made the world far more interdependent and interconnected. Here is the linkage, and hence the need for a mind-set that understands and deals with this very new world order.

To be specific: unseen or ignored today is that events having to do with Russia, Ukraine, NATO, and Europe are directly related and connected to events involving Iraq, Syria, IS, and the Gulf states, including Iran. These interconnections lie in common interests in defeating terrorists and preventing one region's destabilization from contaminating the other. That is, events in the Persian Gulf cannot be separated from those of Europe, or vice versa. Past White Houses failed to grasp the nature of a post-Westphalian world, too often resorting to twentieth-century thinking.

What else constitutes sound strategic thinking, and how might it be implemented? "Shock and awe," described in chapter 6, aims to affect, influence, and control the will and perception of the adversary. In simple terms, we employ it to coerce or convince the other person to do what we want or to stop doing what we find objectionable. Force is but one tool, not the only one, and not necessarily sufficient in itself. Unfortunately, in the second Gulf war "shock and awe" was turned into a sound bite and not a strategy, and it was discredited by this misusage. The short statement above of the true intent of "shock and awe," however, should be the centerpiece of a brains-based approach.

"Shock and awe" posits four prerequisites: extensive knowledge and understanding of the enemy at all levels, brilliance in execution, rapidity, and sufficient control of the environment in all dimensions to impose our will. These criteria, particularly the knowledge requirement, can form the basis for any brains-based approach.

What must be done first to create, implement, and then sustain this brains-based approach to sound strategic thinking? And how can intellect, innovation, and creativity become permanent aspects of this approach? What is needed is institutionalized operational, intellectual, academic, and educational transformations. Implanting a twenty-first-century mind-set means understanding that many of the concepts and tools of the twentieth century and Cold War no longer work or are simply obsolete. But who will lead in this?

Politics in America today have become transfixed on winning elections and not on governing. Worse, too often, newly elected presidents appoint senior staff on the basis of contributions to the campaign and not ability actually to govern. This is particularly true for White House staff. For candidates, strategic thinking is an afterthought in an arena dominated by winning and not the prospect and needs of governing. Congress lacks the institutional basis to become the home for strategic thinking. And too many think tanks are creatures of the "left" and "right" to be seen as analytically objective.

Hence, what must be established is a constituency that makes the case for sound strategic thinking. The first concerted effort to advocate a brains-based approach occurred in Britain in 2015, at the Royal United Services Institute's annual Land Warfare Conference, sponsored by the British Army. I have been a regular attendee since 2010. The last two chiefs of the general staff have chosen a brains-based approach in their army's strategic thinking.

The crucial starting point in this effort must comprise knowledge and understanding. The mandate to know the adversary—real and potential—is older than Sun Tzu. So, how might this be achieved when the "enemy" may range from thirteen-year-old female recruits who live in Birmingham or Boston or Berlin to the "faceless" members of al Qaeda, al Nusra (i.e., al Qaeda in Syria), and, of course, IS?

Many agencies and organizations are utilizing "data mining" to derive information and knowledge on potential enemies. What is needed is a far larger and more focused effort. One model can be derived from World War II, the famous code breakers of Bletchley Park in England. It was Bletchley Park and its American counterparts that broke the Enigma and Purple codes of Nazi Germany and imperial Japan, greatly contributing to victory. What is less well known is that the Germans were at least as good at cracking the Allies' codes, but of course ultimately they were defeated by overwhelming force.

A twenty-first-century equivalent of Bletchley Park must be created to employ against our adversaries, new and old—to understand them better and to use that knowledge to defeat them. This capability can be achieved by exploiting "big data," social media, the universally available Google Earth, and other public platforms. Examples of how this is being done at present are numerous.

The Atlantic Council, with which I am affiliated, presented a brilliant demonstration of these techniques in an analysis providing incontrovertible proof of the presence of Russian forces in Ukraine in 2015. The analysts traced through YouTube videos, "selfies," and other social media a young Russian paratrooper from his home in Siberia to the battle zone inside eastern Ukraine, three thousand miles west. Similar results in both government and nongovernmental agencies are common and constitute "proof of concept." The State Department, Pentagon, or intelligence community may be the appropriate place for this new Bletchley Park.

Obviously, the amount of data is nearly infinite. Further, adversaries can take countermeasures: preventing texting or the posting of videos, and hiding or camouflaging available data. Unlike in other wars, the Bletchley Park code breakers of today are vulnerable to electronic discovery and at risk of being attacked on the Internet or even in person. Indeed, social media of four-star officers have already been hacked in retaliation or for disruptive purposes.

The British Army, nevertheless, has already begun. Two brigades—77 Brigade and 1 ISR (that is, Intelligence, Surveillance, and Reconnaissance)—have been formed for this effort. The former is tasked with employing nonkinetic forms of war to achieve military purposes. The latter exploits open and civilian sources of information to gain knowledge. These could serve as models for the United States and a new Bletchley Park.

The second step in institutionalizing sound strategic thinking is recognizing that present international and national security organizations reflect the twentieth century, even the Cold War specifically. American national-security activity remains based on a law first passed in 1947 (though amended since). The UN, Bretton Woods, the International Monetary Fund, the World Bank, NATO, and other agencies stem from that period. While new organizations and structures have been created—such as the EU, the International Court of Justice, and various international agreements—a new mind-set also must include new organizations.

The National Security Council has become simply too large to control effectively all the actions of government, and it must be properly adapted. Within the military, the Unified Command Plan and the Pentagon organization likewise must be modernized. One way to begin imposing a brains-based approach to strategic thinking is to separate the Joint Chiefs from the service chiefs. Such a separation would remove the new Joint Chiefs of Staff from service-specific interests and needs that may not be in the overall national interest and can present a conflict of interest. The Joint Chiefs' full-time task, then, would be to offer genuine strategic thinking, too long missing from the making and conduct of national security policy. A related step is to streamline the geographic and functional commands and engage them more in broad strategic dialogue.

The third stage would be a revolution in national-security education, vital for the whole executive branch. The Pentagon is the largest consumer of education, in terms of quantity, quality, and expense, in the government. However, the vertical structure of the Department of Defense, in which age and seniority equate to educational requirements, is a relic of the twentieth century. In many cases, officers cannot wait until their fifteenth or twentieth year of service to be eligible for senior war college selection. Additionally, in view of the growing importance of enlisted personnel, advanced education must be made available to this cohort as well.

Socialization among peers is a very important (and too often seen as minor) rationale for advanced education. However, online education, virtual and distance learning, must also be strengthened. The military, with its vast array of war colleges and postgraduate facilities, from Monterey to Mobile, is clearly the most likely venue for this revolution.

An example of new ways to inject strategic thinking into military education is the website CompanyCommander.com, invented by the U.S. Army in Iraq over a decade ago. The purpose was to provide operational linkages and connectivity among young officers, who could exchange real-time tactical information and intelligence and elicit the experiences of those who were serving or had served in specific war zones. CompanyCommander.com should be replicated, adapted, and expanded across government departments to broaden strategic thinking on national security. For members of cohorts who are already connected not physically but digitally, transitioning to a modernized form of CompanyCommander.com will be natural. This exchange of actionable and relevant information and data can reinforce and be reinforced by the new Bletchley Park.

Fourth, all the executive-branch departments, especially the White House, must be prepared to specify and then strenuously test the assumptions that go into all levels of strategic, operational, and tactical planning, beginning with recognition that this is the twenty-first century and many rules of the Westphalian system no longer apply. This implies a permanent "red team" to carry out this testing and a permanent means to inculcate in all ranks the habit of sensibly challenging assumptions, with the purposes noted above. A "red team" must be located in the White House. However, all other departments and agencies should establish "red teams" of their own, at the secretarial or directorial level.

For example, in the fight against IS, we assume that for Iraq to prevail, if the government in Baghdad cannot field an army to defeat IS, no outside force can. But what if Iraq's government is incapable of resolving its sectarian splits and hence of defeating IS? Or what if the only regional state capable of defeating the Islamic State is Iran? Both are possible alternatives. What should the United States do then? Challenging assumptions is critical to policy success.

Regarding political leaders, war games and equivalent seminars are critical in preparing for crises and increasing knowledge and understanding of contingencies. Inserting these exercises into already overfilled schedules will be difficult. There will also be great resistance even to conducting them. Here, Congress and distinguished former senior persons can be helpful, persuading the White House at least to sample these exercises.

Fifth, twentieth-century definitions of containment and deterrence no longer apply and must be modernized. Strategy and policy must focus on specific actions against specific and relevant dangers and threats and not become rhetorical statements. Russia is not going to invade NATO states. It may use intimidation, tactics that have been misnamed "hybrid war." Cyber, hacking, propaganda, economic leverage, and the inflaming of ethnic populations are weapons that must be blunted. NATO must generate deployable capabilities for this purpose. That means NATO needs to broaden itself from a strictly military alliance to one with a greater political thrust. For NATO members on the flanks, a "porcupine" strategy is essential. The strategy would be, with ground-based antiair missiles, antitank weapons, and armored vehicles to bloody badly any Russian intervention. NATO would provide assets to check the nonmilitary tools Russia might use. This requires a new iteration of the "Harmel Report," which transformed NATO in 1967.

For dealing with China, expanded partnerships are vital. A new containment policy would see that our partners have the military capacity to prevent China from breaking out beyond the so-called first island chain, to keep its blue-water aspirations merely that. Direct attack on or invasion of China are bad ideas. But preventing or restraining China from deploying large military forces globally is not.

Sixth, the bandwidth problem must be resolved. To ensure continuity after normal working hours, the NSC should have three deputies. The three would rotate, with small staffs, around the clock. They would, most importantly, respond to incidents and events with immediate recommendations, not simply alerting principals in the watches of the night of impending crises. Further, specific area experts must be senior members of the NSC. In all, however, no more than between seventy-five and a hundred senior staffers should be needed. The NSC as it was under Brent Scowcroft offers the best model.

Seventh, Congress must be engaged at the beginning of decisions and not merely informed. This can be done in two ways. Senior members of both houses—the Speaker/president and majority leader—can be de facto NSC members or at least observers. Alternatively (or additionally) the president of the Senate—the vice president—could preside over a congressional version of the NSC comprising no more than a dozen senior members of Congress. This council would discuss and advise on key issues, so that the administration would be keeping Congress on board for the policy takeoff as well as for the landing.

Finally, with respect specifically to defeating IS, it must be understood that the fight is not against an organization but an idea and a movement. The latter two characteristics of the Islamic State make it highly adaptive. For example, as financial resources have been denied and some territory has been retaken, IS has responded by recruiting child bombers. This is not a new tactic. Child soldiers have too often been put into service, from Vietnam to Africa. It is far more difficult to disrupt and destroy an idea and a movement than to defeat a standing army. This reality has not been fully assimilated. Also, solutions here will not work without the support of the bulk of the Islamic world. This will require skillful and tough diplomacy. For example, radicalism in Saudi Arabia and Pakistan are two very real dangers. Yet in neither country has effective action been forthcoming. Changing this mind-set within such countries' leaderships must be a top priority.

◆

To summarize these recommendations, consider the notion of "black holes." Black holes are not merely matters of physics. Strategic black holes may be even more confounding than those found in deep space. The United States and its allies must deal with three of them. That the United States will do so is far from certain.

The first black hole regards strategy. While administrations wrestle with writing national security strategies, too often these documents become aspirational and unconnected to aims, means, ends, and resources. And it is much more daunting to cope with threats varying from the Islamic State and Islamist radicalism to North Korea's pursuit of nuclear weapons and long-range rockets than with those of the last century. Then the world was largely defined by two opposing blocs—whether allies versus the Central Powers in World War I or Allies against the Nazis and Fascists in World War II, or during the Cold War, when it was East versus West.

The second black hole regards the failure to deal with Russian "active measures." That is separate from the first black hole and requires a political strategic, not a military, response. Russian interference in the domestic politics of many democracies is now common knowledge. So too is Russia's use of propaganda and "fake news" across the entire information spectrum from the Internet to television and social media.

The third black hole is the failure to avert a "hollow force." Uncontrolled internal cost growth represents a threat to the American military far greater than the Islamic State, Islamist radicals, North Korea, or even Russia or China.

These strategic black holes must be filled. This book has offered recommendations for dealing with each.

✦

What happens if these warnings are ignored and remedial actions recommended above are not taken? Be prepared for the worst!

Whether we like it or not—and absent a debacle, miscalculation, or crisis such as September 11—defense budgets will not keep pace with costs. Because of the increasing expense of people in a professional military force—from pay and incentives to retirement and health care—and of ever more capable weapons, cost asymmetries favor adversaries who do not need elaborate conventional forces. The consequences are self-evident. The West is facing the return of the dreaded "hollow force" that plagued America after the Vietnam War.

We need to think our way out of this conundrum, not substitute dollars for brains or rely on obsolete constructs. October 2015 marked the six-hundredth anniversary of the battle of Agincourt. Henry V's army of five to ten thousand defeated a force many times larger, thanks to the longbow and a battlefield that turned into an impassable quagmire and halted the French cavalry literally in its tracks. A brains-based approach to strategy, drawing on that battle, would ask, What are the new "longbows"? And how do we shape future geostrategic battlefields so that the enemy, not us, is trapped in them?

A brains-based approach will not guarantee favorable outcomes. But the absence of one, combined with failure to embrace a twenty-first-century mind-set or recognize fiscal constraints, will guarantee for the United States future battles and conflicts too easily lost and a hollow, impotent military. That would mean more potential Vietnams, Afghanistans, Iraqs, and failing wars on terror. But who will listen, and who will lead? There can be one and only one answer to these questions—the president of the United States. If there is a single lesson of history, it is this: every time our presidents have used military force in conflict or interventions that we started or provoked, we have lost or failed.

That warning does not mean force can never or should never be used. Force was critical in winning World War II and, in a different way, the Cold War. It was critical in driving Saddam Hussein from

Kuwait in 1991. In the battle against IS and other violent ideological forces, military power is necessary. But as Afghanistan, Iraq, and Libya should have taught us, military power is not sufficient in itself. A whole-of-government approach is required, and we have not done well in fashioning one.

Further, decisions on the use of force cross and stress excruciatingly legal, moral, and political boundaries. Employing torture, for example, is destructive to American values and does not work, no matter what its proponents assert. Drones are very capable of killing enemy combatants and terrorists, but with unavoidable collateral damage that no doubt increases recruitment by organizations that wish us ill. In any case, and most important, we can never kill our way to victory; even high-level "snatch" missions have grave downsides. Lawyers cannot be given ultimate responsibility for making military judgments; commanders and the commander in chief must retain that. However, the guidelines are now blurred and may never be clarified. That too is a reality of the twenty-first century.

A second warning is also important. President Trump has declared that the United States needs to rebuild its military. That is quite a statement, as the U.S. military is the most formidable in the world. This is not 1975. But it is true that the military has been stretched. Modernization of weapons systems has been delayed by the need for short-term spending on operations. Increasing the size of the military may strike many as important, given the resurgence of China and Russia on the international scene, the former militarizing tiny islets in proximate seas and the latter intervening into Ukraine and Syria. But the Defense Department is facing a far more dangerous, internal threat. This threat is the return in twenty-first-century form of the "hollow force" that followed the Vietnam War. This book has offered this warning before, but it is important to repeat it.

The Trump plan as portrayed on his campaign website is to increase the ground forces, the Army and Marine Corps, by some 90,000, to a total just under 700,000; to add 1,200 more fighters to the Air Force; and to grow the Navy from 280 to 350 ships. The defense budget for 2017 is about $600 billion, with another $40 billion from

OCO to fill shortfalls. The Trump plan will lead to defense budgets of between $700 and $800 billion a year, if not more.

Spending more money will not work by itself. Make no mistake: unless action is taken now, the U.S. military will become "hollow" again. After Vietnam, the culprit was the diversion of money to non-defense purposes. The major culprit this time is uncontrolled internal cost growth. Today, the United States faces a wide array of challenges and threats, ranging from potential peer adversaries such as China, Russia, and North Korea to Islamic terrorists. Iran too is considered a major threat, in its region. There must be appropriate responses. But Congress is unlikely to approve yearly increases beyond inflation *and* fund a larger force. The symptoms of a hollow force are already visible; readiness, modernization, and maintenance are in decline.

Many reasons explain the persistence of internal real cost growth. Highly trained, well equipped, all-volunteer forces are very expensive. So too is the new technology that provides extraordinary military capability. Myriad acquisition regulations to limit abuses are obscenely costly in time and money. The refusal of Congress to pass serious base-closing and other efficiency measures likewise contributes to systemic cost growth.

Indeed, it is a wonder that the Pentagon works as well as it does. It has to put up with the insanity of "sequestration," caps on defense and domestic discretionary spending mandated by the Budget Control Act of 2011. If these limits are exceeded, arbitrary cuts are imposed on domestic and defense accounts, on a fifty-fifty basis, and must be taken equally across all line items. One asks how the nation can buy 10 percent less of a tank, aircraft, or warship. Yet this is how the law works. Members of Congress fully understand the irrationality of sequestration. However, like so many other consequences of bad legislation, sequestration is still the law of the land.

Fortunately, internal cost growth can be contained. Before the new administration's defense increases are initiated, careful analysis must determine why a larger force is vital, how it will contribute to national security, and, critically, how it will be paid for and sustained. Congress must be part of the solution; the streamlining and consolidating of defense acquisition regulations and a serious new base-closing round are essential. The Defense Department must change its personnel accounts—pay, health care, and retirement—to lower costs. In addition, it must control "requirements creep" and cost overruns in approved new weapons systems; unless program success or failure is at stake, changes in requirements must not be made.

Unfortunately, the political-bureaucratic-defense-industrial complex that defines the what, why, and how of "raising an army and maintaining a navy" is not merely indifferent to this destructive interaction. It is largely the cause.

◆

Erecting a framework for sound strategic thinking and ensuring that all issues are engaged with sufficient understanding and knowledge, so as to promote good decision making, will not automatically correct all the vagaries, idiosyncrasies, and irrationalities of the present process. They alone will not heal a government that is badly broken. However, rest assured that in this era of No World Order, without sound strategic thinking and thorough understanding of facts and realties, a tragic outcome is inevitable. The United States will be far less secure, far less prosperous, and far less able to remain engaged and relevant.

The choice is ours to make.

FINIS

Selected Bibliography

Caro, Robert A. *Master of the Senate: The Years of Lyndon Johnson*. New York: Alfred A. Knopf, 2002.

Chollet, Derek. *The Long Game: How Obama Defied Washington and Redefined America's Role in the World*. New York: PublicAffairs, 2016.

Halberstam, David. *The Best and the Brightest*. New York: Random House, 1972.

International Institute for Strategic Studies. *The Military Balance*. Published annually.

Powell, Colin, with Joseph E. Persico. *My American Journey: An Autobiography*. New York: Random House, 1995.

Ullman, Harlan K. *A Handful of Bullets: How the Murder of Archduke Franz Ferdinand Still Menaces the Peace*. Annapolis, Md.: Naval Institute Press, 2014.

Woodward, Bob. *State of Denial: Bush at War. Part III*. New York: Simon & Schuster, 2006.

Index

Names starting with "al" or "al-" are alphabetized by the subsequent part of the name.

About the Author

A prolific author with eight previous books to his credit, **Harlan Ullman** is an internationally recognized innovator and strategic thinker credited with creating the concept of "shock and awe" as well as a "brains-based approach to strategic thinking" and the thought-provoking idea of an era of No World Order. In addition to chairing two private companies, he is Senior Advisor at both the Atlantic Council and Business Executives for National Security (BENS) and is UPI's Arnaud deBorchgrave Distinguished Columnist. While serving in the U.S. Navy, his past experience includes 150 Swift Boat combat operations in Vietnam, two years in the Royal Navy, command at sea, and a number of senior Pentagon assignments ashore.